PHILOPONUS
On Aristotle On Coming-to-Be and Perishing 1.1-5

PHILOPONUS

On Aristotle On Coming-to-Be and Perishing 1.1-5

Translated by C.J.F. Williams

Introduction by Sylvia Berryman

B L O O M S B U R Y
LONDON • NEW DELHI • NEW YORK • SYDNEY

Bloomsbury Academic
An imprint of Bloomsbury Publishing Plc

50 Bedford Square
London
WC1B 3DP
UK

1385 Broadway
New York
NY 10018
USA

www.bloomsbury.com

First published in 1997 by Gerald Duckworth & Co. Ltd.
Paperback edition first published 2014

British Library Cataloguing-in-Publication Data
A catalogue record for this book is available from the British Library.

ISBN HB: 978-0-7156-2852-2
PB: 978-1-7809-3869-1
ePDF: 978-1-7809-3868-4

Acknowledgements
The present translations have been made possible by generous and imaginative funding from the following sources: the National Endowment for the Humanities, Division of Research Programs, an independent federal agency of the USA; the Leverhulme Trust; the British Academy; the Jowett Copyright Trustees; the Royal Society (UK); Centro Internazionale A. Beltrame di Storia dello Spazio e del Tempo (Padua); Mario Mignucci; Liverpool University; the Leventis Foundatic the Humanities Research Board of the British Academy; the Esmée Fairbairn Charitable Trust; the Henry Brown Trust; Mr and Mrs N. Egon; The Netherlands Organisation for Scientific Research (NWO/GW).

Typeset by Ray Davies

Printed and bound by CPI Group (UK) Ltd, Croydon, CR0 4YY

Contents

Preface

Richard Sorabji

This commentary is one of four which Philoponus describes as being from the voice of, i.e. based on the lecture of, his teacher Ammonius. But in three cases, including this one, he adds that there are reflections of his own. What reflections? We can only guess which are his.

In this volume, covering the first part of the commentary, some of the most striking reflections are those on the identity of people and things over a period of time. The question is particularly acute for living things, because their matter is always changing and, indeed, expands or contracts. The Stoics had postulated a unique bundle of qualities which lasts a lifetime. Others had said that, although the same primary matter does not persist, the same secondary subject does, or that the soul persists, or an essence consisting of matter and form.[1] Philoponus elsewhere records the view that individuals are unique bundles of qualities as if it were Aristotelian.[2] But it is not obvious that this is equivalent to the answer given here by Aristotle, and commented on by Philoponus, which is that the same form persists. Aristotle compares how a tube persists, even though different volumes of water flow through it, expanding or deflating it.[3]

Philoponus raises the question, if the form has its being in the matter, will it not pass away when the matter does? His answer is that it would if the matter passed away all in one go, but not if it passes away gradually.[4]

The problem can be raised about inanimate things too, like the notorious ship of Theseus.[5] If all its parts have been replaced over time by exactly similar parts, would it not be the same ship? But here there is the complication that another ship might be formed out of the discarded parts. Philoponus takes the example of an inanimate thing, a statue, whose foot, hand and head are replaced. But he has in mind replacement by differently shaped parts, so that the form is lost, and hence the identity, as well as the matter.[6]

Although Philoponus, like Aristotle, takes it that identity over time does not require the same matter to persist, he comments that there is an independent reason to think that some of an animal's matter needs to persist. For if it could all be safely replaced, we should be immortal.[7]

There are many other interesting reflections along the way. To name one more, Philoponus highlights a remark of Aristotle's so brief that the best known modern commentary on *De Generatione et Corruptione*, Joachim's, misses the relevance and thinks it must be inauthentic or misplaced. The point is that cause need not be straightforwardly like effect. What is actually cold may make something actually hard. The two things need not at any stage have hardness in common and hardness is not transferred from one to the other. At most, they must belong to the same very broad genus, and what is transferred is not actual hardness, but mere actuality (*entelekheia*), since what is actually cold produces what is actually hard. Aristotle puts his point as follows (I shall adapt Williams' translation used below):

> One thing comes to be *simpliciter* from another thing, as has been determined elsewhere, being caused to do so by something in an actual state either of the same genus or of the same species (fire e.g. by fire, or a human being by a human being) or by an actuality, for a hard thing is not cause to come into existence by a hard thing.[8]

It takes Philoponus to see the force of the last 19 words, and the reason why the hardening exemplifies causation by mere actuality. The general point that cause is not in every case just like effect was well known in the period of the commentators, and is already illustrated by the commentator Alexander by the case of rubbing causing heat.[9] But he presents that as his own example.

Later in the commentary, Philoponus adds restrictions of his own to the principles of causation. Blackness in ebony does not have the right material substrate to affect the whiteness of milk.[10]

It is sad to record that Christopher Williams died after completing two volumes of translation. This volume covers *GC* 1.1-5, the next *GC* 1.6-2.4. He had received comments on the translation of 1.1-4 and had time to revise that part. But the rest of the translation was in a good state. Suggestions for revising it were collected and coordinated by Sylvia Berryman, who added much of the annotation and the introduction. I want to thank the scholars who commented on the translation, Luc Deitz, John Ellis, David Furley, Frans de Haas, Alan Lacey, Donald Russell. I also thank Nicole Ooms for supplying the indexes, and most especially Sylvia Berryman, who has ensured that Christopher Williams' labour will bear fruit. It is a pleasure to his friends that this major two-volume work can be added to what he has given us.

Notes

1. See Richard Sorabji, 'Soul and self in ancient philosophy' in James Crabbe, ed., *From Soul to Self*, London, forthcoming, ch. 2.
2. Philoponus *in An. Post.* 437,21-438,2.
3. Aristotle *GC* 1.5, 321b24-8; 322a28-33; Philoponus in *GC* 105,18-26
4. Philoponus *in GC* 106,3-11.

5. Plutarch *Life of Theseus* 23.
6. Philoponus *in GC* 106,18-23.
7. Philoponus *in GC* 107,3-7.
8. Aristotle *GC* 1.5, 320b17-21.
9. Alexander *in Metaph.* 147,15-28. Further references will be given in our Sourcebook on the Philosophy of the Commentators, in preparation.
10. Philoponus *in GC* 149,11-12.

Introduction

Sylvia Berryman

In his 1981 translation and commentary for the Clarendon series, *Aristotle's De Generatione et Corruptione*, Professor Williams remarked that of commentaries on Aristotle's text, 'more rewarding, philosophically, than any other I have read is that of Philoponus, and it is pleasant to acknowledge a debt of assistance received across so many centuries'.[1] Here is Williams' translation of Philoponus' commentary.

Scholars place this commentary early in Philoponus' career, before he undertook the defence of Christian views that are at odds with Aristotelian doctrine, and before he fully developed his own novel views on such questions as space, void, projectile motion and matter.[2] Throughout much of the early chapters of the commentary, Philoponus confines himself to a close exposition of some rather difficult arguments in Aristotle's text. Philoponus frequently refers to the interpretation of Aristotle by Alexander of Aphrodisias.[3] He sometimes summarizes a section of Aristotle's argument before turning to detailed commentary.[4] On some points, Philoponus builds a substantial digression, but even there he often presents himself as interpreting some remark of Aristotle's or spelling out a consequence Aristotle leaves out as evident.[5] The most interesting passages lie disproportionately in chapter 5, the discussion of growth: there, Philoponus' own preoccupations with issues about the relationship of space, void and change show through. Some of the most interesting doctrines Philoponus develops later in the commentary are anticipated in these chapters.

A central issue of the present text, *On Coming-to-Be and Perishing*, is the transformation of the four elements – earth, air, fire and water – into one another. There is much debate among modern scholars whether Aristotle thinks that there is an additional 'prime matter' underlying these transformations, or whether, as some have argued, the qualities out of which elements are composed – hot, cold, moist and dry – can serve as the 'matter' of the transformation.[6] Philoponus, like other Neoplatonists, does think that Aristotle posits 'prime matter,' and reads this doctrine as systematically present here.[7]

Monism vs. pluralism

Philoponus' Proem to his commentary refers the reader to Aristotle's work *On the Heavens*, which, Philoponus argues, should be understood as the background to this text. Philoponus approaches the current treatise as the deferred proof of much that was assumed in *On the Heavens* concerning the nature and interrelationships of the four elements. It is against the background of difficulties in Presocratic views, especially those of Empedocles, Anaxagoras and the Atomists, that Aristotle justifies his own position.

In pointing out the limitations of his predecessors' views on change, Aristotle refers to his own view that there are four irreducibly different kinds of change: coming-to-be and perishing, change of quality, growth and diminution, change of place. In his view, the monists – early natural philosophers who think there is only one fundamental element taking on different forms – effectively identify coming-to-be with alteration. If everything is made of a single element, then the change from, say, air to fire would be only an alteration of the single persisting substratum. By contrast, the pluralists, who recognize the existence of more than one element, would be able to differentiate coming-to-be from mere alteration – change of quality in a substrate that persists – whether or not they in fact do so.

One group of pluralists reduce all change to spatial rearrangement of smallest parts. The atomists think that the elements, the smallest unchangeable atoms, do not come to be or perish, but merely rearrange themselves into different macroscopic objects. Alteration is mere spatial rearrangement of imperceptible smallest parts; coming-to-be or perishing of things in the ordinary world of experience is really a combination and segregation of atoms. Democritus' view, Philoponus explains, differentiates coming-to-be from alteration, inasmuch as the one is an aggregation, the other a rearrangement, of atoms.

There is more controversy concerning Aristotle's view of another pluralist, Empedocles. Alexander and Philoponus differ on whether Aristotle thinks that Empedocles *should* admit alteration but in fact makes it impossible, or that Empedocles *intends* to allow for the distinction but that his theory of alteration fails. Williams follows Philoponus and reads Aristotle as making the latter claim. The reason why Empedocles' theory of alteration is said to fail is that the qualities which might be thought to admit alteration are 'specifying characteristics' of elements, and as Empedocles' elements do not change into one another, the qualities defining them cannot be said to change. Williams points out that this criticism of Empedocles would only hold if *any* property individuates some substance so that any change of property is a substantial change: he finds this a strange view to credit to Empedocles.[8] Philoponus does think this is what Aristotle is crediting to Empedocles: that Empedocles reduces alteration to substantial change by employing too many of the qualities in his specification of the elements, thus leaving too few of the qualities whose replacement, in Aristotle's view, produces mere alteration as opposed to substantial change. Any change of such definitive properties would amount to the coming-to-be of a new substance. Empedocles fails to distinguish the constitutive qualities of substance from ordinary qualities that alter while the substance persists.

Philoponus clearly thinks the criticism is specific to Empedocles, not to pluralism generally. Anaxagoras' view is opposed to Empedocles' in that the former makes earth, air, fire and water composed out of homoeomers. Homoeomers are stuffs that have an undifferentiated structure: every part of blood or bone, say, is also blood or bone. Aristotle reports that Anaxagoras holds that earth, air, fire and water must be composed of homoeomers, because the four are the *panspermia* or seedbed that can give rise to, say, blood or bone. While this allows for change amongst what Aristotle regards as the four elements – earth, air, fire and water – Aristotle says that Anaxagoras' view makes the homoeomers 'elements'. Philoponus points out that Aristotle is inaccurate here, since in Anaxagoras' view not only are earth, air, fire and water treated as homoeomers, but also that every homoeomer is considered to be composed out of parts of any other.[9] The real difference is that Empedocles took the four elements as *arkhai* or principles where Anaxagoras took the homoeomers.

Infinite divisibility

To justify Aristotle's rejection of atomism, Philoponus considers why it is absurd that something having size should come to be from something not possessing size. In Aristotle the issue comes up in his response to one of the difficulties motivating the atomists, how it is possible to have a continuous magnitude. The atomists say the only alternative to their position is infinite divisibility, and pose the following dilemma. If a magnitude is infinitely divisible, let it be divided: whatever remains – if anything, perhaps sizeless points – could not possess size. How, then, is a magnitude constructed from these?

Philoponus rejects an argument by analogy that tries to show that it is not so absurd for sizeless entities to compose bodies having size. While Philoponus does not accept the atomist argument, he does think there is a genuine difficulty how a sizeable body can be composed from sizeless parts. He anticipates a comparison to the way prime matter and form, though both bodiless, together compose bodies.[10] He rejects the analogy because the prime matter in question never pre-exists in itself: it is only separated in thought, while always existing as an actual body.[11] The analogy to form and matter, then, cannot be the answer to the atomists.

Like Aristotle, Philoponus rejects the suggestion that infinite divisibility means that a magnitude will ever, in fact, be divided at every point *in actuality*, however much it may be at every point divisible *in potentiality*. It is also absurd, Philoponus thinks, to suppose that points should exist in themselves, separated from an extended magnitude, and to conceive of a magnitude as composed from points. A further objection to the composition of magnitudes out of points is that points cannot have a place – on the Aristotelian definition of place – and *a fortiori* cannot change place or have natural places and the natural motions that Aristotle thinks are characteristic of the elements. These difficulties are aspects of the general problem that something composed of points would have difficulty exhibiting the characteristics Aristotle wants to attribute to body. If a whole is said to be composed of parts, this raises a problem whether the characteristics of the whole can be attributed to the parts.

Philoponus illustrates the general problem of assigning the characteristics of a whole to its parts by referring the reader to Aristotle's discussion of infinite in *Phys.* 3.6. Aristotle draws an analogy to a day or the games which are present, not by all its parts occurring simultaneously, but by a part only being present. Philoponus draws the analogy that only a finite number of parts of a division are present simultaneously: Aristotle does not need to claim that an infinite division ever actually takes place, since its 'parts' need not be present all at once. The analogy is tricky. If the 'parts' of the division means parts of what is actually divided, these would be simultaneously present in a spatial magnitude but not in a temporal one, unsettling the parallel. But other ways to read the analogy would sustain Philoponus' point. Either an infinite number of *potential* parts isn't present all at once, since the division hasn't actually been made; or the analogy focuses on the parts of an infinite series of *acts* of dividing, thinking of division as a succession of acts of which the whole series is never completed.[12] Philoponus seems to have the last in mind: the analogy is not so much between spatial and temporal magnitude *per se*, but between a series of acts of dividing and the passing of time. Philoponus thinks we should talk not of division *into* infinite parts but of divisibility *to* infinity. The action of division, like the passing of time, need never cease.

Coming-to-be and alteration

Philoponus draws the real difficulties surrounding Aristotelian coming-to-be out of the first sentence of *GC* 1.3. There are three main problems: one is how anything can come to be from what is not. The solution, distinguishing what is not *actually* but is *potentially*, gives rise to the second: does this potential individual have any characteristics? If it has none in actuality, there seems to be coming-to-be from nothing, but if it does have characteristics in other categories than substance, this seems to attribute separate existence to nonsubstantial characteristics like quality, quantity or relation. The third is the problem applied to souls in Plato's *Phaedo*: if things perish into nothing, why doesn't the cosmos give out in infinite time?[13]

Philoponus interprets this third question as a search for an everlasting material cause underlying the continual series of coming-to-be and perishing, that will, because it is everlasting, ensure that the series of coming-to-be will not give out. This material cause will solve the second difficulty too. The solution is that the matter underlying the coming-to-be and perishing of individuals need not subsist separate from all form. The thought is, presumably, that since it never actually exists separately, questions about the separate existence of its characteristics do not arise.

The distinction of coming-to-be from alteration leads Philoponus to allude to a problem about the relationship between substantial and non-substantial qualities. The specifying or species-determining qualities of substances must have a different relationship to the individual than that of other qualities, because otherwise substantial change would be mere alteration. Philoponus addresses the objection that coming-to-be is merely alteration because it is simply a case of one of a pair of qualities changing. He considers the reply that in different elements, the qualities constitutive of an element are specifically different even if generically the same. He thinks that even if someone rejected this idea, he would be forced to accept that the instances of qualities are at least numerically different when one element changes to another. Nothing persists through interelemental transformation except prime matter.

Philoponus has relatively little to add at this point to the discussion of alteration itself: the key problems arose for him in differentiating alteration from coming-to-be. One problem he does try to clarify is how a quality can be at one time involved in mere alteration, when a change in the quality with the same name can also bring about substantial change for that element. Ordinary water can be said to alter, becoming hotter or colder; yet when the element water changes to air, the cold and wet becomes hot and wet. This shows that a specifying quality in an element, say cold, is no mere affection of the element, nor is it an affection of the other specifying quality together with which it forms the element. If this were so, then substantial change – the change from water to air – would be a kind of alteration, much like water getting hotter.[14]

Growth

Philoponus clearly considers growth an important problem. While in Aristotle, chapter five is a little over a quarter of the combined length of the first five chapters, Philoponus devotes nearly half of his commentary on this section to growth. The main problem is that of distinguishing the features uniquely applicable to growth, and, in particular, of deciding what it is that grows. Two digressions are introduced to consider what, in the case of growth, should be thought of as the 'matter', and how this is different from the matter in other categories of change, especially coming-to-be. Philoponus explains his own view that the matter of growth needs to be something that is inherently quantified. He also seeks to undermine Alexander's interpretation, according to which Aristotle claims that the matter of growth is the same as that of coming-to-be.[15]

From the very beginning of the chapter Philoponus stresses the issue about the matter of change. Aristotle's first question is whether different kinds of change differ in one respect or in more. He seems to be asking whether more can be said about the difference amongst kinds of change than merely listing the different respect of change, that is, change in substance, quality, quantity or place. Philoponus draws an analogy to artistic production: some skills are differentiated by the matter they work in, others by the form produced from the matter, yet others in both respects. Kinds of change, he insists, are differentiated by both. Thus Philoponus wants to focus on the matter (*hulê*) of change at a point where Aristotle wonders whether kinds of change in fact differ in manner (*tropos*).

Philoponus points out that growth bears a peculiar relationship to place, unlike alteration, but that this relationship is a different one from that involved in change of place. Aristotle's own account of place is something of a hindrance here. He wants to say that a growing thing changes its place, although in another sense it remains: rather than saying, as elsewhere, that the body is now in a larger and hence different place (*Phys.* 4.4, 211a16), he says instead that the whole remains but the parts change place, but again not in the way that a revolving sphere remains while the parts change place. In growth, the parts come to occupy a larger place. This raises a problem about the relationship of parts to whole.

A long proof is developed to show that the 'matter' of growth is actually body. In order to underlie quantitative change, he argues, the matter of growth must be three-dimensional, which implies that it is in place. But anything that is in place will also be above and below other bodies, in other words, in spatial relationships; hence it also has accidents in the category of relation.[16] And being above and below other bodies, it is either so by nature or against nature; either answer to this (Aristotelian) dichotomy means that the thing in question is composed of earth, air, fire or water. In other words, anything in spatial relationships must be a bodily substance. This proof strategy is analogous to an argument discussed in the Proem, that the elements must come to be from one another.[17]

The issue in question is really whether the matter of growth is something that could have an existence separable from other bodies. Aristotle in fact argues that the matter of any change whatsoever is always embodied. Prior to any change the matter will exist as part of some body, although not necessarily the one which it becomes. The argument for this is that a body could not grow by the addition of bodiless entities – void, dimensionless points or imperceptible body – because these are either impossible or can have no independent existence. It must be from something having quantity. And whatever has quantity is not separable from body but exists in some body. Moreover, the quantity cannot be 'in' a body merely in the sense of being contained.

Aristotle rejects the idea that the matter of growth has no size in actuality, only in potential. It is, rather, the characteristic of the matter of coming-to-be to exist in potential and not in actuality. Philoponus reads this as endorsing the view that coming-to-be has a completely formless matter – prime matter – whereas the matter of growth, i.e. of quantitative change, is already determined in the category of quantity. Philoponus raises some objections against Alexander over the question whether Aristotle means certain passages to refer to coming-to-be or to growth specifically.

Aristotle simply poses the dilemma that growth by an incorporeal addition implies that there must have been some previously void space into which the growth took place, while growth by the addition of body seems to imply that two bodies are in the same place. After a rehearsal of problems with considering incorporeals as the matter of growth, Philoponus turns to problems with considering body as the matter of growth. These concern the way in which the accretion is absorbed into the growing body and what aspect of the latter is considered to have grown.

Philoponus anticipates a further dilemma that if the growing thing is said to increase in every part by the addition of body, either the receiving body must have void passageways throughout or there will be two bodies in the same place. Aristotle does not specifically address this problem until *GC* 1.8. In a long digression on void, Philoponus considers whether a more general problem might not be urged against coming-to-be as well as growth. In both cases, it is suggested, the resulting body may take up more space than the bodies from which the change occurs, so that either kind of change might be used as an argument for the existence of void. The problem is that if one body expands, there must have been some void space, unless we accept the consequence that another body necessarily decreases simultaneously by the same amount. Some think it absurd that when water expands on becoming steam, somewhere else in the universe a converse contraction necessarily takes place. In *Physics* 4.9, 216b25, where this problem is advanced, a third option – that the universe bulges – is also offered.

Philoponus takes the option of showing how reciprocity is not in fact absurd. He says, first, that reciprocal changes of volume need not be as extreme as elemental transformation – that air can compress, as when currents are caused by wind, without changing to water. It is easier to suppose that compensatory compression or expansion takes place if it does not require reciprocal elemental transformation. Second, he points to a case where we can see reciprocal transformations taking place, when steam expands and rises, reaching the roof, and condenses when it has no further space to expand. Philoponus elsewhere draws out implications of this idea that bodies adapt to fill a fixed quantity of space.[18] Here, in aid of his first point, Philoponus cites the case of a vessel from which the air is sucked out to show that air can in fact rarefy without elemental transformation.[19] The idea of the 'force of the void' is usually used to explain the movement of fluids or bodies to prevent gaps forming: Philoponus does refer to such a case a little later. But here he uses this idea to explain how it is reasonable that compensatory expansion or compression takes place.

This is all looking forward: what Aristotle rather focuses on at this point is the problem about mixture and how, when two bodies combine, one of them can be said to have grown. He clarifies the problem by stressing that merely expanding is not the issue. Food might expand by turning into *pneuma*, but it is not this that is said to have grown. What is said to grow is the body which persists, i.e. stays the same in form while becoming larger. This raises a difficulty in cases where it is not clear which element persists: when water mixes with wine, say. Aristotle says that it is the wine which grows because its characteristics prevail in the mixture. Philoponus expresses some reservations about this solution, pointing out that the term 'growth' is a bit stretched here. Problems about mixture are also discussed more thoroughly later, in *GC* 1.10.

Aristotle compares growth to alteration and says that the origin or *arkhê* of growth is in the thing which grows, which need not be the case with alteration. The reason is that the added matter of growth is destroyed. Where Aristotle was merely trying to sort out which is the proper subject of growth, Philoponus sees an issue about the cause of growth. Of the four kinds of cause in Aristotle – material, efficient, formal and final – he thinks the 'origin of change' is the efficient cause. This idea leads Philoponus to discuss the relationship between the cause and the body undergoing change. He finds it curious that substantial change and alteration of natural things are instigated by external cases, while the things themselves are the cause of growth and change of place. Philoponus addresses this apparent anomaly by explaining why things can't be the cause of their own coming-to-be and perishing or alteration. Natural things cannot cause their own coming-to-be or perishing, in the first case because they don't yet exist and in the second because nature does not allow of self-destruction. This latter restriction is extended to apply to the case of alteration, on the grounds that excessive states of certain qualities are destructive.

The underlying principle invoked is that nature does nothing in vain, which Philoponus extends into the stronger claim that nature does nothing harmful or excessive. The Aristotelian formulation justified looking for a purpose of natural processes, whereas Philoponus' version, implying that the results are necessarily beneficial for the organism, would have more powerful implications.[20] Philoponus himself acknowledges the need to explain why it is that organisms eventually dwindle in power and die, and attributes this to the failure of the matter to keep its form. He uses the idea that something can't cause its own destruction in discovering the efficient cause of growth. After arguing that the nutriment could not be the efficient cause of growth because it would then be instigating its own destruction, he concludes that the growing thing must cause the assimilation to it of the nutriment and so be the cause of its own growth.

It is in connection with this discussion about the cause of growth that Philoponus talks of the powers or capacities for growth and nutrition. Todd has suggested that Philoponus' emphasis on the role of 'powers' in the discussion of nutrition and growth may be due to his awareness of medical ideas on this topic.[21] Philoponus discusses the conditions for the power of growth when he claims that a proportionality must hold between the power and the matter it acts on. This proportionality is offered as the explanation why the power is normally unaffected while acting on the matter, but can be extinguished if the quantity of matter present exceeds the power to act on it. The ways in which change is limited by the quantity of matter will be important in the chapters that follow, where it becomes relevant to the discussion of mixture. Philoponus recognizes that the amount of growth is determined by the quantity of the bodies concerned, and that quantity of matter affects what changes can occur.[22]

Philoponus tackles the problem about how a body as a whole can be said to grow when new matter is added to one part of it. It is the form that is said to grow by being deployed over a larger quantity of matter. The distinction between form in the sense of substantial form and form in the sense of shape introduces a possible complication. He discusses a potential problem with an irregular shaped long bone that might be able to grow by accretion in width, but because of the discontinuities in its shape lengthwise it is not obvious how addition to one end could be assimilated in a way that would preserve the shape.

The discussion of growth, with its emphasis on form, highlights the distinction between homoeomerous masses like flesh and bone on the one hand, and anhomoeomerous parts like a hand on the other. Aristotle refers here to a notion discussed by J.L. Ackrill, the claim that parts of a living body like a hand or an eye only retain their identity when they are actually parts of a living organism: the body of a dead person is only a body in name.[23] This has raised considerable controversy amongst modern scholars as to the value of Aristotle's account of living things.[24] Philoponus says here that this applies to anhomoeomerous parts, rather than to the homoeomerous substances: the reason he gives is that the actualization of the form of the homoeomeries is less evident. He echoes Aristotle's remark that in homoeomeries the form is less distinct from the matter, and seems to take this to mean that while in anhomoeomerous parts there may be nothing other than an actual hand that is potentially a hand, homoeomeries, by contrast, seem more to retain their nature apart from the living body.[25]

*

Professor Williams was completing his translation of *Philoponus On Aristotle On Coming-to-Be and Perishing 1.1-5* and *1.6-2.4* at the time of his death in Spring 1997. He had already received comments on and revised some chapters. Where the translation was not yet completely polished, the suggestions and comments of vetters have proved particularly invaluable. Notes to the translation have been supplemented in some cases, particularly in the later chapters: these are marked by initials. Quotations from Aristotle's text, which Philoponus does not usually cite in full, have been filled out in square brackets. Here Williams' own translation from the Clarendon series has been used as much as possible to supplement the lemmas, modified in the light of differences in Philoponus' version of Aristotle's text and of Williams' own changes in translation style. Oxford University Press kindly gave their permission to draw on the Clarendon translation. I am especially grateful to Richard Sorabji for his assistance throughout.

The companion volume of Williams' translation is appearing simultaneously in this series. In chapters 1.6-2.4, Philoponus continues some of the themes discussed in this volume, and develops some fascinating views, especially on mixture, qualities, and their ability to act on one another.[26]

Notes

1. *Aristotle's De Generatione et Corruptione*, Oxford 1982, p. vi. In his translation for the Clarendon series, Professor Williams left the title of Aristotle's work in Latin, *De Generatione et Corruptione*, and generally rendered the Greek terms *genesis* and *phthora* as 'generation' and 'corruption' respectively. Following standard usage, the title of Aristotle's text is abbreviated as *GC* in this series. However, as Williams uses 'coming-to-be' and 'perishing' in this translation, the title is translated accordingly.

2. See Richard Sorabji, 'John Philoponus', in R. Sorabji (ed.), *Philoponus and the Rejection of Aristotelian Science*, London and Ithaca N.Y. 1987, 1-40, for an overview of Philoponus' work. For more specialized discussion of the chronology of Philoponus' work, see, e.g., Koenraad Verrycken, 'The development of Philoponus' thought and its chronology,' in R. Sorabji (ed.), *Aristotle Transformed: The Ancient Commentators and their Influence*, London 1990, 233-74, esp. pp. 254-7. Verrycken takes the acceptance of an eternally moving cosmos – which emerges in the latter part of *in GC*, not in this volume – as evidence that this commentary is the work of what he calls 'Philoponus 1'. Frans de Haas, *John Philoponus' New Definition of Prime Matter*, Leiden 1997, pp. xiii-xvi, surveys the scholarly literature concerning the ordering of Philoponus' writings on matter.

3. For Philoponus as a source for Alexander's lost commentary, see Robert B. Todd, *Alexander of Aphrodisias on Stoic Physics: A Study of the De Mixtione with*

Preliminary Essays, Text, Translation and Commentary, Leiden 1976. See Richard Sorabji's Preface to the companion volume for new material from Arabic sources.

4. On the structure of *theôria* and *lexis* – exposition and detailed commentary – see Raymond Vancourt, *Les Derniers Commentateurs Alexandrins d'Aristote: L'école d'Olympiodore Étienne d'Alexandrie*, Lille 1941, pp. 7-16; Erich Lamberz, 'Proklos und die Form des Philosophischen Kommentars,' 1-20 in H.D. Saffrey (ed.), *Proclus. Lecteur et interprète des Anciens*, Paris 1987; and the discussion of Vancourt's thesis in W. Charlton, *Philoponus On Aristotle on the Intellect*, London and Ithaca N.Y. 1991, p. 7, in this series. Clearly there is no formal structure of lectures here, but there may be traces of an informal distinction between summary and detailed comment: cf. 29,2; 45,21-2.

5. Passages where the Philoponus seems to feel himself to be departing from mere exposition include 28,15-29,2, which uses material from Aristotle's *Phys.* 6.1 to stress that the hypothesis of dividing to infinity is in fact impossible; 35,13-36,10, which recommends more careful phrasing to avoid the suggestion of dividing into infinite parts; 39,25-40,13, spelling out why parts aren't in contact; 70,12-71,3, on whether different varieties of change differ in matter, form, or both; 73,6-75,24, where he spells out an argument; 91,30-94,7, arguing that reciprocal change is not implausible; 97,15-100,24, considering whether the efficient cause of alteration is internal; and 104,32-111,13 on growth.

6. Williams discusses the controversy between King, Charlton, Solmsen and Robinson in an appendix to his Clarendon translation: *Aristotle's De Generatione et Corruptione*, pp. 211-19. For more recent scholarship, see, e.g., M.L. Gill, *Aristotle on Substance: The Paradox of Unity*, Princeton 1989, pp. 42-6; David Bostock, 'Aristotle on the transmutation of the elements in *De Generatione et Corruptione* 1.1-4', *Oxford Studies in Ancient Philosophy* 13, 1995, 217-29.

7. De Haas discusses differences between Philoponus' understanding of prime matter in this text and the view traditionally attributed to Neoplatonists, in *John Philoponus' New Definition of Prime Matter* p. 145; cf. Richard Sorabji, *Matter, Space and Motion: Theories in Antiquity and their Sequel*, London and Ithaca N.Y. 1988, ch. 1.

8. *Aristotle's De Generatione et Corruptione*, p. 62.

9. On the particular interest for Neoplatonists of Anaxagoras' view that everything has a part of everything, see Carlos G. Steel, *The Changing Self. A Study of the Soul in Later Neoplatonism: Iamblichus, Damascius and Priscianus*, Brussels 1978, p. 26.

10. A similar argument strategy appears in the *Mantissa* 121,21ff., where the compound of incorporeal matter and form is profferred to undermine the absurdity of substance coming-to-be from parts that aren't substances. On the authorship of *Mantissa*, see Robert W. Sharples, 'Alexander and pseudo-Alexanders of Aphrodisias, *Scripta minima*. Questions and problems, makeweights and prospects', 383-403 in W. Kullmann, J. Althoff and M. Asper (eds), *Gattungen wissenschaftlicher Literatur in der Antike*, Tübingen 1997. A translation by R.W. Sharples is forthcoming in this series.

11. Those who suggest the analogy seem to regard prime matter as sizeless. Philoponus himself eventually develops the view that three-dimensional extensionality is the substratum of change. On the relationship between his new view of prime matter and the present chapters, see De Haas, *John Philoponus' New Definition of Prime Matter*, p. 137ff.

12. I am grateful to Richard Sorabji for help in clarifying this distinction.

13. Philoponus later comes to develop criticisms of Aristotle's views on the eternity of the world and the indestructibility of the heavens: for a discussion of the argument in *contra Proclum* and probably *in Phys.*, which allows for matter to come-to-be and perishing into nothing, see, e.g., Richard Sorabji, *Time, Creation and the Continuum*, London and Ithaca N.Y. 1983, p. 249; Christian Wildberg, *John Philoponus' Criticism of Aristotle's Theory of Aether*, Berlin 1988; essays in Richard Sorabji (ed.), *Philoponus and the Rejection of Aristotelian Science*, London and Ithaca N.Y. 1987.

14. Philoponus returns to this problem in later chapters with his discussion of the 'range' of qualities: see the companion volume, C.J.F. Williams (trans.), *Philoponus On Aristotle On Coming-to-Be and Perishing* 1.6-2.4

15. De Haas sees this as one of the three main themes of the chapter: distinguishing growth from coming-to-be, developing the implications both for void and for Philoponus' own ideas on 'fitness' and 'latitude': *John Philoponus' New Definition of Prime Matter*, pp. 137-64. The terms *epitêdeiotês* and *platos* are translated 'suitability' and 'range' by Williams: these concepts will occur more prominently in the chapters following *in GC* 1.5. (The only explicit use of *platos* in these chapters is at 110,3.26, in a nontechnical sense.)

16. cf. Philoponus *in Cat.* 83,13-19, where he defends the claim that quantity is prior to quality in that body receives three dimensionality before qualities and relations.

17. Philoponus' discussion of being in contact and why it can't strictly be said of mathematical objects echoes this strategy: see the companion volume.

18. In his commentary on Aristotle's *Physics*, Philoponus turns to cases where bodies seem to be adapting to fill the space available as evidence that place or space must be independent of the particular bodies occupying it. See esp. *in Phys.* 569,18-572,6, translated for this series in *Philoponus Corollaries on Place and Void* with *Simplicius Against Philoponus On the Eternity of the World (Fragments)*, trans. David Furley and Christian Wildberg, London and Ithaca N.Y. 1991; see David Furley, 'Summary of Philoponus' Corollaries on Place and Void', 130-9 in Richard Sorabji (ed.), *Philoponus and the Rejection of Aristotelian Science*, London and Ithaca N.Y. 1987, and David Sedley, 'Philoponus' conception of space', 140-53 in *Philoponus and the Rejection of Aristotelian Science*.

19. This example is, curiously, also cited by advocates of void with quite the reverse aim, to show that there must be void spaces between the particles of air. On its use by Hero of Alexandria in the Introduction to his *Pneumatics*, see De Haas, *John Philoponus' New Definition of Prime Matter*, pp. 159-60. For literature on antecedents to Hero, see, e.g., H.B. Gottschalk, 'Strato of Lampsacus: some texts', *Proceedings of the Leeds Philosophical and Literary Society* 9, 1965, 95-182.

20. On global teleology in Philoponus, see Michael Wolff, *Fallgesetz und Massebegriff: zwei wissenschaftshistorische Untersuchungen zur Kosmologie des Johannes Philoponus*, Berlin 1971, pp. 62ff. Sambursky notes a context where the principle that nature does nothing in vain is understood to mean avoiding excess: Olympiodorus *in Meteor.* 272,5 takes the fact that the reflection of light is at equal angles, the shortest course possible, as an instance of nature doing nothing in vain: S. Sambursky, 'Conceptual developments and modes of explanation in later Greek scientific thought', 61-78 in A.C. Crombie (ed.), *Scientific Change: Historical Studies in the Intellectual, Social and Technical Conditions for Scientific Discovery and Technical Invention, from Antiquity to the Present*, London 1963, pp. 75-6.

21. R.B. Todd, 'Galenic medical ideas in the Greek Aristotelian Commentators', *Symbolae Osloenses* 52 (1976), 117-34; also R.B. Todd, 'Some concepts in physical theory in John Philoponus' Aristotelian commentaries', 151-70, *Archiv für Begriffsgeschichte* 24, 1980, pp. 168-9.

22. For more on this, see the companion volume *Philoponus On Aristotle On Coming-to-Be and Perishing 1.6-2.4*.

23. J.L. Ackrill, 'Aristotle's definition of *psychê*,' *Proceedings of the Aristotelian Society* 73, 1972-3, 119-33.

24. For some implications of this problem see, e.g., Richard Sorabji, 'Body and soul in Aristotle', 43-64 in J. Barnes, M. Schofield and R. Sorabji (eds), *Articles on Aristotle 4. Psychology and Aesthetics*, London 1979; M.L. Gill, *Aristotle on Substance: the Paradox of Unity*; M.F. Burnyeat, 'Is an Aristotelian philosophy of mind still credible?' in M. Nussbaum and A. Rorty (eds), *Essays on Aristotle's De Anima*, Oxford 1992, 15-26; S. Marc Cohen, 'Hylomorphism and functionalism', in *Essays on Aristotle's De Anima*, pp. 57-73; Jennifer Whiting, 'Living bodies', in *Essays on Aristotle's De Anima*, pp. 75-91; David Charles, 'Matter and form: unity, persistence and identity,' in T. Scaltsas, D. Charles and M.L. Gill (eds), *Unity, Identity, and Explanation in Aristotle's Metaphysics*, Oxford 1994, 75-106; Frank A. Lewis, 'Aristotle on the relation between a thing and its matter, in *Unity, Identity, and Explanation in Aristotle's Metaphysics*, 247-78.

25. Aristotle usually talks as if this problem applies to parts of the body only: hand, eye, foot, finger. He does extend it to homoeomeries in *GA* 2.1, 734b24-34, but here and in *Meteor*. 4.12, 390a2 Aristotle says that homoeomerous masses are less dependent on their function or end than are parts of an organism. Philoponus' explanation here may draw on the *Meteorology* passage.

26. I am grateful to Richard Sorabji and Frans de Haas for their helpful comments on earlier versions of this introduction.

Textual Emendations

3,26	Reading *kath' hên*, as Vitelli suggests, rather than the MSS' *kath' has*
4,5	Reading *esti* with a paroxytone accent
8,13	Reading *huperkeimenois* in place of *hupokeimenois*
9,2	Retaining *ho Têlemakhos pros ton patera hupo tês Athênas metablêthenta*, which is deleted by Vitelli
10,20	Inserting *hoti* at this point, as suggested by Vitelli
13,21	Following Vitelli, who suggests reading *ephasken* rather than *phaskôn*
14,3	Following Vitelli's suggestion and deleting the word *auto* at its first occurrence
14,9	Deleting Vitelli's comma between *menontos* and *tou hupo-keimenou*
18,4	Reading *hêi* with Aristotle's MSS, rather than *ê* given by Philoponus
21,17	Reading *oude* with Vitelli, which is the modern Aristotle text, rather than *ouden*, the reading of the Philoponus MSS.
28,3	Reading *moriôn*, which Vitelli suggests for *monadon* of the MSS
28,16	Reading *stigmas* rather than *atoma*
29,32	Reading *ouk an eiê*, with the Aldine, rather than *hama* with Vitelli
33,14	Following the Aldine editor in omitting the repetition of 'he says'
37,3	Following Vitelli in inserting *morion* here
40,2	Vitelli indicates a lacuna, while noting that one MS inserts *kai houtôs*
51,8	Vitelli follows the Aldine editor in supplying *ti* at this point
55,31	Following Vitelli, who suggests *prostetheike* instead of *pros-titheika*
57,23	Following MSS G and T here and reading *to* rather than *tôi*
58,25	Reading *to hou heneka toû heneka tou* with MS Z
61,26	Vitelli follows the Aldine editor in inserting *hê de genesis* in the text
61,28	Reading *aporêseien an tis* which is missing from Philoponus' MS
63,9	Following Vitelli's insertion of *legei*

63,16 Following Vitelli's insertion of *sêmainei. kata to hupokeimenon* here

64,19 Omitting *ei* with MS Z

67,12 Retaining *de*, which Vitelli follows the Aldine Editor in deleting

69,25 Reading, with the Aldine Editor, *phoras* rather than *phthoras*

70,24 Inserting *poteron kath' heteron monon* following the Aldine editor

75,9 Following the Aldine editor and one MS, omitting *kai* after *megethos*

76,6 The Aldine editor supplies *poteron phêsin*

76,26 Reading *autou* for the MSS' *toutou* at Vitelli's suggestion

79,3 Reading *hautê* with (G)a. Vitelli prints *autê*

81,25 Reading *oute* instead of *oude*, as Vitelli suggests

82,5 Reading *auto kath' hauto* for *autas kath' hautas*, as Vitelli suggests

83,22 Reading *panti adunaton* with Plato's text, at Vitelli's suggestion. The MSS of Philoponus have *pantêi adunaton*

86,25 Vitelli here prints *atopô*, but this must be a misprint for *atopôi*

88,24 Following the Aldine edition and reading *ta dê kata koinên ennoian* in the place occupied by the lacuna, and supplying *ektithetai*

89,3 Vitelli follows the Aldine editor in inserting *hôste* here

91,18 Vitelli follows the Aldine editor in supplying *gar*

98,26 Taking *to dunamei* to be written in error here for *tên dunamin*

107,27 Reading *epeisiousa* where Vitelli prints *epeisousa*

118,3 Following the Aldine editor in reading *meta touto* for *meta toutou*

118,15 Vitelli reads *holon men gar hôs holon ouketi. oude gar panti moriôi tês sarkos hê prosthêkê meizôn gegonen, hekaston mentoi morion tês hulês gegonen;* I have translated the reading of R, which transposes *ouketi … prosthêkê* to follow *mentoi morion*

119,14 Reading *kai hotioun* where the MSS have *kai hoti kai*

Philoponus
On Aristotle On Coming-to-Be and Perishing 1.1-5

Translation

Lecture Notes taken by John the Philologist of Alexandria from the Course given by Ammonius the Son of Hermeias with some Observations of his own on the First Book of Aristotle's *On Coming-to-Be and Perishing*

PROEM

Aristotle dealt in the *Physics* with the principles of natural phenomena, that is, matter and form, and with the things which accompany all natural <phenomena> alike, place, time and change.[1] He then made it his aim in the following treatises to deal with natural things themselves.[2] Some natural things are incapable of coming-to-be or perishing, others are capable of coming-to-be and perishing. Of those which are imperishable and eternal, some are eternal both as wholes and in respect of their parts, like the things in the heavens, whilst others are eternal as wholes, but capable of coming-to-be and perishing in respect of their parts, as are the four elements.

He dealt with those natural things which are eternal – not only the ones which are eternal as wholes and in respect of their parts as well, but also the ones which, though like this as wholes, are perishable in respect of their parts – in his work *On the Heavens*. For his teaching about the four elements is not irrelevant, as one might think it was, to his theory about the heavens, since the description 'the heavens' means 'the whole world' in the usage of earlier periods.[3] Plato for one says in the *Timaeus*,[4] 'Let this be our name for the whole heaven, or world, or however else it may be most acceptable to name it', and in the *Statesman*,[5] 'that which we call the heavens or the world'. So when Aristotle entitles his work *On the Heavens,* he does not mean to refer to the heavenly bodies only, but to the whole world.

In that treatise, as has been said, he deals with the things which are said to be in any way eternal, whilst in the treatises which follow he deals with everything else, that is to say, with things subject to coming-to-be and perishing and everything that accompanies them. Again, some of the accompaniments of things subject to coming-to-be and perishing accompany all of them alike, some are peculiar to things of certain kinds. Of the accompaniments which are peculiar to things of certain kinds, some accompany peculiarly terrestrial things, others superterrestrial things, i.e. to things situated between the earth and the heavens, which we refer to as 'meteorological phenomena'. Where terrestrial things are concerned, some accompany things *qua* animate, some things *qua* inanimate. Of those which are characteristic of things *qua* animate, some are characteristic of things *qua* sentient, some of things *qua* insentient.

Aristotle therefore divides his physical[6] treatises in a way that corresponds to these distinctions. For just as in the *Physics* he deals with what accompanies all natural <phenomena> in general, so in the present work he is going to discuss what accompanies all things subject to coming-to-be and perishing. In the *Meteorology* he deals with the things which are formed above the earth, and what accompany them, in the biological works (which are very numerous on account of the great variety of species encountered in the domain of living things) with what accompany things *qua* animate and sentient, in *On Plants* with animate but insentient things, and in *On Metals*[7] and the fourth book of the *Meteorology* with inanimate things.[8]

Natural phenomena and those of Aristotle's treatises which deal with them are divided up in a summary fashion in the way described. But since there is a considerable degree of continuity between the present work and *On the Heavens*, as the 'on the other hand' at the beginning of the work makes clear (he writes 'On the other hand, about <the causes and definitions of> coming-to-be and perishing') as though referring back to the 'on the one hand' placed at the end of *On the Heavens* (for we get a single continuous sentence if we join together the end of that work with the beginning of this one, like this: 'This, then, is the way in which, on the one hand, we decide the issues concerning heavy and light and their essential characteristics, while, on the other hand, about <the causes and definitions of> the coming-to-be and perishing of things the nature of which is to come to be and perish, etc.') – since, therefore, as has been shown, there is continuity between the present treatise and that one, it is reasonable for us not to be unmindful of the doctrine of *On the Heavens*, but to run over in a somewhat summary fashion the teachings of that work.[9]

We should know, therefore, that in the first two books he discusses the things which are eternal, and in the remaining two the things which come to be and perish. In the first book he enquires about the substance of the celestial body, saying that it is different in nature from the four elements, being incapable of coming-to-be and perishing, not only in respect of its entirety, but also in respect of its parts, and admitting no change except that of place. He enquires also whether it is infinite or finite, and demonstrates that it is finite by an argument of this sort, as well as by many other elegant arguments: he says that calling a circle infinite is like calling a cubit infinite; for just as calling something a cubit is to speak of it as measured and finite, so calling something a circle both names its shape and with the thought of this takes in also its limits. So having shown that the celestial body is finite, he further demonstrates that outside it there is not only no body, but no place and no void either. For, in his view, it is not in the nature of the things there to be in a place,[10] nor does time make them grow old.

This, then, is his teaching in the first book. In the second his topic is the shape of the heavens as a whole and of the stars that are set in them, which he says is spherical, and the motion these bodies exhibit, which he says is circular. Finally, after this, we have his teaching on the four elements taken as a whole: he enquires what is the shape of these too, and shows that it is spherical. On the subject of the earth he gives a lengthy account, dealing with four questions: its size, its shape, its position and its motion. As for size, as against the bulk of people, who think it has infinite size, he holds that it is finite and smaller than most, indeed almost all, the stars, with the exception of the moon. In shape, he shows that it too is spherical. Where position is concerned, it is situated in the centre. It needs no force to hold it up, as one might think. On the contrary, it would need force to move it from the central position, being immoveable in its own place.

This set of enquiries about the heavens and the four elements taken as a whole,[11] in which respect they are incapable of coming-to-be or perishing, occupies the first and second books. He next intends, beginning with the third book, to set out his teaching about the four elements, in so far as they are capable of coming-to-be and perishing (and they have this character, obviously, in respect of their parts; for it is out of the parts of the elements that the things which come to be do so, and into these that the things that perish perish). So, meaning to discuss, in respect of the things that come to be and perish, what elements and how many elements go to make them up, he enquires first whether there is such a thing as coming-to-be at all. For perhaps there *is* no such thing at all as coming-to-be, as those maintain who suppose that there is no movement or change, like the school of Parmenides. And he shows that there is such a thing as coming-to-be, on the one hand refuting and solving the paradoxes that have been brought to bear upon coming-to-be, and on the other hand calling in evidence the obviousness of the fact that things come to be and perish. He enquired generally where the people who put forward this view ever got the idea that there was no such thing as coming-to-be. He says that, since they were convinced that there was such a thing in the world as knowledge, and said that knowledge was of things which were static and always in the same state, they put forward the view that everything that is stands still. But against this he shows that while it is true both that there is[12] such a thing as knowledge and that this is indeed of things that are static and always in the same state, nevertheless we are not compelled to suppose that everything is static and to get rid of movement. For it is possible to suppose that of all the things there are, some are static and eternal and these are the objects of knowledge, while others are capable of coming-to-be and perishing and it is in these that movement takes place. But even in the generated things themselves there is something static and permanent, in respect of which they too can be objects of knowledge. I mean form. For the form of the things which, one by one, perish and change is always preserved by succession.[13]

In these and similar ways he demonstrates the existence of coming-to-be and of the things that come to be and perish. He then asks what the things that come to be come to be from, whether from something incorporeal or from some corporeal element, and shows that it is not from something incorporeal. For one or other of two absurd conclusions will necessarily follow: either it will be a vacuum[14] which receives that which comes to be from something incorporeal, or, if there is no such thing as empty space, a body will pass through a body. It remains that the things which come to be do so from a corporeal element.

At this point[15] he also defines ‘element’, saying that an element of bodies is that into which composite bodies are ultimately dissolved, either potentially or actually existing within them (which of these two is the case is for the moment unsettled), and which itself is indivisible into things differing from each other in form. He has left unsettled the question whether the element exists in the body actually or potentially, because he has not yet explained the way in which coming-to-be takes place. For if coming-to-be and perishing come about by way of aggregation and segregation, the elements will exist actually within the things they compose; but if by way of a change of substance, <they will do so> potentially and not actually.

So having shown that things come to be, not from something incorporeal, but from something corporeal, which he calls an element, he enquires next whether there is just one such element or more than one, and whether they are finite or infinite. It is impossible, he says, for there to be just one. From what would the great variety amongst things that come to be be derived, if they came to be from just one thing? And where would the different and opposite movements come from, some things being upwardly mobile and others having a downwards tendency? For opposites cannot exist in one and the same thing. Even Hippocrates says, ‘If man were just one thing, he would not be in pain; and even if he were in pain, there would be <just> one thing which would heal him.’[16]

So it is not from just one, but from more than one. But not from an infinite number, since it has been shown that it is impossible for the infinite to exist actually. I do not mean that it is impossible for the elements to be infinite only in number and not also in size; for if the heavens which encompass everything have been shown to be finite, it could hardly be the case that one of the elements was infinite.

So the elements are finite and more than <just> one. Without going on to state how many there are or what they are, but taking it as agreed that there are four, and allowing the investigation into whether they are capable or incapable of coming-to-be to contribute to the demonstration that this is their number, he transfers the discussion to this topic; and having shown that they are not incapable but capable of coming-to-be, especially from the obviousness of the fact (for we see all water perishing and coming-to-be air, and the same in the case of the others), he proceeds to enquire what they come from, whether from each other or from some other substratum,[17] as was supposed by those who posit the intermediate body between water and air. And he shows that it is not from some other <element>. For that other element, since it is a body, must necessarily exist in a place.[18] So it will either be in the upper regions or in the lower; and if in the upper, this must be so either naturally or unnaturally. Likewise in the lower regions: either naturally or unnaturally. If, then, it is in the upper regions naturally, it will be fire or air, and if it is in the upper regions unnaturally, it will be either water or earth. The same will follow conversely if it is supposed to be in the lower regions: if it is in the lower regions naturally, it will be earth or water, if unnaturally, fire or air.

Moreover, this body will certainly not be without quality or form, which would be impossible. For that[19] is a feature of matter, which is incorporeal,[20] but we have agreed that it is corporeal elements that we are looking for. So if it is something that has qualities, either it will be hot or it will be cold, and either dry or wet.[21] If, then, it is hot and dry, it will be fire, but if hot and wet, air; and if it is supposed to be wet and cold, it will be water, but if cold and dry, earth.

It is not, therefore, from something else that they come to be; so it is from each other. And if from each other, either as pre-existing potentially within each other or as doing so actually. But if they are brought into being from each other as pre-existing actually within each other, the coming-to-be will take the form of separating out, as Anaxagoras' school supposed. This, however, he declares impossible. For if, he says, it is by separating these things out from each other that they are brought into being, air, for example being brought into being from water through homoeomerous[22] particles of air actually pre-existing in the water, and the same with each of the others, either coming-to-be will at some time have to come to a halt, the remaining homoeomerous particles having been used up (I mean air and fire and earth), and the particles of water only remaining, since it will no longer be possible for anything else to be separated out from the 6,1
elements ….[23] So either this result which has been described will come

about, namely, the halting of coming-to-be, or, if indeed you grant that the elements for ever come to be from one another, it will be necessary to posit an infinite number of bodies actually existing in the same thing; and that is impossible.

So it remains that the elements are brought into being from each other in virtue of the fact that they pre-exist potentially in each other. They pre-exist in each other potentially either by being broken up into primary elements which are common to all of them, which some called 'atomic bodies' (like the followers of Leucippus and Democritus) and some 'surfaces' (like Plato); or by being able to change into each other. He showed that it was not by their being broken up into the primary elements. (For it is not possible for there to be atomic bodies. And it is silly, in his view, to <think that you can> break up body into surfaces; for by the same token bodies could be broken up into surfaces, surfaces into lines and these into points, so that bodies would be composed of points, which is the ultimate absurdity.) It remains, therefore, to suppose that the elements come to be from one another in some other way.

Seeking to find the way in which they come to be from one another, he moved to the account of their powers and affections and movements. At the end of the third book he says that it is necessary to go through all the differences which distinguish them from each other; both those <differences> which involve their powers or tendencies and those which involve qualities – both active and passive – are examined. Then, in the fourth book, he discusses heaviness and lightness, which determine their natural movements and the allotment to each of its proper place.

It is his intention to speak about their other differentiating powers too, in respect of which their change into one another takes place, and which serve both to clarify the manner of their coming-to-be from one another and to make evident their number, both how many there are of them and which they are. This being so, it is reasonable for him, before <he deals with> the elements' coming-to-be out of each other, to set out in the first book of the present treatise his teaching about coming-to-be and ceasing to be *simpliciter*, not asking whether there is such a thing as coming-to-be (he has given us his view of this in *On the Heavens*), but explaining what it is and how it differs from the other sorts of change, alteration and growth. Having worked out everything the person giving an account of coming-to-be and perishing in general needed to discover, he next sets himself the task of dealing with the coming-to-be from one another of the simple bodies, which are the elements of all the composite bodies which are in process of coming-to-be and perishing.

Since for the explanation of these things an account is needed of contact, of action and passion[24] and of mixing, he first undertakes an enquiry into these matters. This completes the first book. The second discourse includes his teaching about the elements. He investigates their differentiating characteristics, both active and passive, and by their means, as has already been said, he discovers the manner of 7,1 their coming-to-be from one another and the demonstration that the elements are this many and no more. For from the start, in *On the Heavens*, he took it as agreed that there are four, and left until later the proof of these matters.

< 1.1. MONISTS AND PLURALISTS>

> **314a1** On the other hand, about coming-to-be and perishing of those things that come to be and perish in the course of nature, [in respect of all of them alike ...]

He is right after writing 'coming-to-be of those things that come to be' to add 'in the course of nature'. For some things come to be through <people's> skill or choice: through choice, things like friendships and enmities; through skill, things like houses and ships. But the discussion is not about these, but about the things that come to be and perish in the course of nature. And not just some of these, but, as he says, 'in respect of all of them alike': i.e. the enquiry is general and deals with all the things which come to be and perish. For it is said right at the start that it is not about these or those particular things that the present treatise is concerned, but generally about all things subject to coming-to-be and perishing. For special teaching about parts of this area is given in the treatises which follow, first those which deal with the characteristics of meteorological phenomena, and then others which concern animals and plants.

> **314a2** ... we must distinguish both the causes and the accounts <of them>.

We must distinguish, he says, 'the causes' of the things which come to be and perish, speaking in the plural, not the singular. For the substratum[25] is a cause, and <so is> the form itself and the source from which change begins, i.e. the efficient cause, and that-for-the-sake-of-which is a cause, namely, the end. For he is going to speak about all of these. The phrase 'the accounts of them', despite being in parallel with it, would not mean the same thing, as the connective 'both' makes clear. Rather, some people have understood 'causes' to mean the universal causes common to all the things that come to be (e.g. What is the universal efficient cause of perishing and coming-to-be? What is the matter common to them all? And so on for the rest[26]), and 'accounts' as the particular, proximate causes belonging to each

<kind of> thing. (What is the matter of animals? Answer, perhaps: the four humours. What is the matter of meteorological phenomena, rain, hail, snow, thunder, lightning, winds? Answer: of the first group, namely, rain, hail, dew, snow, the moist exhalation;[27] of the rest, the
8,1 dry exhalation. And in the case of metals, etc.: What is the matter of each? And similarly, what is the proximate, efficient cause for each, and what the form?)

In my view, however, by 'causes' he means the four we have mentioned, whether the common ones or the proximate ones for each of the things that come to be, while by 'accounts' he means accounts in terms of efficient causality of how each thing comes to be or perishes. For instance, it is because the sun moves away and the mist becomes cold that condensation occurs, and this results in a change to water, or, if the cold intensifies, in freezing; and if there is a freezing of water, it produces hail or ice, but if of mist, <it is> snow <that> comes to be. Similarly in the case of lightning and thunder, because the wind trapped in the clouds, or dispersed from the upper part of the clouds by their natural motion in an upward direction, condenses them on that side because they are deprived of warmth, and then through the compression of this part the wind trapped in the lower parts is squeezed out, then, being shot forth and dashed against the clouds which lie on top of it,[28] it produces the sound as a result of the impact, and the lightning as a result of the rapid movement and the friction which sets it on fire.[29]

So it seems that Aristotle calls these explanations of the things which come to be and perish 'accounts'. For it is not enough to say that the wind is the matter of lightning and thunder, nor that the motion of the heavenly bodies is their efficient cause, but one needs to add as well the account according to which, when the one acts and the other is affected, the things that come to be come to be or the things that perish perish.[30]

314a3 And secondly <we must> investigate growth and alteration,[31] asking what each of them is …

The discussion of these matters is both useful to the natural scientist in its own right (for both growth and alteration are natural changes of a kind and themselves types of coming-to-be, as will be explained in what follows) and moreover contributes to the explanation of coming-to-be strictly so called, as he himself makes clear through what he infers <from it>. For whether alteration and coming-to-be are the same or different, as their names differ, is something we shall discover more easily when we have discovered what alteration actually is.

> **314a4** … and whether we are to suppose that the nature of alteration and of coming-to-be is the same [or different, as they are certainly distinguished in name].

Coming-to-be is change in respect of substance from not being to being, whereas alteration is change in something which already has a form in respect of one of its accidents. Thus even Homer uses the word 'alteration' for the change in Odysseus' accidents:

> Stranger, you seem altered now from what you were before. 9,1

Telemachus addressing his father who has been changed by Athena.[32] Notice how he does not say 'other', but 'altered'. For coming-to-be makes something something else, e.g. makes water fire, whereas alteration makes it qualitatively different, for example, makes something white black. So, he asks, are coming-to-be and alteration different only in name, or is there a distinction in reality corresponding to the difference in names?

> **314a6** [Of the old philosophers] some say that what is called coming-to-be *simpliciter* [is alteration, some that alteration and coming-to-be are different.]

Alteration is a sort of coming-to-be, but not coming-to-be *simpliciter* or in the full sense, but, with an addition: <it is> a *sort* of coming-to-be.[33] This is why he added '*simpliciter*'. And first, as his custom is, he gives a survey of the opinions held by the old philosophers about coming-to-be, so that by examining these he may establish his own views. He says that some of them supposed that coming-to-be in the strict sense was the same as alteration, and others that it was different. And he goes on to inform us who the leaders were on either side of this dispute.

> **314a8** Those who say that the universe is some one thing and make everything come to be from one thing [are obliged to say that generation is alteration …]

His aim is to set forth the opinions of <thinkers> of the past about coming-to-be and alteration. What he says is something like this: of the past <philosophers>, he says, some posited one element of all things, some more than one. Those who posit one reduce coming-to-be and alteration to the same thing; but the way this comes about must be explained. Since they laid down that the first element of all is one and that all other things come to be from this, it is absolutely necessary that it should remain the same in substance[34] while it produces the other things; for if it were changed in substance, it would not be the first element, but would have prior to itself something in which the change would have occurred which itself would remain the same and unchangeable – the sort of thing that we ourselves suppose the formless matter to be.[35]

If, therefore, the element exists already possessed of form (as they themselves suppose) and is unchangeable in respect of substance, since there will no longer be a primary element, it remains that the change which it undergoes in producing everything will no longer be change in respect of substance. This being so, clearly it will not be coming-to-be but alteration; for, as I have said,[36] coming-to-be is change in respect of substance from not being to being, whereas alteration is change in something already possessed of form in respect of one of its accidents.[37]

Consider whether we have not been forced to attribute this view to them. For coming-to-be is not of the substratum and the matter, whether it remains unchangeable or not, but of that which is composed of it together with the form. So we too say that coming-to-be is something that arises in prime matter, which remains unchangeable (because the primary substratum must always remain), but nevertheless we produce the elements out of it and the qualities which supervene on it. So what prevents its being the case that we too make the primary element unchangeable without on this account getting rid of coming-to-be? Let it be, then, that it is the coming together of this sort and this number of qualities in the primary element which brings things into being, and that it is in these things that alteration happens later on. Nevertheless, <we shall be in trouble> unless we say this: that we make the primary substratum formless and by the qualities' meeting together give it form and thus produce things, whereas they, supposing it to be possessed of form and unchangeable, * * *[38] since even what is first cannot bring into being from itself some other form while remaining unchangeable, unless the change they ascribe to it occurs in its accidents.

In this way, then, those who posit one element are compelled to reduce coming-to-be to the same thing as alteration, while those who posit more than one element can distinguish between coming-to-be and alteration, supposing coming-to-be and perishing <to be brought about> by aggregation and segregation, alteration by change of position and arrangement, as the followers of Leucippus and Democritus supposed. However, speaking also of *all* those who, by positing more than one element, could preserve both coming-to-be and alteration, he says <that>[39] they did not all in fact preserve them. Empedocles, for instance, though positing four elements, got rid of alteration, since he said that the elements are incapable of being affected and that the qualities that are in them are unchangeable; so that coming-to-be alone is admitted on <Empedocles'> hypothesis, even if in a different manner from that in which we posit it, as will be shown in what follows.

'Those who say that the universe is some one thing': to explain what it means to say that the universe is one, he added 'make everything come to be from one thing', i.e. 'posit one element of all things'.

314a10 ... and that what, in the strict sense, comes to be, alters.

What above he called 'coming-to-be *simpliciter*' he now, with greater clarity, described as 'coming-to-be, in the strict sense'.

314a11 Those who assert a plurality of matter [such as Empedocles, Anaxagoras, and Leucippus – for these it is different.] 11,1

Those, he says, who assert a plurality of matter, speaking of what in their view are the primary elements as 'matter' (for according to them these are matter, since they suppose them to be unchangeable and unalterable) – according to them, he says, coming-to-be is different from alteration. Although he does not say who the people are who hold that the element is one, he did add the names of those who say there are many, mentioning Empedocles (he posited four elements, fire, air, water and earth), and Anaxagoras, who posited an infinity of homoeomers,[40] and Leucippus: for the latter, together with Democritus, posited an infinity of bodies, infinite both in number and in variety of shape. And there are indeed those who make the substratum one, as Thales treats water, Anaximenes and Diogenes air, Anaximander the natural stuff[41] which lies in between air and water and is infinite, and Heraclitus fire.

314a13 In fact, however, Anaxagoras forgot in one passage what he said in another:[42] [he says that coming-to-be and perishing are the same thing as altering ...]

After saying that for those who assert the plurality of the elements of the things which are, it follows that coming-to-be is different from alteration, he blames Anaxagoras for improperly using the word 'alteration' to apply to coming-to-be. For he made the homoeomers elements, which, according to him, are infinite and unchangeable, and he produced coming-to-be[43] by aggregating, segregating and separating out these <homoeomers>, but called <real> coming-to-be and perishing 'altering'.

314a15 … yet like others he says that the elements are many. [For Empedocles makes the corporeal elements four, but in all, with the sources of movement, his elements are six in number, whereas Anaxagoras' are infinite, as are those of Leucippus and Democritus. (Anaxagoras regards the homoeomers as elements, i.e. bone, flesh, marrow, and whatever else is such that we can apply the same name in the same sense to a part of it as to the whole. Democritus and Leucippus say that there are invisible bodies out of which everything is composed, infinite both in number and in variety of shape …]

Next he mentions those who posited more than one element, and amongst whom is Empedocles. He posited, on the one hand, the four bodies as material and, as it were, passive, and, on the other hand, Strife and Love as active and producers of change. Anaxagoras and the school of Leucippus posited an infinity of bodies. But Anaxagoras' are the homoeomers (and he himself[44] goes on to tell us what a homoeomer is, saying that they are the things any part of each of which is the same in name and definition[45] <as itself>. Any part of flesh is flesh, and the same again with bone and sinew, but the parts of a hand and the other anhomoeomers[46] are not the same in name and definition with the whole, for the parts of the hand are not called hands.) Democritus and Leucippus, on the other hand, posited atomic[47] bodies infinite, not only in number, but also in the variety of their shapes, so that it is a consequence of the latter's theories that there is something more infinite than the infinite, because they claim that each of the shapes exists, not in just one atom, but in a plurality <of atoms>.

The school of Epicurus, according to Alexander, ceased in this respect to be in agreement with Democritus: they maintain that in number the atoms are infinite, but in variety of shape indefinite, rather than infinite. But they too are forced to multiply the infinite. For let the number of shapes of the atoms be finite: it is absolutely necessary that each of the shapes exist in a finite number of atoms or in an infinite number. If each shape provides the form for a finite number of atoms, the plurality produced from all of these combined will also be finite. So either it is not necessary that all the atoms have a shape, or, if all of them have shapes, they will be finite in number. It was laid down, however, that they were infinite in number. So it is impossible that each of the shapes should exist in a finite number of atoms.

Either, therefore, each exists in an infinite number, or some of the shapes exist in an infinite number and some in a finite. If they all exist in an infinite number, the infinite will be multiplied; and if some exist in an infinite number and some not, either once again the infinite will be multiplied, even if three only, or two, shapes exist in an infinite number of atoms, or in any case something larger than infinity will exist, even if only one shape exists in an infinite number. For the plurality made up of all of them combined is more numerous than the atoms <grouped> under a single shape. So if each of these is impossible, and it is absolutely necessary that one of them follows, given that the atoms are infinite in number, the hypothesis about the number of the atoms being infinite has to be false.

> **314a23** ... and that they differ from each other in respect of these components, [and in respect of the position and arrangement of these components.)]

What he is saying 'differ from each other' are not the elements, as one might think from the way he speaks, but the things composed of the elements. For the reference of 'they' is not to the immediately preceding subject, but the one further up, I mean, to 'everything else', which indicated the composite things. These composite things, he says, differ from each other in three ways, according to Democritus: first from the fact that the atoms that are their components differ in shape, which his 'in respect of these components' indicates. For fire and earth are not composed of the same atoms, but fire is composed of spherical atoms, whereas earth is <composed>, not of atoms like these, but perhaps of cubic ones.

But the composite things also differ from each other, he says, 'in respect of the position and arrangement' of the atoms. For often the difference between two particular things composed of the same atoms will be in respect of the arrangement of the atoms, in so far as in this one, for the sake of argument, the spherical atoms are put first in order and the pyramidical ones last, but in the other, conversely, the pyramidical ones are first and the spherical ones later, as occurs in the case of the syllables OS and SO. The way in which the same letters[48] are arranged is what makes the difference. Similarly, the difference between the composite things occurs also in respect of the position of the atoms, sometimes being on their sides, sometimes upright, and in other cases upside down: thus the difference between the letter Z and the letter N is only in respect of position, as well as that between Γ and Λ. But it should be recognised that the first of the three differences that have been mentioned, involving things' being composed of different sorts of atoms, makes the composite things other and altogether different things, whereas those which involve arrangement and position <make them> have different qualities, rather than <making them> different things.[49]

314a24 The followers of Anaxagoras and those of Empedocles clearly maintain contrary positions: [the latter say that there are four simple elements, fire, water, air and earth, rather than flesh and bone, and other such homoeomers; but the former regard the homoeomers as simple and elementary, and earth, fire, water, and air as compound, since they are a seed-bed[50] of the homoeomers].

Anaxagoras, he says, held a view about the elements contrary to that held by the followers of Empedocles. For Empedocles says that the four elements are first and most simple, and the homoeomers, bone and flesh, are brought into being by the aggregation of these. But Anaxagoras, conversely, said[51] that the four elements are composed out of the homoeomers; for he said that the homoeomeries[52] of bone and sinew and each of the others belonged to fire and water and the others, since he saw everything coming-to-be out of these. But in the same way that he spoke of homoeomeries of bone and flesh and the others, which we say are composite, so he spoke too of <homoeomeries of> fire, air, water and earth. Indeed everything was in everything, though each thing appeared as, and took its name from, the dominant component. So in fact his view was not contrary to that of Empedocles' followers; for he said that the elements were no more composite than flesh and bone and the others. The difference lies in the fact that Empedocles called the elements principles of the others, whereas Anaxagoras called the homoeomeries principles of everything, and <said> that each thing appeared to be and took its name from the dominant component, since after all the anhomoeomers have to be composed of the principles.

14,1 **314b1** Those who construct everything out of one thing [necessarily identify coming-to-be and perishing with alteration …].

He sets out clearly how, for those who posit one element, alteration is the same thing as coming-to-be, while for those who posit more than one it is something different. Above he had done no more than this:[53] announce what followed from each of the hypotheses. Now he demonstrates just this.

314b3 … for the substratum remains one and the same throughout.

Because, as we have said, the primary matter has to be unchangeable.

314b3 And this is just the sort of thing we call 'altering'.

Namely, changing while the substratum remains one and the same.[54]

> **314b4** Those who allow a plurality of kinds [have to distinguish alteration from coming-to-be, since for them coming-to-be and perishing occur when things come together and separate. Accordingly Empedocles in fact speaks in this way: 'There is no such thing as the birth of anything, but only mixing and separating of what has been mixed.']

He calls the elements 'kinds'. For these people, he says, who posit more than one element, coming-to-be is different from alteration, given that they say that coming-to-be is achieved through aggregation. For the things which are composed of different things are not the same; so aggregation cannot be alteration. Evidence is provided by Empedocles for the claim that coming-to-be occurs through aggregation, when he says that none of the composite things has a nature of its own, but that all these things have their being[55] in the aggregation of the things that are mixed together. For there is no such thing, he says, as the birth[56] of anything, but only mixing and separation of what has been mixed.

> **314b8** It is clear, then, that what they say in speaking thus is in accordance with <their> position ...

Clearly, he says, the statement that coming-to-be is different from alteration is in accordance with the hypothesis that there is more than one element, and clearly they do speak in this way, i.e. maintaining that the elements are more than one. Alexander, however, interpreted this in a way more closely tied <to Empedocles' philosophy>. The statement which claims that coming-to-be and perishing come about in this way, i.e. by segregation and aggregation, is in accordance with the hypothesis that there is more than one element, because they[57] are forced to distinguish coming-to-be from alteration. And clearly Empedocles has said that coming-to-be takes place by aggregation, given his words 'There is no such thing as the birth of anything, but only mixing and separation of what has been mixed'. And the school of Democritus maintained that it was by aggregation of atoms that coming-to-be took place, and perishing by segregation. But Anaxagoras too held that it was the homoeomeries' being separated out and coming together with one another that obviously produced flesh or bone, since the nature of flesh did not so much come to be as manifest itself, when a number of homoeomeries of flesh came together in the same place.

314b10 … and that they do speak in this way;

That they do say that coming-to-be takes place in this way, i.e. in the way described, is clear, he says, both from the line of Empedocles which says 'but only mixing and separation of what has been mixed', and from Democritus' remark about composite things' 'differing in the things out of which they are <composed>'.

314b10 … but they too are bound to admit the existence of alteration [as something other than coming-to-be, although this is impossible according to what they say.]

He has shown that they say that coming-to-be is something different from alteration, since they maintain that it takes place by way of aggregation. He next shows that, while they too are bound to say that alteration exists and is not the same as coming-to-be, it is, nevertheless, impossible in the light of their theories for alteration to exist. This is a point which he makes, not now equally against all those who bring about coming-to-be by aggregation, but specifically against Empedocles. First, however, he shows that it is necessary <for him> to say that alteration exists and is something distinct from coming-to-be, then that by their own arguments[58] they abolish alteration.

314b12 It is easy to see that this statement of ours is correct. [For just as, whilst the substance stays the same, we see change in it in respect of size – what is called growing and getting smaller – so we also see alteration.]

He shows that they are bound to say that alteration <exists>, moreover as something distinct from coming-to-be, and why they are bound to say this, and that it is impossible according to their own remarks for alteration to exist. This is how he shows it. In the same way that we can see, and it is evident, that change of size occurs without substance being lost, it is equally evident that change of quality occurs without substance being lost; but this is what alteration is. So they are bound to admit that alteration exists because it is evident. He goes on to show that it is impossible according to the arguments of Empedocles' own <theory>.

This is Alexander's interpretation <of the passage>. But it is possible to interpret differently the remark 'they too are bound to admit the existence of alteration', and what follows. Those who posit more than one element, <Aristotle> says, are forced by their hypothesis to introduce alteration, as something distinct from coming-to-be and perishing, since they explain these by aggregation and segregation, as has been said earlier, but alteration by something other than the explanations involving aggregation, sc. by position and arrangement. Nevertheless, he says, although the hypothesis makes room for both things, coming-to-be and alteration, some <philosophers>, Empedocles being one of them, have produced theories of a kind which make it impossible to preserve alteration. For the qualities,[59] in terms of which the change which is alteration is explained, are said by him to be the differentiating features which endow the elements with their forms, supposing the elements to be imperishable and unchangeable.

'It is easy to see that this statement of ours is correct.' 'This statement' <refers to the claim> that, although their[60] hypothesis contains the idea both of coming-to-be and of alteration, he himself put forward theories which abolished alteration. Then, intending to show that by what he says Empedocles abolishes alteration, he first recalls what alteration is, namely, change in a substance which remains the same.[61] He uses the parallel of growth, in his remarks 'For just as, whilst the substance remains the same,[62] we see etc.' He takes growth to be evident and <its existence to be> admitted by everyone. For against alteration, perhaps, someone might fight against the odds, as Protagoras did, saying that nothing whatsoever had a determinate nature, but that the differences between sensible qualities were relative to the state of the perceiver. But no one could argue against growth, since it is quantitative change of the underlying substance which remains unchanged, from which it is possible to infer the conclusions about alteration.

> **314b15** But nevertheless it is a consequence of what is said by those who posit more than one principle [that alteration is impossible. For the affections, in respect of which we say that alteration occurs, are the specifying characteristics of the elements; examples are hot and cold, white and black, dry and wet, soft and hard, and each of the others, just as Empedocles says: 'The sun is white to see and hot all over, but rain is dark and cold all through'; and he similarly assigns qualities to the other elements. If, therefore, it is impossible for water to come into being from fire or earth from water, it will be equally impossible for anything to come to be black from white or hard from soft, and the same reasoning will apply to the other qualities; but precisely this is what constitutes alteration.] 17,1

He begins to explain how those who posit a plurality of principles in their theories deny alteration through what they say. For they say that 'the affections, in respect of which we say that alteration occurs, are the specifying characteristics[63] of the elements', and being their specifying characteristics, they always remain with the elements to which they belong. For the specifying characteristics are, according to them, unchangeable and incapable of being affected.

Not all those who posit a plurality of principles deny alteration: only Empedocles. Setting out the remarks in which Empedocles makes this point, where he assigns whiteness and heat to the fiery body and to the Sun (for he thought that celestial things were made of fire), and blackness and coldness to water, he says that he makes similar claims about the other affections, e.g. wetness, dryness, density, and, in a nutshell, the rest of the affections – 'similar' in the sense that they are the differentiae of the elements and give them their specifying characteristics, themselves remaining the same.

So, according to Empedocles, as has been shown, alteration does not exist. According to Anaxagoras the homoeomeries have these affections as their specifying characteristics,[64] while according to the school of Democritus the specifying characteristics of the elements are their shapes, and they are insusceptible of the other affections, like heat and cold, whiteness and blackness, etc., in which the composite things merely seem to participate in virtue of their relation to us. As for these affections, which they seem to us to have, but which do not really[65] exist in bodies – some of them correspond to the bodies' being constituted by the aggregation of atoms of certain kinds, as heat seems to belong to fire from the spherical atoms which compose it on account of the ease with which spherical objects can be moved (for it is this ease with which it penetrates <things>, caused by the fact that a sphere moves around a point, which, in his view, makes heat seems to exist, as, conversely, the cube <accounts for> cold by its solidity and the difficulty with which it is moved). Other affections, without change in the aggregated bodies, maintain the appearance of change as a result of change in the position or arrangement of the atoms, which we say corresponds to alteration. For the same body seems at one time white and at another time black, or cold or hot, according as the atoms in the composite body change their position or their arrangement.

Of course fire always seems to stay the same, because the atoms out of which it is composed, even if they change their position, always have the same relation to us on every side owing to their being spherical. Now things made of triangular <particles> are not like this, since they will have the bases on the outside and the apices on the
18,1 inside, or vice versa. But all affections generally, both those that are always retained, like heat in fire, and those which are changed from time to time in different ways, only, in their view, seem to be there, but are not really[66] present in any way in bodies.

314b26 This[67] shows that it is always necessary to posit a single matter for contrary qualities, [whether the change that occurs is locomotion, growing and getting smaller, or alteration.]

The substratum in respect of each change he calls 'matter'. Having shown how those who say there are many elements deny alteration, he next infers this as a corollary. For if the reason why Empedocles cannot admit alteration is his supposing that the primary substances are unchangeable, and yet alteration is an evident fact, there must therefore be some one thing which persists and changes from contrary to contrary. So if there is such a thing as alteration, and change in general, the substratum is one, and if the substratum is one, there has to be such a thing as change. For the things which are are not all of one kind, as obvious facts bear witness. So if there is one substratum, clearly it is this which changes in respect of the contrary qualities. And he regarded this argument as applicable without distinction to every sort of change.

314b28 Furthermore, it is equally necessary for this to exist and for alteration to exist; [for if there is alteration, both the substratum is a single element and there is one matter for all things capable of changing into one another, and if the substratum is one there is alteration.]

He says that the existence of the common substratum and that of alteration are equally necessary. That is to say, as it is necessary to posit a common substratum, so it is necessary also to posit alteration, since each is implied by the other, alteration by the common substratum, and the postulation of the common substratum by <that of> alteration. He adds the words 'for all things capable of changing into one another' on account of the celestial bodies, for he has in mind the fact that the latter change only in respect of place.

315a3 Empedocles seems to contradict both the phenomena and himself. [At one and the same time he maintains *both* that none of the elements comes to be from any other, whilst everything else comes to be from them, *and* – when he has gathered together the whole of nature except Strife into one – that from this One everything once again comes into being. Clearly, then, it is by their being separated out from some one thing by various differentiae and affections, that one thing came to be water, another fire, just as he calls the sun white and hot, the earth heavy and hard. So if these differentiae are removed (and they are removable, since they came to be) obviously earth must come to be from water and water from earth, and similarly with each of the others, not only then, but also now – given that they change in respect of their affections. And that they can be added and again removed follows from what he said, particularly since the battle between Love and Strife still continues. Which is why they were generated then too from one thing.]

After explaining the consequences of positing just one element, namely, the failure to distinguish coming-to-be from alteration, and those of positing many, namely that this hypothesis implies recognition of a difference between coming-to-be and alteration, even if <the thinkers in question> did not themselves notice this and did not distinguish between coming-to-be and alteration, he especially reproaches Anaxagoras with forgetting in one passage what he has said in another, by calling coming-to-be and perishing 'alteration',[68] and again now he especially attacks Empedocles too for contradicting both the phenomena and himself. He contradicts the phenomena by denying the existence of alteration, which is an obvious fact, and he contradicts himself because he says on the one hand that the elements are unchangeable and do not come to be from one another but other things from them, and on the other that under the domination of Love all things become one and produce in the end the Sphere which exists without qualities, so that in it neither the particularity of fire nor that of any of the other <elements> is retained any longer, since each of the elements loses its particular specifying characteristic, so that it is clear that he supposes that it is possible for the differentiae which are the specifying characteristics of the elements to be lost by them.[69]

Again, from the same considerations which led him to say that they can come to be, he infers that they can be separated. He says that they come to be when, after the Sphere has come to be and all things have come together in it, Strife again becomes dominant. Then, he maintains, out of the Sphere, which is a single and undifferentiated body, the four elements come to be, evidently through the addition to the one of certain differentiae [and affections],[70] some in one part of it, some in others, and these enable the elements which come to be out of it to be marked off from one another. So if they have come to be, they could be removed, 'particularly since the battle between Love and Strife still continues'.

So they could also come to be from one another. For if the body of fire, which was first in the Sphere in an unsegregated state with no demarcation between it and anything else, has later after receiving the differentiae become fire, so the differentiae of fire too could have come to exist in any other part of the Sphere where, let us suppose, the differentiae of water and earth and air have now come to exist, in exactly the same way as, by coming to exist in this part of the Sphere, they produced the fire. This being so, it is clear that it is in their nature to change into one another. For this is what it is for the elements to be able to change into one another, namely, that the differentiae which are the specifying characteristics,[71] now of this, now of the other <element>, should be able to come to be in turn in one and the same substratum.

For it cannot be said that the very same body of fire which joined the others in the coming-to-be of the Sphere later itself received the differentiae of fire and has become fire. For this is a random matter: the Sphere was undifferentiated body, specifically identical[72] with itself, and a common substratum for everything. For if someone were to say that it was not possible for the differentiae which are the specifying characteristics of each element to come to be in any part of the Sphere whatsoever, it would be clear that he is not maintaining that the body of the Sphere is undifferentiated, nor that it is one but is bestowing different peculiarities on different parts of it, which cause fire and none of the others to arise in this part and something else in another part. So, if he supposes that the body of the Sphere is altogether undifferentiated, and that, in turn, now Strife is dominant and produces the elements, now Love is dominant and produces the Sphere, it is absolutely necessary on these suppositions for all the elements to change into each other.

315a18 For the universe was not, presumably, fire *and* earth *and* water when it was one.

When, he says, 'the universe', i.e. the Sphere, 'was one', there was neither fire in it nor any of the others in actuality, since it would no longer have been one; but it is clear that each of the elements was divested of the being that belonged to it, and that all combined to produce the single being of the Sphere.

315a19 It is not clear whether one ought to make [the One or the Many] the principle – [that is to say, fire, earth, and the others in the list. In so far as it is like the underlying matter out of which earth and fire come to be by a process of change caused by the movement, the One seems to be elementary; in so far, however, as the One comes to be through the coming together of the Many, and they through its breaking up, it is they who are more elementary and prior in nature.]

Again, he brings objections against Empedocles on the grounds that he posits things which do not accord with each other. It is not clear, he says, what sort of thing one ought to regard as a principle on the basis of what he says, whether the Sphere is the principle of the elements or they of the Sphere. In so far as the four elements come to be out of the Sphere, as if out of some matter without qualities,

<serving as> a common substratum, changing and receiving their specifying characteristics[73] in accordance with the change caused by Strife – thus far he would seem to cast the Sphere in the rôle of principle and matter (for the first principle has to be without qualities). But in so far, conversely, as he said that the Sphere comes to be from the combination of the four elements being aggregated by Love, and these from the dissolution of the other, one might cast the four elements in the rôle of principle. For it is the property of a principle to be simpler, and the elements are simpler than the Sphere that is composed of them; for the Sphere is composite with these as its components.

<1.2. INFINITE DIVISIBILITY>

> **315a26** Our subject then is coming-to-be and perishing *simpliciter* considered generally, [whether or not there is such a thing and how it exists.]

He has discussed the opinions of his predecessors about coming-to-be, both those who reduced it to alteration and those who distinguished it. He now returns to his proposed topic, i.e. the account of coming-to-be, and takes up the question whether coming-to-be exists, and the way in which it exists, and the question of the other natural changes. For the discussion of these is particularly necessary, since we find none of the philosophers of the past saying anything on these subjects which deserves discussion.

None of the earlier philosophers, then, has left an account of the complete set of natural changes, i.e. coming-to-be, growth and alteration. Plato, however, had something to say, but only about coming-to-be, and not every sort of coming-to-be, but only that of the elements (for he produces them from surfaces), but he has nothing further to say about how the composite things come to be from the synthesis of these. The proof of the fact that Plato gives an account of the coming-to-be of the elements but none of coming-to-be in general, is to be found in the impossibility of extending his account of the coming-to-be of the elements to cover the coming-to-be of flesh and bones. For he says that the elements have come to be from triangular surfaces; but, although he proposes to speak about the coming-to-be of bones, he does not in fact go on to explain it in terms either of the combination of surfaces, or of that of the things which come to be from the surfaces, i.e. the elements. For he says, 'The Demiurge shaped pure earth and kneaded it to make it smooth and moistened it with marrow. Then, after this, he places it in fire, and after *that* bathes it in water, and again in fire, and again in water; and by transferring it in this way frequently from one to the other he rendered it insoluble by either.'[74] But marrow, from which together with earth he makes bone, is neither an element nor a surface. It is change of quality and affection which produces bones, and quality and affection cannot be produced from the surfaces. <Aristotle> is going to say himself in a later passage 'They do not even[75] attempt to produce an affection from the surfaces',[76] because the specifying characteristics of the elements are their shapes, not qualities or affections.

Without bothering to raise objections to this theory, since it is absurd, Aristotle says that <Plato> has said nothing at all about the coming-to-be of bones, since, if Plato did say something of this sort, it is altogether implausible in the light of the appearances. For if marrow were prior to bone, it too would necessarily have been bone: Plato himself at all events calls marrow 'bone-begotten',[77] in so far as it has its being in the latter. So before bone came to be, bone was. Moreover, be it never so true that the Demiurge made the said original bone in this way, the bones that come to be naturally in animals do not come to be in this way. So Plato had this much and no more to say about coming-to-be, and of the others no one had anything to say, 'except superficially, apart from Democritus'. For <Democritus>, he says, more than any of the others can be seen to have given thought to everything and posited principles which he could apply to everything.

> **315a27** And about the other movements,[78] [e.g. growth and alteration. Plato investigated only coming-to-be and perishing, and how they apply to objects; nor did he treat of every case of coming-to-be, but only that of the elements; there was no discussion of the case of flesh or bones or the rest of the things of this sort, nor yet of alteration and growth and the way in which they apply to objects. Altogether no one seems to have paid attention to any of these things except superficially, apart from Democritus. He seems to have given consideration to them all ...]

He uses the word 'movements' in place of 'changes'.[79] For coming-to-be, as he says himself in the *Physics*,[80] is a change, but not a 22,1
movement. And he uses one case in place of another, the accusative in place of the genitive; for he ought to have said 'about the other movements (genitive)'.[81] This is a mode of speech found in archaic writings, e.g. in Homer:

> Leaders in mourning, who the echoing sound[82]

in place of 'Leaders of mourning'. Aristophanes too in the *Ecclesiazusae*:[83]

O pourer of gold, as for the bottle which you made,
While my wife was dancing in the evening,
The stopper has fallen out of the mouth.

He uses the accusative 'as for the bottle' instead of the genitive 'of the bottle';[84] for the stopper had fallen out of the mouth of the bottle.

315a35 ... but it is in the 'how' that he really excels. [For none of them laid anything down about growth, as we are saying, beyond what the man in the street may have to say, namely, that things grow by the accession of like to like. There was still no discussion of how this is effected ...]

By 'in the "how" ' he means 'in the way'. For though he postulates <that> both coming-to-be and alteration <occur, he does> not hold that they occur in the way in which we[85] do, but thinks that coming-to-be exists by way of aggregation and segregation, and alteration by change of position and arrangement. About growth too the others said just what might be said by the man in the street – nothing more and nothing less – namely, that growth comes about through something being added (but on how it is added, whether through channels or by way of a body passing through another body, they have nothing further to say; for all these give rise to problems, and the same problems arise in connection with acting and being acted upon, in what way the one acts and the other is acted upon), but he has more to say later in the book about Democritus' findings on the subject of growth.[86]

315b4 ... nor about mixing, [nor, practically speaking, of any of the other topics such as action and passion – how one thing acts and another is affected by natural actions. But Democritus and Leucippus, having got the figures, get alteration and coming-to-be from these: coming-to-be and perishing by their aggregation and segregation, alteration by their arrangement and position.]

Either mixing is the same as mingling (mingling is, for example, what happens in the case of liquids, when different masses lie side by side and their qualities work on each other and spread through each other), or else mixing covers more cases than mingling. One sort of mixing is mingling, as in the case of wine-honey, another is juxtaposition, as in the case of the *panspermia*,[87] and another is interlocking, as in the case of matter and form. The person who is discussing coming-to-be needs to say something about these things too, in order to know in what way that which comes to be does so, and whether any of these are needed for coming-to-be or not.

315b9 But since they thought that truth <lay in> appearing [and that the appearances were infinite and contrary to each other, they made the figures infinite]. 23,1

According to him, their view is that every appearance is true, and that as each thing appears to be, so it actually is, but, as the same thing often gives some people contrary appearances, the followers of Democritus are able on their own principles to preserve the view that such appearances relating to the same object are still true, by assuming that the shapes of the elements are infinite. For by dint of altering their arrangement and exchanging positions these things offer a different appearance at different times to different people even in the case of the same object in virtue of their relation to, and their distance from, the observers. Thus the neck of a dove, struck by the sun's rays, offers an appearance of different colours. Corresponding to different positions of the eye it appears to some blue, to others gold, to others black, and other colours[88] to other people. Of shapes also, squares appear rounded from a distance, and a disk placed at a distance, if we observe it end on, is seen by us as straight. Honey appears bitter to the person with jaundice and sweet to the healthy; and Z is seen either as Z or as N according to its relation to the person looking at it.

315b11 So by the changes of the compound thing [the same thing seems to give contrary appearances to different observers.]

By 'compound' he is not referring to the composite thing, but to that which puts the composite thing together.[89]

315b13 The admixture of a small particle would effect a transposition, and if one component were transposed, he says, <the compound> would appear utterly different.

Not only does repositioning and rearrangement of the atoms alter the appearance of what is seen, but another relationship and a different appearance comes into being corresponding to the outflow of atoms from the composite things and their impact on those who see <them>. This at least is how Alexander interprets it. But perhaps it might be said that this fits change by way of growth; for the followers of Democritus claimed that growth and diminution took place through the outflow and admission of atoms, and they said that this change was not apparent, as it is in alteration. In the <case of> outflow, a small particle flowing out makes the whole different. If you remove just the 'im' from 'impossible', you produce 'possible'.[90] Thus a small outflow has made what is left the contrary of what you started with.

24,1 **315b14** For comedy and tragedy come to be out of the same letters.

This is an illustration of what he has just said. The same letters[91] rearranged in this way and that produce results that are widely divergent, viz. tragedy and comedy.

315b15 Since almost all of them think that coming-to-be and alteration are different, [and that whereas things come to be and perish by being aggregated and segregated, they alter by having a change in their affections. So we must concentrate on these topics in our thinking; for they include a number of well-argued dilemmas. For if coming-to-be is aggregation, many impossible consequences follow. But again there are compelling arguments on the other side, which it is not easy to escape from, that it cannot be otherwise; and if coming-to-be is *not* aggregation, either there is no such thing as coming-to-be at all or it is alteration – or else we must try to escape this dilemma too, difficult though it is.]

Since, he says, the majority (for <this is true of> both Democritus and Leucippus, and Anaxagoras and Empedocles as well) thought coming-to-be and perishing <took place> by way of segregation and aggregation, and made a distinction between this and alteration, as do the followers of Democritus, it is necessary to treat of these <philosophers>; for their account raises a number of problems. Many absurdities will follow from the supposition that coming-to-be occurs through aggregation; for we will abolish the affections and the continuity of bodies. And it is not easy to refute the arguments which set out to prove that 'it cannot be otherwise' than by aggregation that coming-to-be exists. Moreover, in addition to the strength of the arguments which tend to show that coming-to-be is aggregation, and the difficulty of refuting them, if we actually make the assumption that coming-to-be is *not* aggregation, it becomes doubtful whether there is any such thing as coming-to-be at all, or, if there is, whether it is not the same thing as alteration. So this too must be examined, despite the difficulty there is in solving these problems.

315b24 Basic to all this [is the question whether the things there are come to be and alter and grow and undergo the contrary of these things because the primary existences are things which have size and are indivisible, or whether nothing which has size is indivisible; this makes a great deal of difference.]

Basic, he says, to the proposed enquiry whether coming-to-be is or is not aggregation is the examination of the possibility of atomic bodies' existing. If there are such things as atomic bodies incapable of being affected, coming-to-be will necessarily take place by aggregation. If, on the other hand, it is not possible to posit the existence of atomic bodies, whilst the necessity for coming-to-be to take place by way of aggregation will be removed, the impossibility of its doing so will not be entailed. For if atoms do exist, coming-to-be necessarily takes place by way of aggregation; but if atoms do not exist, aggregation is not got rid of altogether. For coming-to-be could take place by way of aggregation even if elements were not atoms, as Empedocles' theory shows. So if atomic bodies do not exist, all that goes is the necessity 25,1
that coming-to-be should take place by way of aggregation, and the necessity having gone, the question of greater plausibility will now have its place. Since, therefore, affirmation of the existence of the atoms entails acceptance of the view that coming-to-be takes place by way of aggregation, while denial of the atoms does not entail denial that coming-to-be takes place by way of aggregation, it is reasonable for him to say, in respect of the proposed investigation of the question of atoms, that it makes 'a great deal' of difference, rather than that it makes all the difference.

315b28 And again, if they do have size, <are they bodies,> as Democritus [and Leucippus teach, or planes, as in the *Timaeus*?]

For the investigation of coming-to-be it is necessary to enquire into the existence of atomic things possessed of size, and if they exist, the question immediately arises whether they are bodies, as in Democritus, or planes, as in Plato. Then, having alluded to the absurdity of this view (he has discussed it at greater length in the account given in *On the Heavens*),[92] he passes on to the question whether there can be indivisible bodies, as alleged by Democritus. He says that this theory involves a great deal of absurdity; nevertheless, in comparison with Plato's theory it comes out as much more persuasive and much more scientific,[93] since Democritus' theory can save both coming-to-be and alteration, whereas Plato's, by making planes the principles of bodies, might be thought somehow to save coming-to-be, but does not even begin to attempt to produce quality and affection.

He goes on to set out the reasons why the principles which Democritus proposes are more persuasive than those in the *Timaeus*. Study of mathematics, he says, has made philosophers of this school inexperienced in scientific matters,[94] and with this 'lack of experience' he contrasts 'being at home with nature', i.e. having had much experience of it.[95] For the followers of Democritus, having trained themselves well in scientific matters, put forward principles better able to preserve agreement with what happens in nature. To corroborate what he has said he develops the arguments of both sides, by use of which they attempt to prove that there are indivisible things possessed of size; and he shows the marked superiority of Democritus' arguments over those of Plato where persuasiveness is concerned, and that the absurdity of the latter is manifest, whereas those of Democritus are difficult to refute.

315b30 This latter doctrine, as we have explained elsewhere, is in itself unreasonable – to halt the analysis at planes. [Thus it is more reasonable to hold that what are indivisible are bodies, but a great many unreasonable consequences are involved here too.]

By 'this' he means either that it is absurd to analyse bodies so far, i.e.
26,1 until you arrive at planes (for it is impossible for the division of bodies to proceed thus far), or that it is absurd, if you are analysing bodies into planes, to stop at this point and not analyse these into lines and lines into points. For the same relation obtains between body and surface as between the latter and line and between this last and point. In this case everything will turn out to come from points. He has given his response to this theory in *On the Heavens*, Book 3.[96]

315b35 [But these philosophers are able, as has been said, to produce alteration equally with coming-to-be by transposing the same thing] in respect of position and order[97] [and by the differences between the figures, as Democritus does. (This is why he says there is no such thing as colour: position determines colour.) But this is not similarly possible for those who analyse bodies into planes; for when these are put together, nothing comes into being except solids; for they do not even attempt to generate any affection from them.]

Rhusmos, tropê and *diathêkê* belong to the dialect of Abdera,[98] and they are used by Democritus, who calls shape *rhusmos*, position *tropê*, (e.g. the base of the pyramid's being underneath and the apex on top; or vice versa) and order *diathêkê* (the fact that these <atoms>, for instance, come first and these others later). It has earlier[99] been said that, in <Democritus'> view, the aggregation of the shapes effects coming-to-be, whereas their transposition and rearrangement effects what appear as affections. For it was his teaching that colours and other affections were nothing in reality: it is by *tropê* that he says colouration occurs.

316a7 [The cause of comparative inability to see the agreed facts as a whole is inexperience. That is why those who are more at home in physical investigations are better able to postulate the sort of principles] by which they are able to connect together a wide range of data ...

By making use of principles of this sort, they are able to connect together and explain a wide range of natural phenomena. If the *hai* were written without the *s*,[100] 'are able to' would be being predicated of the principles, i.e. 'The principles are able to connect together a wide range of data'.

316a8 ... those whom much attention to concepts [has diverted from study of the facts come too readily to their conclusions after viewing a few facts. One can see from this too how much difference there is between those who employ a physical and those who employ a logical mode of inquiry.]

By 'concepts'[101] he means mathematical <concepts>, since they have being only in thought. Those, he says, who have studied mathematics, from lack of experience of existing things, i.e. of things that have subsistence[102] and existence, for example natural things,[103] easily jump to conclusions about their principles, and thus are easily refuted.

316a12 [Concerning the view that there are indivisibles which have size,] the latter say 'Because[104] <otherwise> the Triangle itself will be many', [whilst Democritus seems to have reached his conclusions from more germane, i.e. physical, considerations. What we are saying will be clear as we go on.]

Plato used these arguments to show that there were atomic things possessed of size. If, he says, every thing possessed of size is divisible, the Triangle itself, i.e. the idea of the triangle, will also be divisible; and thus there will be things prior to the Triangle itself, into which it can be divided. That is impossible – that there should be something prior to the idea. If therefore the Triangle itself is not divisible, it is not the case after all that every thing possessed of size is divisible. So if not every thing possessed of size is divisible, there will be some things possessed of size which are indivisible. There is nowhere where Plato is known to have said this, that there are atomic things possessed of size, but either Aristotle is reporting this from unwritten lectures,[105] or, what is more likely, these are arguments put forward by people who claim to be Platonists. For it is improbable that Plato, who was such a practised mathematician and knew that it was possible for any given straight line to be cut in two, would say that there were indivisible things possessed of size, unless he was saying that the triangles were indivisible in this way, namely that they could not be changed and dissolved into other shapes. For all the rectilinear figures can be broken up into triangles (the square can be cut into two triangles by the diagonal, and the pentagon into three, and the others in the same way).

However, the triangle itself is not divided into other figures, but into straight lines. So perhaps it is in this sense that he was saying that there were indivisible things possessed of size.

To this argument one should reply that the idea of the triangle is not a thing possessed of size at all, but the concept of a thing possessed of size. So this <concept> is, arguably, indivisible, but what we are saying is that things possessed of size are divisible. And there is no need for there to be an indivisible thing possessed of size just because the concept of *thing possessed of size* is indivisible.[106] For there is no need for things to be exactly as their concepts are, since the thought of the house and the concept with which the builder builds it are incorporeal, but the house is not incorporeal.

> **316a14** A dilemma arises if one maintains that there is some body possessed of size which is everywhere divisible, [and that this is possible. For what will there be to survive the division?]

He sets out on one side the arguments which led Democritus to posit atomic bodies, and goes along with the persuasiveness and reasonableness of the opinion. He makes an initial assumption, saying that it is the same thing for the division of the continuous to go on to infinity and for the continuous to be able to be divided everywhere simultaneously, and from this he derives absurdity in the following way. If it is possible for each of the parts[107] that are continually coming into existence as a result of the cutting again to be further divided, clearly the body is everywhere divisible. If the body is everywhere divisible, he says, that is, that it is possible for it to be everywhere divided, it is possible for it to be everywhere divided simultaneously. Everything that is in potentiality can be supposed without absurdity to have come about in actuality; for, generally speaking, if one supposes that what is in potentiality has come about in actuality, falsehood will[108] follow, but not impossibility.

So, if it is not impossible, let us suppose that it has been everywhere divided. But if it has been everywhere divided, the thing possessed of size[109] will have been divided, not into things possessed of size, but either into points or into nothing. For if it has been divided into things possessed of size, it would no longer be the case that it had been divided everywhere. But if everywhere, it will have been divided either into points or into nothing, and will be composed of these. For everything is composed of the very same things into which it is divided. So the thing possessed of size will be composed of nothing or of points, which is absurd. So it is not possible that the thing possessed of size should have been everywhere divided. If so, then there are some things possessed of size which are atoms.

Such, then, is the line of argument. If saying that the thing possessed of size is divided into nothing or into points[110] entails that the thing possessed of size is composed either of points or of nothing, he proves that this is in every way impossible, namely, that a quantity should come to be out of points. For if the points are added to the quantity, they make it neither greater nor less; for we see that when a given quantity is divided into a number of <different> ones, so that a number of points come to be in actuality (for points are the limits of that which is divided), and is put together again, the whole does not become any larger in being put together, nor in being divided does it become smaller than it was in the beginning before it was divided. And if this number <of points> is not going to make the thing possessed of size larger by being added to it, since that which is without parts and has no size does not have it in its nature to produce something possessed of size, obviously, even if all <the points> in the thing possessed of size into which, by our supposition, it has been divided are put together again, it will not produce something possessed of size.

And in general it is not possible to produce any quantity by putting point together with point. For it is necessary either that the points that are being put together touch each other in respect of the whole of themselves, or that they touch each other in one respect and not in another. If, on the one hand, it is in respect of the whole <of themselves> that they coincide, all will again be one point. But if, on the other, they are united by touching in respect of one part <of themselves>, but do not touch in respect of another, the point will have a part and will not be without parts, which is impossible, because we 29,1
shall be destroying the concept of a point.[111] After making these remarks, let us return to the text.[112]

316a17 For if it is everywhere divisible, and this is possible, it might be at one and the same time in this divided state, [even though the divisions had not taken place at one and the same time; and if this were to come about there would be no resulting impossibility.]

If, he says, it is everywhere capable of being divided, it might at some time be divided everywhere at once. Now there is nothing absurd in supposing that what can happen has come about in actuality; for it does not have the impossible as a consequence, as he says further on, because, if we suppose the thing possessed of size to have been divided 'ten thousand times into ten thousand pieces', even if it has not yet been <so> divided, nor perhaps could ever be, owing to the weakness of the dividing agent, the supposition is not impossible, nor yet absurd. So it is not absurd to suppose this. But he understands 'being everywhere divisible' as entailing 'being at one and the same time everywhere divisible', and we must recognise that it is here that the argument goes astray, as he goes on to demonstrate. For the statement that the continuum is divisible *ad infinitum* does not entail that it is at one and the same time everywhere divided; for, generally, the statement that the process of cutting up a thing possessed of size never comes to an end but will increase[113] *ad infinitum* seems to leave no room for its having been everywhere divided at one and the same time. For once it is divided, the process of cutting up *ad infinitum* comes to an end. This will be examined more closely in what follows, where he himself sets out the difficulty that attends on the solution.

316a19 And in the same way by bisection [or by any method whatsoever, supposing its nature is to be everywhere divisible, if it has been divided, nothing impossible will have happened; since even if it is divided ten thousand times into ten thousand pieces nothing impossible follows, albeit no one would, perhaps, so divide it. Since, therefore, the body is everywhere such, suppose it to have been divided. What then will be left? Something possessed of size? That is impossible; for there will then be something which has not been divided, but *ex hypothesi* it was divisible everywhere.

Well then, if no body or thing possessed of size is left, though division does occur, it will be the case either that the body is formed out of points and the things out of which it is composed are without size, or that they are nothing at all; so that it would both come to be out of nothing and be composed of nothing, and the whole of itself would presumably be nothing else than appearance.]

It applies generally too, he says, if it is in the same way both everywhere divisible and at the middle. This is explicative of 'division occurs everywhere'. For at any time each part which comes to be from the division can again be further divided at the middle. This is why, by way of making the point more clearly and giving it a more comprehensive interpretation, he continues 'or by any method whatsoever, supposing it to be everywhere divisible, if it has been divided, nothing impossible will have happened'.[114] For if what is possible is supposed to occur, a falsehood may perhaps follow, but nothing impossible. For example, it is possible for it to rain in summer: if therefore we suppose that it rains in the summer, we may perhaps be supposing something false, but not impossible; and if not impossible, it could occur; and if it is possible that it should occur, it would actually occur over a long period.[115]

> **316a29** Similarly if it is composed[116] out of points, it will not have quantity; [for when the points were in contact and there was just one thing possessed of size and they were together, they did not make the whole the slightest bit larger.]

Just as that which is formed out of things that are not would not be[117] something which is, so too if something is composed out of points, which is the same as to say 'out of things without parts', it will not have quantity; for points do not have quantity. For when they were together in the thing possessed of size in its undivided state and were united, i.e. what he calls 'touching', the thing possessed of size did not come to be in any degree larger because of them. It is to provide a demonstration of this that he proceeds to his next remarks.

> **316a31** For when it is divided into two or even more [parts it was not the slightest bit smaller, nor indeed larger, than it was before. So even if all the points are put together they will not produce size.]

When the continuum, he says, is divided into a number of parts and put together again, neither will the whole be larger in the united state because the points have come together, nor will it be smaller in the divided state. And this is true even though he actually says both things in each case; for neither in the joining together nor in the dividing does the whole become either greater or smaller, which shows clearly that the addition of the points contributes nothing to <any> increase in a thing possessed of size, nor the division to <any> decrease. So even if they were put together that would not create <any> quantity or thing possessed of size.

> **316a34** Again, even if something like sawdust comes into being during the division [of the body, and in this way some body gets away from the thing possessed of size, the same argument applies: how is the new body divisible?]

Just as when wood is being sawn up particles of sawdust come to be, which, although they are corporeal, cannot be sawn up further, and the whole comes to be smaller on account of these being worn away, if someone were to make a similar suggestion in the case of things being divided, so as to say that the divided thing is used up in the production of tiny particles, the same argument applies. For the sawdust particle, given that it is not a point but a thing possessed of size, will itself be divided, if that which is possessed of size is everywhere divisible. And if it is not divided, Democritus' statement is true, namely, that there are atomic bodies, and that it is from the aggregation of these that other things come into being, and that a thing possessed of size is not everywhere divisible.

> **316b2** And if it is not body but inseparable form [or affection which has got away, and the thing possessed of size consists of points or contacts affected by this, it is absurd that something with size should be formed out of things which lack size.]

Or 'separable'; for both readings are found.[118] 'Inseparable' means being incapable in itself of subsisting in separation from a substratum, but existing always in the compound, like all the enmattered forms. If, however, 'separable' were what was written, it would mean something which by its nature can be separated when its substratum perishes. Both readings have the same force and refer to the same thing.[119] This argument differs from the previous ones, because ear-
31,1 lier he took something possessed of size, and dividing it discovered that points were left from which a thing possessed of size could not come to be. Here, on the other hand, he says that if someone were to suppose that a thing possessed of size were put together, not out of things possessed of size, but out of points which take to themselves in the <process of> putting together some form and affection and thus produce something possessed of size, the said form or affection being separated in the division so as to leave the points behind, the same absurdities would follow, namely, the production of something possessed of size from things not possessed of size.

And if someone is at a loss to know how he infers this as something absurd, namely, producing something possessed of size from things not possessed of size (for body is also made to come to be from things that are not bodies by those who say that prime matter accomplishes the production of body by taking form to itself)[120] – let such a one recognise that if we do say that bodies are put together from matter and form, it is not from matter which has previous existence by itself that we say body comes into being. For it is only in thought that we separate it from form and consider it in its own right, since it is never capable of subsisting by itself. For it is always by such and such a body changing into such and such that the coming-to-be and perishing of bodies takes place, and in general, matter and form belong to the category of relatives and neither can exist in separation from the other. Those who say that the points are left behind from the division after the form has been separated off, as well as generating something possessed of size from sizeless things actually pre-existing in an sizeless state, also resolve something possessed of size into sizeless things actually subsisting by themselves; and this is absurd. Moreover, even if matter is incorporeal by its own definition, nevertheless it is potentially body, existing everywhere without form, whereas points are not without form, nor do they have size potentially, nor can they be the substratum for something else, since they themselves need another thing in order to exist; for they have their being in a line, not having existence by themselves. So how will something possessed of size find in them the ability to exist?

316b5 Furthermore, where[121] will <the points> be? And will they be motionless or in motion?

This sentence can be construed both as a question and a statement. As a question, in this sense: What kind of place[122] or what kind of motion will you assign to the points? Neither the <place> above (for they are not fire or air), nor the <place> below, since they are not water nor yet earth. And in the same way you assign them neither motion nor immobility. For if they were immobile, they would not, after being divided, come together to produce coming-to-be. If, however, we suppose them to be in motion, first, it is absurd for something in motion not to be body; and next, what sort of motion will they have assigned to them? The argument is the same as that with respect to place.[123] If, however, you understand the sentence as a statement, you
will be saying that it is necessary for them to be somewhere. For if 32,1
they do not occupy a place when they have come to be from the dissolution of a body, <the space> which was occupied by the body which has been resolved into them will be a vacuum. But this again is impossible. For how are these incorporeal and completely unextended <points> to occupy a spatial extension?[124]

316b6 And any one contact always involves two things, [since there has to be something else besides the contact or division or point. If, then, someone asserts that a body, whatever it may be and whatever its size, is divisible at every point, these consequences will follow.]

Every contact is a limit, but not every limit is therefore also a contact. So if you call positions and points 'limits', it is impossible for there to be a limit without there being something which is limited; and if <you call them> 'contacts', they will be contacts of things that are in contact. The fact that the things that are in contact are different from the contact or the point or the division (for these all mean the same) is shown by the contact's being one while the things that are in contact are two. The argument, then, can be understood in this way, as indicating that it is impossible to resolve body into points. But it is also possible to understand the argument as directed to establishing that it is not possible by putting together points to produce something possessed of size. For how is it at all possible for them to be put together, since they are unable to touch one another? For things that are in contact touch one another in respect of some part of themselves, so that there are parts of them over and above the <part that is in> contact, but points cannot touch one another in respect of some <part of themselves>.

316b9 Moreover, if I divide a piece of wood and put it together again, [it will once more be equal and one thing. So it is clear that the same thing happens if I cut the wood at any point whatsoever.]

He further establishes this by means of an argument he used earlier,[125] namely, 'A thing possessed of size comes to be by the putting together of the things into which it has been divided'. For he accepted earlier the point that if it is into points that bodies are divided, the putting of these together again produces something possessed of size. So he provides further support for the view that this must necessarily be the case by giving an illustration. For, if I take some wood or some other thing possessed of size and make a division in a certain part <of it>, and then put it together again, that which comes to be from the putting together of the divided portions comes to be equal to the original.

In just the same way, if I divide the wood everywhere (for it is given that it is possible for it to be divided everywhere) so that there is nothing <left> other than points (for he uses the word 'division' to describe the points at which the division and the cutting takes place), it will be necessary that, just as with the earlier cutting, when the parts into which it is divided are put together what is produced is equal to the original, so too, if I divide it everywhere so as to leave nothing but points, then, when the points are put together, they make what is put together out of them equal to the original divisible thing 33,1 possessed of size. But this has been shown to be impossible. For even if an infinite number of things without parts are put together, they are unable to produce a thing possessed of any size whatever. So it is not possible for things possessed of size to be divided into points. If so, things possessed of size are not everywhere divisible; for their being so entails their being divided into points. And if they are not everywhere divisible, there are indivisible bodies.

> **316b11** So potentially it is divided everywhere. [What, then, is there besides the division?]

His quickness of thought has led him[126] to a compressed mode of expression. What this means is this: If the thing possessed of size is potentially divisible everywhere, let this division be carried out in actuality. For the supposition is not impossible; it has already been said that the possible may at some time actually come to pass. Given this, there follows the absurd consequence that has been mentioned, namely, that things possessed of size be composed of points.

> **316b12** For even if there is some affection, [how, notwithstanding, is the thing broken up into these, and how does it come into being out of these? And how are these separated? So if it is impossible for things possessed of size to be formed out of contacts or points, there must needs be bodies and things possessed of size which are indivisible.]

Again he takes up what had been said before. For if, he says, there is some affection in the continuum, how[127] will the thing possessed of size be resolved into these, i.e. into an affection and points? And how can it be composed of these? How is it possible for these to be separated out from each other so that the points subsist apart from the affection? For suppose they are related as matter to the affection, and this in its turn is their being, as is intended by the theory that holds things possessed of size to be composed of points and affections: well then, matter, in so far as it is matter, being something relative, cannot exist apart from the form of which it is the matter, as we said earlier. So it is impossible for points to exist by themselves apart from form.

> **316b16** However, consequences just as impossible follow for those who posit these. Discussion of this it to be found elsewhere.

[Nevertheless a solution has to be attempted: so we shall have to state the dilemma once more from the beginning.]

There is a discussion of the many absurd consequences entailed by
34,1 the theory which posits indivisible things possessed of size in *On the Heavens* 3,[128] *Physics* 4,[129] and also in the work entitled *On Indivisible Lines*,[130] which some attribute to Theophrastus. But now, he says, the problems raised by Democritus must be solved, which he uses to refute the division *ad infinitum* of things possessed of size. So it must be noted that his purpose now is not directly to prove that there are no indivisible things possessed of size (for the impossibility of this theory is demonstrated in the books just mentioned), but to refute the arguments by which indivisible things possessed of size are introduced. So he summarises Democritus' argument and <then> articulates it more fully, and in this way reaches the refutation <of it>.

316b19 There is nothing absurd in the view that every perceptible body is both divisible at any point whatsoever and undivided, [for divisibility will belong to it potentially and undividedness actually. Being simultaneously everywhere potentially divisible would seem, however, to be impossible.[131]]

His purpose is briefly to recapitulate the difficulty that has been set out in a variety of ways so that he can in this way produce the solutions. And first he distinguishes the way of taking the statement that body is divisible everywhere according to which the aforementioned absurdities follow, from the way of understanding it in which it entails nothing absurd. Naturally he makes this distinction first in order to show which signification the phrase 'everywhere divisible' must bear if absurd consequences are to follow so that he can direct his solution against the argument taken in this sense.

To summarise, the points made by the passage as a whole are of this sort. The sentence 'The continuum to be everywhere divisible' has two meanings: (i), which signifies that it is divisible in any part, i.e. it is not the case that it can accept division in this part <of itself> but not in <some> other, but everywhere without distinction, since there is nothing in the continuum to prevent the division. For even if it accepts division in actuality in this part first, the division which exists in potentiality in another part and which has not so far taken place none the less could have taken place earlier than the one which has already been performed. To put it briefly, that body is said in this sense to be divisible everywhere which is able to accept all the divisions, where 'all' is taken as meaning 'any one you like out of all of them', not 'all simultaneously'. It is as though one were to say that a man is capable of acquiring every science: one would not mean that

he can succeed in all of them simultaneously, but rather in any one of all of them, not specifically in this or that. Understood in this way, he says, nothing absurd follows if we suppose that which is undivided in actuality to be divisible everywhere *qua* being capable of accepting 35,1
division in any part <of itself>. For if it is understood in this way, it does not follow that a thing possessed of size is simultaneously divisible everywhere.

This (ii) is the second significance of the phrase 'divisible everywhere', namely, that the body is 'simultaneously everywhere potentially divisible', which is impossible. For it cannot come to be divided simultaneously everywhere in actuality, and that which, if it is supposed to happen, implies the impossible, did not in the first place obtain in potentiality either. That it is impossible for anything to be simultaneously divided everywhere in actuality is clear from this: if division takes place at positions[132] and points, and no point is next to another point, but, given that you take any two points there is always a thing possessed of size between them, it is quite obvious[133] that it is impossible that something should be simultaneously everywhere divisible. It was by taking the phrase 'everywhere divisible' in this sense that Democritus constructed his *reductio ad absurdum*, making difficulties for the supposition he had made himself, not refuting the one that was in question.

When these things have been thus stated, a doubt might still, perhaps, be raised about what we are saying when we say that a thing possessed of size is in potentiality divisible *ad infinitum*. For it is on this basis that the proposition 'It is everywhere divisible' is understood, as we have already said in our earlier discussion.[134] For if in potentiality it is divided *ad infinitum*, it is possible for it to be divided *ad infinitum*, and it is not impossible to suppose that that which can take place should actually come about. So we shall introduce the actual infinite, which is absurd. The division of continuous <things possessed of size>, then, will not go on to infinity, but will come to a halt somewhere. So there will be indivisible things possessed of size.

The solution of the problem is easy for those who have made the appropriate distinction in advance, as is done in the *Physics*.[135] Aristotle says there that we say that a day is present, not in virtue of its being present as a whole, but in virtue of a part of it always being present, and that we say that a sports match is actually present, not in virtue of wrestling and boxing and running and jumping and the rest all being performed simultaneously, but in virtue of some part of it being present, either some jumping or other or wrestling or one of the other events. Just so, we say that a thing possessed of size is divided *ad infinitum*, not in virtue of an infinite number of segments of it being able to come to be simultaneously subsistent, but by taking some <different> segments from the infinite number of segments and

<different> parts of the infinite.[136] The segments that are taken at any given moment from the division of continuous are limited, but from the fact that those that have been taken can again be divided, the division is said to go on *ad infinitum*, because the division does not give out and because there is no part that is taken which is not capable itself of accepting division. In this way we also say that
36,1 number can be increased to infinity, not in virtue of its being able by being increased to come to be infinite in actuality (for whatever number you take is always finite), but because, while its increase never gives out, it is always possible to take another one greater than the one that is being taken.

If we are to observe clear distinctions in our speech, <we should say that> the thing possessed of size is not divisible *into* an infinite number <of pieces>,[137] even in potentiality, since the division into an infinite number of pieces can never take place (given that one point cannot even come next to another point, for that which is between two points is always a thing possessed of size). However, <we can say that it is divisible> *to* infinity,[138] because the division in potentiality never gives out. This, then, was the sense in which we spoke of the thing possessed of size as being 'everywhere divisible', in that it could be divided in every part <of itself> and there being no part we could take that would be indivisible in potentiality. For this is why it is possible for division to occur indifferently anywhere at all, on account of no part being indivisible in potentiality.

As for being simultaneously everywhere divisible and being divisible into an infinite number of pieces,[139] both <these claims> are false. For the one implies that the thing possessed of size is divided into points and is composed of points; and <the other, namely,> that it is divisible into infinity, <implies> that the infinite is indeed actually subsistent, which is absurd. For the infinite exists *qua* coming-to-be and never reaches the stage of existing *qua* subsistent. He himself puts this another way in the *Physics*,[140] saying that attaching 'whole and all <there is>' to 'infinite' is not attaching linen to linen, because that which is 'whole and all <there is>' is complete, and that which is complete has an end,[141] whereas the infinite has no end. That is 'whole and all <there is>' outside of which is none of its parts, whereas that is infinite outside of which there is always something . So 'all there is' and the infinite are not the same. When we say 'everywhere divisible', therefore, we show by the very expression we use that we are not saying that things possessed of size are divided up into an infinite number <of pieces>,[142] but into a finite number, each of the parts being itself everywhere divisible.

We seem, he says, when we say 'everywhere divisible', to understand the 'everywhere' as meaning that nothing remains undivided as a result of the division, which is false and the contrary of what is said by us.[143] For we say that a thing possessed of size is divisible to infinity, and everywhere divisible in this sense, namely, that every part you take can be divided and that <procedure> never gives out. If, therefore, it were so divided as to allow division to give out through there being nothing left that was capable of being divided, it would no longer be divisible to infinity. For that which <goes on> to infinity never gives out. So if it gave out, it would not <go on> to infinity, nor would it be everywhere <divisible> in the sense that a part that results from the division[144] can always itself be divided.

<What about the remark> 'There is nothing absurd in the view that every perceptible body is both divisible at any point whatsoever and undivided'<?> He said 'perceptible', i.e. physical, not implying that the other bodies are not also divisible (for the mathematical <body> is also like this), but because it is with this that the argument is concerned. Or else by 'perceptible' he means 'existing in actuality'; for that which does not exist in actuality is not divisible. This is how matter is, according to his own definition; for it too is body, only not perceptible <body>, but body in potentiality. Intending to recapitulate Democritus' problem in a summary manner, he first determines the sort of meaning 'everywhere divisible' must have if nothing absurd is to follow and the sort of meaning it must have if it is to imply the absurdities which are derived <from it> by Democritus. And he says that it is true to say that that which can be divided in any <part>[145] whatsoever is everywhere divisible even if it has not yet been divided, and that this has nothing absurd following from it. (For that which is undivided in actuality can in this way be said to be everywhere divisible. It is clear from the fact that you can take a point anywhere at all on the continuum that there will be a <possible> division too in every part of the continuum.) On the other hand, it is absurd to say that <a thing is> everywhere divisible, *qua* capable of being divided everywhere simultaneously. And he again adds his account of how it is absurd and why, recapitulating Democritus' problem. And then, later, he produces the solution, saying that Democritus had committed a fallacy by not refuting the thesis that a thing possessed of size is everywhere divisible, but understanding the phrase 'everywhere divisible' according to some private interpretation of his own.

316b23 For if it were possible, it could come about (not so as to be simultaneously both these things [in actuality, undivided and divided, but so as to be divided at any point whatsoever). There will then be nothing left and the body will have vanished into something incorporeal, and could come to be once more, either out of points, or absolutely out of nothing. And how is this possible?]

This, he says, is absurd, namely, saying that <something> is simultaneously divisible everywhere in potentiality. For if it is so in potentiality, it could come about in actuality too – come about, not in such a way that it would be divisible in the same respect both in potentiality and in actuality (for that is obviously absurd and needs no argument <to show its absurdity>, to suppose the same thing <to be> simultaneously undivided and divided). What I mean, he says, is that if it is simultaneously divisible everywhere in potentiality, it could be translated into actuality, so that it would be divided into points. This is the meaning of 'divided at any point whatsoever'. And he goes on next to indicate the extent of the absurdities which follow from supposing that a thing possessed of size is divided into points, going back to Democritus' difficulty. The extent of the absurdity is the same as it was when he began discussing the issue at the start. For if, he says, it is supposed to be everywhere divided simultaneously there is nothing left, except that the corporeal has passed away into the incorporeal. And since a thing is composed out of the same things as those into which it is divided up, he adds that if it were divided up into what is incorporeal, i.e. into points, it would be <a thing> composed of points; and if <it were divided up> into nothing, it would be <composed> out of nothing.

316b28 In fact, of course, it is divided into separable bits, always having smaller [and smaller size as you go on dividing, at a distance from each other and separated.]

This *reductio ad absurdum* disposes of the statement that maintains that body is everywhere simultaneously divided, by showing that this implies that things possessed of size are composed of points or of
38,1 nothing. He now accepts as obvious, arguing as it were on behalf of Democritus, the view that division always takes place into separable, i.e. subsistent, things possessed of size. For even if the division takes place into segments always smaller in size, <it will> nevertheless <be> into things which are subsistent and can subsist by themselves. And if this is obvious, quite clearly the divided <portions> will not simultaneously be infinitely many, nor <will> the division <proceed> to infinity, since there are not infinitely many separable parts in finite things possessed of size. And 'always' in this context (for the remarks are taken from Democritus' summing up of his discourse) does not mean 'to infinity',[146] but it is always divided up into smaller <pieces> 'up to this point',[147] as he puts it in what follows, namely, up to the point where the division comes up against atoms.

316b29 But neither, it is claimed, could division into parts yield a process of disintegration which went on to infinity, nor could the division occur simultaneously at every point, [for this is impossible, but up to a certain point.]

He has already explained why this is impossible. For if it is divided in this way, whether all at once or even piece by piece, it will be divided into points and will be composed of points. But this is impossible. And since it is impossible for a body to be divided at every point, division will not go on *ad infinitum*. For if it were divided into points this would be likely to be the result, because the points that are in a thing possessed of size are potentially infinite in number. Since, therefore, the division does not proceed to infinity and is not <a division> into points, it remains that the division must come to a halt somewhere and atomic bodies be left which can be divided no longer.

316b32 So there must exist[148] atoms possessed of size which are invisible,[149] if indeed coming-to-be and perishing exist[150] by aggregation and segregation respectively.

The interpretation of the text is somewhat obscure. It will appear that what he is saying is this: given that coming-to-be and ceasing-to-be take place by way of aggregation and segregation respectively, it is necessary that there should also be things possessed of size which are atoms. But contrariwise the <existence of> atoms should support the view that coming-to-be takes place by way of aggregation. But, while the aggregation account of coming-to-be does indeed follow from the postulation of things possessed of size which are atoms, there is no necessity to postulate things possessed of size which are atoms, given that coming-to-be is by way of aggregation. Of course it is the existence of atoms that the Democritean argument is thought to prove, not that coming-to-be exists by aggregation. So the theory that coming-to-be exists by aggregation must be derived from the existence of atoms, not the other way round as the text seems to indicate.

It is necessary, therefore, to understand the text in a simpler fashion as arguing in this way: 'So there must exist atoms possessed of size', and then, after heavier punctuation as if from a different starting point, '<So>[151] if indeed coming-to-be and perishing exist by aggregation and segregation respectively'. Or in this way: 'So there must exist atoms possessed of size, <and from these> if indeed coming-to-be and ceasing-to-be exist, which is evident, the one <will be> by segregation and the other by aggregation'. He said that the atoms were 'invisible things possessed of size' to avoid refutation on the basis of what is perceived. For none of the things possessed of size that are apparent <to us> is indivisible. So he said that the atoms are invisible to us on account of their size. And there is nothing surprising in the idea of something that exists, but owing to its small size is not seen. It is like the particles of dust in the air which are invisible to us until, when a ray of light from a window falls on them, they become visible in it because of the brightness of the light.

316b34 This, then, is the argument which seems to make it necessary that there are atoms possessed of size. That it contains a hidden fallacy, and where the fallacy is hidden, is what we must now explain. [Since no point is contiguous to another point, being everywhere divisible in one sense belongs to things possessed of size and another in which it does not. When this is asserted, it is thought that there is a point both anywhere and everywhere, so that the magnitude has necessarily to be divided up into nothing; for because there is a point everywhere, it is formed either out of contacts or out of points.]

He has set out the argument for the proposition that there are atoms and has shown the sense in which 'everywhere divisible' has to be taken if the absurd consequences are to be drawn.[152] It remains for him to supply the solution to the problem by exposing the fallacy on the grounds that it proceeds by using an idiosyncratic interpretation of 'divisible *ad infinitum*'. Once again he sets out the different meanings of the expression 'everywhere divisible'. He says that one of the things meant cannot possibly exist, while the other can. Being 'everywhere divisible', he says, 'in one sense belongs to things possessed of size' and in another it does not. It does not belong – and it is by understanding it in this sense that Democritus constructs his *reductio ad absurdum* – in the sense of being divisible everywhere simultaneously. This is impossible, he says, for the reason that there is no point contiguous with another point. Aristotle takes this to be evident. Indeed it is conceded by the school of Democritus. It is against this that they constructed their *reductio ad absurdum*. But if someone is looking for a justification of this too – I mean of there not being any point contiguous with another point on the continuum, and generally of the thing possessed of size not being composed of points – we must address ourselves to him also.

The points which, according to the hypothesis, compose the thing possessed of size must of necessity be supposed either to be arranged in sequence without there being any question of there being a finite distance between one and another,[153] or to be at a distance from each other, or in one respect to be at a distance from each other while in another be in contact,[154] or to be touching each other with respect to the whole of themselves. If they are at a distance from one another,

they will not be joined together and will not constitute a thing possessed of size. If, however, they are at a distance from one another in one respect and in contact with one another in another respect, they will have parts (but *ex hypothesi* the points are without parts). 40,1
But if they touch each other with respect to the whole of themselves, two points will coincide with one another * * * [155] if all the points out of which the thing possessed of size is held to be composed coincide in this way, the whole thing that is possessed of size will be a single point. So it is impossible for point to be contiguous to point, but this is implied by the hypothesis that a thing which is possessed of size is divisible everywhere simultaneously in such a way that no part which can itself also be divided is left out of the division. For point is not contiguous to point, as has been proved: rather, between any two points whatsoever there is a thing possessed of size. A thing possessed of size, therefore, could not be everywhere divisible in this sense, since the aforementioned absurdities will follow <if we suppose this>. How then, and for what reason, will the property of being everywhere divisible belong to the continuum? The reason is that anywhere at all in the continuum there is a point in potentiality. And if it is possible to find a point anywhere at all in the continuum, it is also possible that division should take place anywhere at all in the continuum. It is in this sense that a thing possessed of size could be said to be everywhere divisible, in so far as it can be divided anywhere.

317a8 [In one sense there is a point everywhere], because there is one anywhere and all are like each one.

That is to say, if someone makes a single cut, he is able to do this anywhere. He says 'one', because it is not possible to find another one next to it. Furthermore, it is possible to perform all the divisions, not in the sense of making them 'all simultaneously', but in the sense of 'anyone whatsoever of them all'. This is what he means by 'all are like each one', i.e. not *this* any more than *this*, and as with any one 'this', so with all the others as well. Each of all <of the divisions> can come about in the same way. Just so indeed a man is capable of acquiring each of the whole collection of the sciences.

317a9 But there are no more than one, [since they are not consecutive …]

There are no more than one consecutive <points>,[156] as is clear from the reason he adduces.

317a9 … so not everywhere.

Add to it 'simultaneously'; for it is not divisible everywhere simultaneously.

> **317a10** For if it is divisible at the middle it will also be divisible at a contiguous point. [For position is not contiguous to position or point to point, and this is division or junction.]

He now constructs a proof to show that it is not everywhere divisible
41,1 in such a way that nothing is undivided. But the text does not fully indicate what is meant. It would be clear and simultaneously the argument would be stated in full if what was said was 'If the continuum were divisible everywhere simultaneously in such a way that nothing of it was left undivided, being divided by bisection or in any other way, it would be divided also at a contiguous point'. And it would have remained <only> to infer the consequence <of this>: 'but this is impossible'. But, although he does not infer this impossibility, he next adds why it is impossible for it to be divided at a contiguous point, saying 'for position is not contiguous to position, and this is division or junction'.[157] That is to say, supposing position to be contiguous to position is no different from saying that a thing possessed of size is merely division and junction and is no longer divided into things possessed of size or composed out of things possessed of size.[158] You could understand the text in this way as relevant to what follows: for it is not possible, he says, for it to be divisible everywhere simultaneously. Why? Because position is not contiguous with position. 'This' means the position,[159] and the division and composition of things possessed of size corresponds to this position. Obviously, if these were not next to each other – the positions, I mean – it would not be divided everywhere simultaneously.

> **317a12** So segregation and aggregation exist, but not into and out of atoms, [since this leads to many impossibilities, nor in such a way that division can occur everywhere (for this would be what would happen if point were contiguous to point), but into smaller and yet smaller parts, and aggregation out of smaller <into greater>.]

It is clear, he maintains, from what has been said, that there is indeed such a thing as aggregation, although there are no things possessed of size which are atoms. He has shown that things possessed of size are both aggregated and segregated. But it is not necessary, given the existence of aggregation and segregation, that on this account things possessed of size which are atoms should exist; nor, if there is aggregation and segregation, will the thing possessed of size also be everywhere divisible in such a way as to come to an end in points or in nothing. But aggregation is always from smaller things possessed of size to larger, and segregation from larger to smaller, and neither to atoms nor from atoms. For many absurdities follow from the supposition of atoms: alteration in the proper sense, continuity, and corresponding affection[160] will all at once be got rid of.

> **317a17** Nevertheless, coming-to-be *simpliciter*, i.e. absolutely, is not defined by aggregation and segregation, as some say, nor is alteration change in the continuous. This is just where all the mistakes are made. [Coming-to-be and perishing *simpliciter* occur, not in virtue of aggregation and segregation, but when something changes from this to that as a whole. These people think that all such change is alteration, but there is in fact a distinction.]

The existence of aggregation and segregation he grants, as something obvious. However, he does not concede that coming-to-be, properly so called, is produced only by aggregation, as is claimed by some, who 42,1
maintain that coming-to-be and perishing are aggregation and segregation, and that alteration is change in the continuous. Those who offer these definitions are mistaken on all counts. For not all change of the continuous is alteration, but it can be coming-to-be. (There is change both of water into air and of lead into white lead, which remain continuous throughout and do not involve segregation or aggregation.) Nor do segregation and aggregation in every case involve coming-to-be and perishing. For if you segregate <the parts of> lead by cutting it up fine, and then reverse the process by melting them and thus bringing them together, you have not brought about coming-to-be or perishing. So what is coming-to-be and what is alteration? – this is what he will teach us next.

> **317a23** For within the substratum there is something which corresponds to the definition and something which corresponds to the matter. [When, therefore, the change takes place in these it will be coming-to-be or perishing: when it takes place in the affections, accidentally, it will be alteration.]

In each thing, he says, there is something which corresponds to the form and something which corresponds to the matter. So when change takes place in respect of these, that, he says, is coming-to-be not alteration. Change takes place in respect of these when the matter is affected in some way and, losing its previous form, changes to another. Change in respect of these is coming-to-be and perishing; but if these remain and the thing changes in respect of one of its accidents, this is alteration.

317a27 However, things do become <more> easily corruptible as a result of being aggregated and segregated: [for instance, the smaller the particles into which drops of water are divided the sooner they become air; if they are aggregated the process is slower.]

Coming-to-be, he says, is not the same as aggregation, nor is segregation the same as perishing, but they do contribute to coming-to-be and perishing. Both <when it is> poured out and <when its parts are> segregated water is more quickly turned to air: for example, if someone pours a little water on to a table. In this way it becomes more susceptible to being affected. And air, when <its parts are> aggregated and <it is> condensed, is more easily converted to water.

317a30 [But this will become clearer in the following pages: it is enough now to have determined the point] that coming-to-be cannot possibly be aggregation – not of the sort some people say it is.

This is in opposition to the view that <coming-to-be is> out of atoms. Again in what follows he will say that in general coming-to-be is not aggregation.

<1.3. COMING-TO-BE *SIMPLICITER*>

43,1 **317a32** Having settled these matters, we must first consider whether there is anything which comes to be *simpliciter* and perishes …

He has refuted Democritus' arguments designed to establish the existence of atomic bodies and has proved that it is not necessarily by way of aggregation and segregation that coming-to-be and perishing take place, and that once this <idea> is dismissed, alteration and coming-to-be will not turn out to be the same. These are all things which he originally set out to investigate. Following on this he says that one must enquire whether, in general, there is such a thing as coming-to-be *simpliciter*, that is, whether there can be a coming-to-be of substance or not. For coming-to-be understood in the strict sense and without any addition – this he calls coming-to-be *simpliciter*. Is there then, he asks, such a thing as the coming-to-be of substance, or does nothing come to be *qua* substance, and is there neither coming-to-be nor perishing of substance? Is it only the accidents of substances which come to be, things which are said to come to be, not *simpliciter*, but with an addition? It is in this sense that that which <comes to be> healthy from being sick comes to be, and that which <comes to be>

large from being small. In all these cases certain accidents come to be attached to, or detached from, some underlying[161] substance. So he is enquiring, as I said at the beginning, whether there is coming-to-be and perishing only of the accidents, but in no way of substance. For the person who wants to explain how coming-to-be and perishing take place ought first to show whether there is such a thing as coming-to-be at all. It would be stupid to go on to explain the second if the first had not been established, just as it would be if someone undertook to construct a proof of the immortality of our body without previously showing that it was in general susceptible of immortality. So in this way here too, before explaining how the coming-to-be and perishing of substances takes place, he deals first with the problem of the very existence of the coming-to-be of substance.

Wishing to make us alert to possible objections and to prevent our accepting unexamined whatever may happen to be said, he first of all attempts to get rid of coming-to-be by means of various persuasive arguments, attempting to prove that there is no such thing. Then, in finding a way out of this difficulty, as a result of the solution itself he encountered another difficulty, only to add a third difficulty; and having enquired how it comes about that coming-to-be never ceases, from his solution of this third difficulty extracts a solution of the second.

He enquires, therefore, to begin with whether there is such a thing at all as the coming-to-be of substance, since it gives rise to this problem: if there is coming-to-be of what is *simpliciter*, given that everything which comes to be X comes to be from what is not-X, the coming-to-be of substance (for this is what coming-to-be *simpliciter* is) will be from that which *simpliciter* is not. But '*simpliciter*' has two meanings: (i) what is first in each category, that is to say, the universal and common genus of each category,[162] and (ii) that which is common to all the categories. When we say that that which comes to be *simpliciter* (i.e. substance) comes to be from that which *simpliciter* is not, we mean either (i) 'from what is not substance', that is, something which is not included in the genus, substance, or (ii) 'from what in no sense and in no way is'. If someone were to say that it is from what is not substance that the things which come to be *simpliciter* come to be, clearly, given that there is no substance there will be no quality or quantity or any of the other categories either; for none of the others apart from substance can subsist. So there will be nothing to serve as the point of departure for the coming-to-be of substance.[163] If, on the other hand, by 'that which *simpliciter* is not' you mean 'what is denied equally of all the categories', and it is from this that the coming-to-be of substance takes place, that which in no sense and in no way is will once again have to serve as the point of departure for the coming-to-be of substance. So whichever interpretation you take of 'that which *simpliciter* is not', the same absurdity results.

In fact 'that which in no sense and in no way is' is not speakable or thinkable, as Plato says in the *Sophist*.[164] For if it were speakable or thinkable or subsisted only in the imagination, like, say, Scylla or the goat-stag, it would not be something that in no way was, since it *is* sayable or imaginable or thinkable. So from what is not in this way, how could anything come to be? Because of this it has been a common opinion amongst scientific writers[165] that nothing comes to be from what in no way and in no sense is.

After raising this difficulty, he provides the solution, saying that that from which that which comes to be *simpliciter* comes to be, is in one sense something which *simpliciter* is not and in another sense something which is *simpliciter*, where what he is hinting at is the matter, for it is this which in one sense *simpliciter* is not and in another is *simpliciter*. In the sense that it is actually nothing, it *simpliciter* is not: in the sense that matter is potentially everything, it could be *simpliciter*. And in this way coming-to-be is from what is. When I say that it 'is actually', this must be understood as meaning 'in existence', since matter, which potentially is everything else, *is* actually matter. For if it were matter too <only> potentially, it would no longer be matter.

Having solved his problem in this way, he generates another problem out of the solution. When, he says, we spoke of the coming-to-be of substance as being from what is potentially substance but actually is not substance, we set ourselves the question whether this 'substance in potentiality' participates in actuality in any of the other categories, or in none. If it does, the affections <of things> will be separable, that is, capable of actually subsisting outside actual substance. If it does not participate in any of them, there will be something subsisting which exists as nothing in actuality, i.e. this formless matter will be something subsisting in its own right,[166] which is absurd.

In this way he poses the problem and brings the discussion to an impasse. Then, before telling us his solution he tacks on another problem – a thing he has a habit of doing often – and by means of his
45,1 solution of the second problem solves the first as well. The second problem goes something like this: How does it come about that there is never an end of coming-to-be? For if, he says, that which perishes vanishes into that which is not, how is it that it has not come about long ago that the things that are have all been used up, bringing an end to coming-to-be? It was proved in the *Physics* that all bodies are limited, both in number and in magnitude.[167] So if that which perishes vanishes into that which in every sense is not, in an infinite time the Universe must give out. What then is the cause of the continuing

sequence?[168] It is the material cause which he is looking for: What do the things that come to be have as their matter, as that which explains the fact that coming-to-be never gives out? Is it, he suggests, because instead of that which perishes vanishing into that which in no way and in no sense is, the perishing of one thing is the coming-to-be of another?

This provides us with the solution for the earlier problem as well. For if the coming-to-be of one thing is the perishing of another and the perishing of one thing is the coming-to-be of another, it is obvious that we are not compelled to suppose that matter exists actually, that is, as a subsisting thing, separate from all form. For it is always <matter> previously occupied by some form that gets rid of the earlier form and changes to another, and what happens is the perishing of the earlier one and the coming-to-be of its successor. So that which is subsistent and existent in reality[169] is already possessed of form[170] and a composite thing of matter and form, and change is not in respect of both of these. For it is not that which is composed of matter and form which underlies coming-to-be and perishing, but the formless matter alone. That is why it is reasonable for us to speak of the coming-to-be of substance as being from matter, which is potentially substance, and of that which comes to be *simpliciter* <as coming-to-be> from that which *simpliciter* is not. For it is as substratum that matter is that from which the coming-to-be of substance <takes place>. Having given these matters preliminary consideration, let us proceed in our examination of the text.

> **<317a32>** ... or whether in <this> strict sense <of 'come to be'> there is nothing which does so, but it is always a case of coming-to-be something from being something. [What I mean is, for example, coming-to-be well from being ill and ill from being well, or small from big and big from small, and all the other cases following this pattern.]

It has already been explained[171] that by 'that which comes to be *simpliciter*' he means 'that which <comes to be> by way of substance' (we say that which comes to be by way of substance 'has come to be' *simpliciter*, without addition: 'A man has come to be', 'A horse has come to be'), whereas 'that which comes to be something' is '<that which comes to be> by way of accident', because we do not express the coming-to-be of accidents without an addition. For when a man, for example, changes in colour, we do not say that the man has come to be, since having come to be *simpliciter* and without addition signifies change in substance, but we say that he has come to be something, say pale or dark. The addition is what shows the difference, e.g. 'The man has become pale', 'Socrates has become musical'.

To show what 'something from being something' means for him he adds 'well from being ill and ill from being well'. So if 'something from 46,1 being something' expresses coming-to-be by way of accident, clearly 'that which comes to be *simpliciter*' signifies that which comes to be by way of substance. For coming-to-be by way of substance is opposed to coming-to-be by way of accident.

> **317b1** For coming-to-be *simpliciter* would involve something's coming-to-be from not being *simpliciter*, so that it would be true to say that[172] not being belongs to some things: [coming-to-be something is from not being something, e.g. from not being white or not being beautiful, whereas coming-to-be *simpliciter* is from not being *simpliciter*.]

He sets out the difficulty which might lead one to suspect that there was no such thing as coming-to-be *simpliciter*. The way in which the difficulty is brought out is something like this: If what comes to be comes to be from something, and from what is not such (for whatever comes to be comes to be from what is not like this, pale from not pale, hot from not hot), and generally speaking, if each thing comes to be from its own denial, it is obvious that that which comes to be *simpliciter* also comes to be from its own denial, that is, from what *simpliciter* is not. If so, then that which *simpliciter* is not is and subsists. For this is what 'not being belongs to some things' means, i.e. 'There belongs[173] to some things not being *simpliciter*', as if one were to say 'Not being an animal belongs to a man'.[174]

> **317b5** *Simpliciter* can signify either what is first in each category of being or what is universal [and includes everything. If the former, generation of substance will be from what is not substance; but where neither substance nor individuality belongs, neither, of course, does any of the other categories, e.g. quality, quantity, or place, for that would mean affections' existing in separation from substances. If, on the other hand, 'not being *simpliciter*' means not being generally, this will amount to a universal denial of everything, so that that which comes to be must needs come to be from nothing.]

That which *simpliciter* is not in each category and that which comes to be from that which *simpliciter* is not are, in his view, said *simpliciter* not to be either[175] because they do not happen to fall within the category under which the thing which comes to be is arranged, e.g. that which *simpliciter* is not in <the category of> quality is that which cannot be subordinated to *quality*. For <the phrase> 'what is first in each category' is indicative of the highest genus. For it is that which is most generic which is first in each category. For the <genus> of pale is colour, that of colour is affection, that of affection is quality, which is what is first in this category. That, therefore, which *simpliciter* is not in <the category of> quality is that which is not such-and-such,[176] and that which comes to be from what *simpliciter* is not is that which does not come to be from the such-and-such. For that which comes to be pale from not being pale does not <come to be> from what *simpliciter* is not (for *pale* is not first in <the category of> quality), but from what is not *something*. For 'something' applies to all the things which fall under the first.

This, then, is one of the things which is meant by '*simpliciter*', that, namely, which he indicates by the phrase 'first in each category'. The other thing which it can mean is that which in no sense is and which is the denial universally of all forms of being, indicated by him by his use of the word 'universal'. These two meanings, therefore, will be considered also in relation to substance. That which *simpliciter* is not in substance <is> either that which does not fall within the category of substance or that which in no way is, and <that which>[177] comes to be out of that which *simpliciter* is not <is> either that which <comes to be> from what is not substance (for if a man <comes to be> from what is not a man, it does not immediately follow that <it comes to be> from what *simpliciter* is not: man is not what is first in <the category of> substance) or from that which in no sense and in no way is.

He shows that whichever of the two meanings you take, saying that what comes to be *simpliciter* and by way of substance comes to be from what *simpliciter* is not leads to absurdity. For if, he says, what is *simpliciter* means the first genus,[178] the coming-to-be of substance would be <said to be> from what is not substance. And what is not substance is not any of the other categories either,[179] since the others have their existence in substance, and what is neither substance nor one of the others will be in every sense nothing. So the coming-to-be of substance will be from what in no sense and in no way is, which is absurd. The same absurdity will follow too, if '*simpliciter*' means the negation of all that is. Once again the coming-to-be of substance will be from what in every sense is not.

It must signify the former only. This is because from the beginning he takes the meaning of '*simpliciter*' to be that which indicates the strict sense of a word (for when I say that that which comes to be by way of substance comes to be *simpliciter*, I use this interpretation, and he himself made this clear by contrast: he contrasted 'not strictly speaking' with '*simpliciter*'),[180] and he goes on to say that that which is *simpliciter* comes to be from that which *simpliciter* is not, no longer understanding 'what *simpliciter* is not' in accordance with the first interpretation, that which makes it mean 'that which strictly speaking is not'.

This is when he says '*Simpliciter* can signify either what is first in each category of being' and the following words. He seems here to change the meaning of '*simpliciter*' so that it means 'universal'. For in general 'that which strictly speaking is' is thought of in terms, not of each category, but only of that of substance, and 'that which strictly speaking is not' means, not the negation of each category, but of substance only. However, even if he had changed the meaning of 'that which strictly speaking is not' to that of 'that which *simpliciter* is not', this does not result in the least in the problem's collapsing. For even if we take that from which we say the coming-to-be of substance takes place to be that which strictly speaking is not, we shall have once again to take this 'what strictly speaking is not' either as the negation just of substance or as the negation generally of all that is. So again by either route we reach the same conclusion, that that which in no way *is*, is the origin from which the coming-to-be of substance occurs.[181]

317b13 The dilemmas that arise concerning these matters and their solutions have been set out elsewhere [at greater length, but it should now and again be said by way of summary that in one way it is from what is not that a thing comes to be *simpliciter*, though in another way it is always from what is; for that which is potentially but is not actually must necessarily pre-exist, being described in both these ways.]

<By 'these matters' he means the problem> of the starting point for the coming-to-be of substance and how coming-to-be *simpliciter* is from what *simpliciter* is not. The solution of this problem, he says, 48,1 has been stated by him elsewhere (and it has <in fact> been stated in Book 1 of the *Physics*). There he enquires about the starting point of coming-to-be, and says that to the extent to which privation is considered in connection with matter, to that extent it is that which is not, whereas to the extent to which matter is something (it is in potentiality that which is coming-to-be), it is that which is. *Qua* something persisting <through the change>, <the starting point is> matter, *qua* something not persisting, privation. And his present results are in accord with what he has said in that place. For in one sense, he says, <the starting point is> that which *simpliciter* is not, since matter, which is the starting point of coming-to-be *simpliciter*, is nothing in actuality and involves privation when considered in itself, so that it would seem to be that which *simpliciter* is not; but in another sense, it is that which is, in that it is in potentiality, since this is what matter is like.

It must be recognised, as was said earlier, that we are now saying that those things which are in reality[182] are things which are in actuality, since even matter, which is in potentiality those other things which have reality and are subsistent in their own right, is matter in actuality. For if you said that it was matter in potentiality, it would no longer be matter. And we must take note of this: namely, how through his solution he has both saved <the possibility of> coming-to-be *simpliciter* and avoided having to say that that which in every way is not is; for it is that which in every way is not in actuality, he said, not that which in every way *simpliciter* is not, which is the origin of this sort of coming-to-be.

> **317b18** But even when these distinctions have been made, there remains a question of remarkable difficulty, [which we must take up once again, namely, how is coming-to-be *simpliciter* possible, whether from what is potentially or some other way. One might well wonder whether there is coming-to-be of substance and the individual, as opposed to quality, quantity and place (and the same question arises in the case of perishing). For if something comes to be, clearly there will exist potentially, not actually, some substance from which the coming-to-be will arise and into which that which perishes has to change. Now will any of the others belong to this actually?]

After solving the first problem and saying how it is that the things that come to be *simpliciter* come to be, namely, from that which is in potentiality but is not in actuality, he says that he has come across another, tougher problem arising from the solution. Does this <being> in potentiality, from which that which comes to be comes to be, have belonging to it in actuality any of the other categories, e.g. quantity or quality or any of the others, or does nothing belong in actuality to this <thing> that in potentiality is substance? For if nothing belongs to it, that which in actuality is nothing, or, as he puts it 'that which is not in this sense',[183] i.e. separable and in actuality subsistent, will be, which is absurd. For he regards it as an absurd conclusion to <have to> call 'that which is not in this sense', i.e. that which is nothing in actuality, separable and subsistent. If someone were to try to escape this conclusion by saying that this <thing> neither exists nor subsists, he would fall into an even greater absurdity by saying that that which comes to be comes to be from nothing pre-existing. This, he says, has been a common anxiety of all philosophers, having to say that the things which come to be come to be from nothing pre-existing.

This, then, is what will follow if none of the other things[184] belong in actuality to that which in potentiality is, and in potentiality is 49,1 substance. If, however, any of the other things existing in actuality does belong to the potential substance, it will result in affections' existing in separation from substance – if, that is, without the substratum being a substance in actuality, these <affections> exist in actuality, which is not possible. For they are affections of that which is substance in actuality, and it is impossible for the affection to exist in separation from that of which it is an affection.

> **317b27** [What I mean is this:] Will that which is only potentially a this and existent, [but neither individual nor existence *simpliciter*, have any quality or quantity or place? If it has none of these, but all of them potentially, that which in this sense is not will consequently be separable, and further, the principal and perpetual fear of the early philosophers will be realized, namely, the coming-to-be of something from nothing previously existing. But if being individual and a substance are not going to belong to it while some of the other things we have mentioned are, the affections will, as we have remarked, be separable from the substances.]

In Aristotle, 'a this' signifies substance.

> **317b33** We ought, then, to work at these problems as much as possible, and also enquire what is the cause of coming-to-be always existing, both coming-to-be *simpliciter* and the partial sort of coming-to-be.

We must enquire, he says, how a solution can be found for the difficulties that have already been raised, and then he tacks on another difficulty, saying that we ought to consider how it comes about that coming-to-be never gives out, but always exists, both that which occurs *simpliciter* and that which is partial. By '*simpliciter*' and 'partial' he means either <the coming-to-be> of substances and that of accidents, '*simpliciter*' applying to substances and 'partial' to accidents, or – and perhaps this has more truth in it – both the '*simpliciter*' variety and the 'partial' variety apply, in his view, to substances. He sets out their distinguishing features a little later, calling the <coming-to-be> of substance in the strict sense simple coming-to-be, and that which is the opposite of this partial. He proceeds to show what each of these is.

> **318a1** Given that there is one cause from which we say change begins and another which is matter, [it is the latter sort of cause that we must speak about. For the former has already been

spoken about in the treatise on movement, where we said that there is that which is throughout time unmoved and that which is always in motion: the former of these, the unmoved principle, it is the task of that other and prior philosophy to clarify.]

His aim is to discover the cause of the fact that the things which come to be never give out, but since there are different kinds of cause for things which come to be, there is no need now for him to speak of them all. What sorts of causes are there of things coming-to-be? And which is the one which it is right to mention at this point? The causes are the material and the efficient: this latter is the one which is the source of the beginning of change. He set out no other causes but these, judging them to be of more use for coming-to-be on account of their existing beforehand, for the formal and final causes come later. Of these causes – I mean the efficient and the material – the efficient, he says, is not the one to talk about now, but rather the material. 50,1

But having mentioned the efficient cause, he touches lightly on his account of it, saying that efficient causes, as he also maintains in *Physics* Book 8, divide into that which is always unchanged and that which is always being changed, and that it is the one which is primarily the cause of change, which he also called principle, that is unchanged. This is that which is a 'principle' in the strictest sense of the word. That is the topic, he says, of the first philosophy (for it belongs specially to theology and the work entitled 'After the *Physics*', although <it should be called> rather 'Before the *Physics*';[185] for the things which are by nature prior are in relation to us posterior; and he spoke of the unchanged cause in *Physics* Book 8 as well), whereas he will speak in the book which follows this one[186] about the body which is in circular motion, which moves everything else by being continually moved itself.

318a8 [The latter, that which moves the other things through being continually moved, we shall treat of later, and determine] which thing of this sort of those we call particular is the cause.

By 'particular things' he means things which are generable and perishable, and it is amongst these that coming-to-be and perishing occur.

318a9 Now, however, let us discuss the cause which is placed in the species of matter. [It is because of this that perishing and coming-to-be never disappear from nature.]

He says 'in the species' rather than 'in the genus', because matter is a genus which in fact includes the matter which underlies substance as a species. And in general, everything in potentiality is matter of that which it is able to come to be. So let us speak of this matter, he says, on account of which perishing and coming-to-be always exist in nature and never give out. For matter, being in potentiality, is receptive of contraries and exists eternally, accepting alternately one contrary at one time and another at another, and is the cause of perishing and coming-to-be never giving out in nature.

318a10 For maybe at the same time as this becomes clear, so will the solution to the dilemma we were faced with just now [as to the correct way of speaking also about perishing and coming-to-be *simpliciter*].

If, he says, this became clear, namely, why perishing and coming-to-be never give out, we might together with it obtain clarification of the dilemma we were faced with earlier, whether or not any of the others[187] will belong in actuality to that which is substance in potentiality.

51,1 **318a13** Enough of a dilemma is in fact involved in the question what is the cause of the continued succession of coming-to-be, [if that which perishes disappears into the non-existent and the non-existent is nothing (for the non-existent is neither something nor suchlike nor so big nor somewhere). If some one of the things which exist is always disappearing, why has not the universe been entirely spent and taken its departure long ago, if, that is, there was only a limited quantity of matter for the generation of each of the things coming into being? For it is certainly not because the matter of generation is infinite that it does not give out.]

By way of showing that there are good reasons motivating the dilemma we have just been talking about relating to the impossibility of the continuous existence of coming-to-be, he sets up an argument for it which goes along these lines: if, he says, what perishes disappears into that which is not, and that which is not is none of the things which are, as he showed in the argument enumerating by genus the things that are (for it is not a this, meaning a substance, nor a quantity nor a quality nor any of the others), how can coming-to-be fail to give out? For if <something>[188] of what is is always disappearing, and what is is finite, the things that are would long ago have been used up <and passed> into that which is not. A proof of the finitude of what is is given in the *Physics*,[189] for nothing is infinite in actuality. For he showed that it is in potentiality that the infinite exists, since the division of something that is continuous <goes on> to infinity in potentiality. So it is only this which was <seen to be> bound not to give out, namely, the division of things that are continuous, since it is in this way only that the infinite <is given>. This <was seen to> come about as a result of the continual reduction of the previously existing size of what is, by means of the parts of it always being taken away and ceasing to exist.

> **318a21** [That is impossible, since nothing is actually infinite] but only in potentiality, in respect of division; [so the only possible inexhaustible coming-to-be would be due to something smaller always coming into existence – but in fact this is not what we see.]

I.e. in potentiality its division goes on to infinity. For number possesses infinity in respect of increase, whilst magnitude <possesses it> in respect of division.

> **318a23** Is it, then, because the perishing of *this* is the coming-to-be of something else [and vice versa, that the change is necessarily unceasing?]

His solution of the dilemma is too concise. Things do not perish, he says, <by turning> into that which is not, as was postulated in setting up the dilemma, but <by turning> into something else which is, and the coming-to-be of one thing is the perishing of another. This then is the interchange and alteration of the substratum, i.e. of the matter which changes in respect of its forms, and this kind of going back and forth is the explanation of the way in which coming-to-be is kept going. And in this way also he would solve the puzzle mentioned earlier about coming-to-be *simpliciter*. For if nothing perishes <by turning> into that which in no way is in actuality, neither would it come to be from that which in no way is in actuality, but whatever comes to be does so from something which is in actuality and is already possessed of form.[190] But that which comes to be comes to be from it, not in so far as it is in actuality, but in so far as <it is> in potentiality. For since it is impossible for that <which is> in potentiality to subsist by itself, this thing which is in potentiality is in actuality another this something, which contributes to nothing except its existence, but stops short <of contributing> also to the coming-to-be from it of that which it is in potentiality. For it possesses actual existence in virtue of its form, but the coming-to- 52,1
be of that which it is possible for it <to come to be it possesses> in virtue of its matter.

318a25 As far as concerns the existence of coming-to-be and equally of perishing in the case of each of the things that are, [this explanation should be considered sufficient for them all.]

Concluding his argument he says that he has given the explanation of the existence of coming-to-be and equally of perishing, using 'equally' in lieu of 'always'.[191] 'In the case of each of the things that are', i.e. in the case of each <kind of> substance, both <that which is> substance *simpliciter* and <that which is> partial <substance>.[192] The next topic is the distinction between these.

318a27 But why some things are said to come to be and to perish *simpliciter* and others not *simpliciter* [needs further consideration, if indeed one and the same thing is both the coming-to-be of *this* and the perishing of *that* and vice versa. Some account of this is needed.]

Aristotle again sets out a problem, another one: why, of comings-to-be, some are called cases of 'simple coming-to-be' and others cases of 'something coming-to-be',[193] and of things that come to be, some are said to come to be *simpliciter* and some not *simpliciter*. There is good reason for regarding this as a problem, as he himself says, given that the coming-to-be of *this* is the perishing of something else, and the perishing of *that* the coming-to-be of something else. For in this way equality belongs to all the things which come to be from each other and perish <by turning> into each other, so there is no reason why *this* should be said to come to be rather than *that*. So it is clear from the way the argument is set up that his concern is only with substances, why some substances are said to have simple comings-to-be, others to have, not simple, but copulative comings-to-be,[194] and <that his concern is> not, as some have thought, with accidents, as though substances came to be *simpliciter* and accidents not *simpliciter*. For he has provided a preliminary discussion of these matters already, and will investigate them in what follows, but for the moment his topic is substances, which do come to be from each other, while accidents neither <come to be> from substances nor substances from them, nor in all cases from each other. For the triangle does not in all cases <come to be> from another figure but also from what is shapeless, and what is coloured also from its privation, should it come to be from air as from <its> matter (for air is colourless), and what is knowledgeable often <comes to be> from what lacks knowledge.[195] So the topic under discussion is not the coming-to-be of accidents, but that of substances. For these in all cases come to be from each other, and it is of these that the comings-to-be in some cases take place *simpliciter*, and are spoken of in this way, and in others involve something coming-to-be. He tries to find the explanation of this usage, and says that the cases of something coming-to-be are to be distinguished from those of simple coming-to-be by three criteria. The first 53,1 criterion distinguishes the more matter-like substance from the more form-like, and of these the school of Parmenides called the more matter-like 'not being' and the more form-like 'being'. For this was why this man gave earth the name 'not being', as possessing the character of matter, and fire 'being', as something active and more form-like. So according to Parmenides, the coming-to-be of fire would be a case of simple coming-to-be, whereas that of earth would be a case of something coming-to-be.[196] Similarly with perishing, that of fire would be simple and that of earth would be a case of something perishing. For Parmenides, these would be paradigms of simple coming-to-be and something coming-to-be, since he supposed that earth is matter-like and fire form-like.

You could say that the same relation held between the coming-to-be of the simple elements and that of compounds. The coming-to-be of the simple elements, being as it were more matter-like and underlying the compounds in the position of matter, <would be a case of> something coming-to-be, whilst that of compounds, like man and horse, would be simple coming-to-be.

However, there is another criterion which applies within the class of the more matter-like things themselves – I mean the simple bodies[197] (for these, as has already been mentioned, are matter for the compound bodies) – and this criterion serves to distinguish some as being substances to a greater degree and superior substances from others which are substances to a lesser degree and inferior substances. Those whose distinguishing features are active are substances to a greater degree and superior substances, those with passive and privative distinguishing features are substances to a lesser degree and inferior. Heat is more forceful and a form, whilst cold is more passive and a privation. So fire will be to a greater degree substance and its coming-to-be will be a simple coming-to-be, whereas earth will be substance to a lesser degree and *its* coming-to-be not simple. When fire changes into earth, this is simple perishing, but a case of *something* coming-to-be. When, on the other hand, earth changes back into fire, this contrariwise is a case of *something* perishing, but simple coming-to-be.

There is a third criterion which can be got from the ideas of ordinary people, though not from the truth <of the matter>. That which is more perceptible seems to ordinary people to be to a greater degree something that is, and that which is less perceptible to be to a lesser degree something that is. So in their view the <coming-to-be> of things which are more perceptible, like earth, is a simple coming-to-be, and that of air is a case of *something* coming-to-be (for air is less perceptible), but in truth it is the other way round. For air is something that is to a greater degree than earth, given that heat is active and more form-like, as already pointed out, whereas coldness is, as it were, a sort of privation.[198]

These are three criteria which are taken into account in making distinctions between substances: one, (a), in terms of simplicity and complexity, or affinity to matter or form; another, (b), in terms of being to a greater or lesser degree substance, or superior or inferior <substance>, and a third, (c), in terms of being more or less perceptible. In accordance with these, things which come to be from one another are said <to exhibit the phenomenon of> simple coming-to-be or of *something* coming-to-be.

After this his investigations cease to be concerned with things which come into being from one another and turn to the unqualified and general question of why, of some of the things which are, we say that they come to be *simpliciter* and without any added qualification, but of others <this is> always <said> with an added qualification and never *simpliciter*, given that they are all the things that are. He says that in this case '*simpliciter*' and 'not *simpliciter*' are defined in terms of the categories. For since some <words> signify a substance, some a quality, and some a quantity, those things which change in respect of substance we say come to be *simpliciter*, but those <which change> in respect of some other category always <do so> with some additional qualification. This is reasonable, since substance is that which, in the strict sense, is. Nevertheless, he says, in all the other categories too, the accidental ones generally, the change to what has greater worth is simple coming-to-be, e.g. alteration <from black> to white, but this is no longer the case for the change to what is inferior, e.g. <alteration from white> to black.

318a31 For we say <on occasion> that now <something> is perishing *simpliciter*, and not merely that *this* <is perishing>, [and that *this* is a case of coming-to-be *simpliciter*, and that of *perishing*.]

He now treats as evidence linguistic usage which distinguishes coming-to-be *simpliciter* from *something* <coming-to-be>, and which does not only speak with an additional qualification of these particular things' coming-to-be, but on occasion omits the additional qualification. So it is worthwhile pursuing the investigation further.

318a34 [Again, this comes to be something without coming-to-be *simpliciter*:] for we say that a person who learns comes to be knowledgeable, not that he comes to be *simpliciter*. [We often

> make a distinction by saying that some things signify a particular individual and others do not. The account that is needed is a consequence of this.]

This has led some people to the view that he is discussing substances and accidents and saying that the coming-to-be of substances is simple coming-to-be and that of accidents the coming-to-be of something. But this is not so: rather the discussion is, as has already been said, about substances, how some are said to come to be *simpliciter* and some with an additional qualification. He brings in the example of the person who is learning as evidence of the fact that our usage makes a distinction and says of some things that they come to be *simpliciter* and of others that they come to be not simply, but with an additional qualification.

> **318b2** It makes a difference what things the changing object changes into: for instance, it may be that the way that leads to fire is a coming-to-be *simpliciter*, but a perishing of something, say earth; whereas the coming-to-be of earth is a coming-to-be of something, <not a coming-to-be *simpliciter*,>[199] but a perishing *simpliciter*, say of fire, in the way that Parmenides speaks of two things, that which is and that which is not, [fire and earth respectively.]

Here he sets out the criterion by which a distinction is made between cases of simple coming-to-be and cases of *something* coming-to-be, 55,1
and we need to investigate what the criterion is; for there seems to be some incoherence in what he says. It may, perhaps, be maintained by someone that this distinction is in terms of the comparison between what is simpler and what is more complex: because the simpler things are more akin to matter and are subordinated to compounds in the relation of matter <to form>, their coming-to-be might be described as *something* coming-to-be and that of the compounds, since they possess the form more distinctly, simple coming-to-be. It is in accordance with this conception that Parmenides, whose theory held that earth and fire are elements and considered earth as forming a substratum like matter and fire as that which contributes form,[200] named earth 'that which is not' and fire 'that which is'. Accordingly, on that criterion, he says, the coming-to-be of fire would be a case of simple coming-to-be, that of earth a case of *something* coming-to-be and not simple <coming-to-be>.

It seems to count against this interpretation that Aristotle nowhere clearly mentions the comparison between what is simpler and what is more complex, but besides there is also the other consideration. For if the simple and the compound differ in virtue of being more akin to matter and form respectively, the criterion will be the same as that which follows, the second to be mentioned, according to which he takes the one to be to a greater degree substance, the other to a lesser degree; for he estimates the degree to which something is substance on the basis of its kinship to matter or form. And he himself clearly indicates this in his remarks about the second criterion, where he says, 'For example, heat is a positive characteristic and a form, but cold a privation', in addition to the fact that he says nothing about being more akin to matter or form in his discussion of the first criterion, but only about what is and what is not.

For this reason I think that Alexander's interpretation is actually more true and is in agreement with the text. He says that the first criterion operates with the contrast between what is and what is not. It is not that this represents Aristotle's own view, but when someone makes the assumption that there is what is and what is not, as Parmenides does, calling fire 'what is' and earth 'what is not', it follows on this assumption that the way to what is not from what is is <a matter of> simple perishing and <of> *something* coming-to-be, whilst the opposite is true of the way from what is not to what is, <this being a matter of> *something* perishing and <of> simple coming-to-be. For Aristotle's overall view is that no substance changes to that which is not. For the perishing of one thing, he says, is the coming-to-be of another. So in the case of substances nothing changes into privation *simpliciter*, but the thing which changes into the privation of *this* changes into another thing which is.

He adds[201] 'in the case of substances' because in the case of acci-
56,1 dents it *is* possible: the musical may change into the unmusical and the privation without taking on, in the process of losing the property of being musical, another form or affection, other than the privation, and that is why being musical or unmusical contributes nothing to the matter's subsisting.[202] In the case of substances, however, privations and the absence of forms render the matter non-subsistent, unless the change takes place to something else which is in actuality, and to some form.

318b7 It makes no difference whether <we postulate> this particular pair or another like it.[203] [What we are after is the manner of the change, not its matter. The way which leads to that which is not *simpliciter* is perishing *simpliciter*: that which leads to what is *simpliciter* is coming-to-be *simpliciter*.]

It makes no difference, he says, whether Parmenides posited fire and earth or some other pair. We are not looking for the substratum to which these distinctions are considered to apply, but for the distinctions themselves and the way in which the differentiation occurs, which determines the distinction between <cases of> *something* coming-to-be and <cases of> simple coming-to-be. For he had already laid down the criteria <for distinguishing> between those things to which changing things change, criteria according to which we differentiate simple coming-to-be and the coming-to-be of something.

> **318b11** In whatever terms the distinction is made, whether in terms of earth and fire [or of some other pair, one of the pair will be that which is, the other that which is not. This, then, is one way in which coming-to-be and perishing *simpliciter* will differ from those which are not *simpliciter*.]

Whatever sorts of things, he says, are used to distinguish that which is and that which is not, whether you should say they are distinguished by fire and earth or by some other pair, of these very things one will be said to be what is and the other what is not.

> **318b14** Another way is by the character of the matter involved. [If the distinguishing characteristics of the matter signify individuality to a greater degree, the matter itself is to a greater degree substance; if they signify privation, not-being. For example, if heat is a positive characteristic and a form, but cold a privation, earth and fire differ in accordance with these distinguishing characteristics. The common view is rather that the difference is in terms of the perceptible and the imperceptible: when the change is to perceptible matter, they say that coming-to-be occurs, when to matter that is not apparent, perishing.]

It is the simple bodies which he is calling matter, on the grounds that they underlie as matter the coming-to-be and perishing of the compounds. And in this way it is the compounds which he seems more to be characterising in terms of form, and the interpretation given earlier, according to which we said that Aristotle set out the first criterion in terms of the comparison between what is more simple and what is more complex, seems to be in accord with the one that is before us. This is because he assimilates the one – the simple – to matter and the other – the compound – to form. Now, however, since the criterion is considered to apply within matter itself, by which I mean the simple bodies, he seems to be setting out the second criterion. The criterion is, as we have already said, the fact that some of the simple bodies are substance to a greater degree and some to a lesser: to a greater, those which are more active and which have distinguishing features to a greater extent and ones which are analogous to form, such as heat. For heat, he says, is 'a category',[204] that is, a <real> 57,1
existence and a positive characteristic, 'whereas cold is as it were a

privation', and things which have it as their form[205] as a result of receiving it are substance to a lesser degree and inferior. Accordingly, he says, since fire and earth are distinguished on these criteria, i.e. in terms of positive characteristics and privations, it is fire which will be substance to a greater extent and earth to a lesser, and the change from earth to fire will be a case of *something* perishing and simple coming-to-be, and vice versa for the opposite change.

> **318b21** They distinguish what is and what is not by their perceiving or not perceiving it, [in the same way as the knowable is what is and the unknowable what is not, for perception has the force of knowledge.]

He has mentioned the third criterion, the one which represents the popular view of the matter, making the distinction in terms of things' being more or less perceptible. He now follows this up by explaining why the popular view is that a higher degree of being belongs to that which is more perceptible. Since they think that perception is the same thing as knowledge, and that what is and what is not are in reality defined by knowledge and lack of knowledge (for that which is is known and recognised, whilst that which is not is unrecognised and unknown), they think that the things which are and the things which are not are distinguished by perception and absence of perception.[206]

> **318b24** Just as they hold that their own life and being consists in perceiving or being able to perceive, so, they think, does that of things.

The other consideration that influences people to think that perceptible things are what are, and imperceptible things things which are not, is the assumption that they themselves exist and live to the extent that they perceive and are able to perceive. Just as they define living and existing for things that perceive in terms of perceiving, so, they say, existing for things that are perceived amounts to their being able[207] to produce perception. For the phrase 'so does that of things' does not stand for 'by perceiving', but for 'by producing perception', so that everything is defined in terms of perception and the absence of perception, but living things by their perceiving and the rest by their being perceptible.[208]

> **318b26** In a sense they are on to something true, though what they actually say is untrue.

It is right to think that the more a thing is knowable the more it is and the less it is knowable the less it is, and generally to define 'what is' and 'what is not' in terms of knowledge and absence of knowledge (for that which in virtue of its own nature is unknowable does not exist either), but a mistake to reduce perception and knowledge to the same thing.

318b27 Coming-to-be *simpliciter* and perishing come out differently on the common view and on the correct view. [By the standard of perception wind and air are to a lesser degree, so they accordingly say that the things which perish *simpliciter* perish by changing into these, and that things come into being when they change into what is tangible, i.e. earth. In fact, however, <wind and air> are individual and <identifiable with> form to a greater extent than earth.]

The correct view is that it is the coming-to-be of that which to a greater degree is which is simple, while on the common view it is not that which to a greater degree is, but that which is more perceptible. These views are at loggerheads with one another. For wind and air in comparison with earth will seem to the many to be of lower worth, since they are less perceptible, and that is why they also say that things which perish <and turn> into air disintegrate into nothing. For example, if water perishes, they do not usually speak of air having come to be, but of the perishing of water. If, however, air perishing produces rain, they call this the coming-to-be of water, not the perishing of air. So earth, which is something tangible and resistant, i.e. solid, is thought to *be* to a greater degree, since it is more perceptible. In reality, though, it is air which is something that is to a greater degree than earth, since it is something which surrounds the earth and has a distinguishing feature, namely heat, which is more form-like.

318b35 [We have now stated the reason why there is such a thing as generation *simpliciter*, which is the perishing of something, and such a thing as perishing *simpliciter*, which is the coming-to-be of something:] and it is due to a difference of matter either in respect of its being substance [or not being substance, or in respect of its being more or less so, or because in the one case the matter from which or to which the change takes place is more perceptible and in the other case less perceptible.]

He recapitulates his discussion of the <various> criteria by which a distinction was made between cases of coming-to-be *simpliciter* and cases of *something* coming-to-be. He mentions 'a difference of matter' as something which all the criteria have in common, as though he were to say that simple coming-to-be is distinguished from the coming-to-be of *something* by differences in the matter of the changing things on one <or other> of these criteria. He then brings forward the three criteria: either <they differ> in respect of being or not being substance (so that he can speak of the first criterion as that which concerns what is and what is not), or in respect of *being* to a greater or lesser degree (which is a way of speaking of being more like matter or more like form), or, generally speaking, in respect of being a superior or inferior substance, respectively, since form itself is superior to matter, as that for the sake of which something else is <is superior> to that which is for the sake of something,[209] or in respect of being more or less perceptible.

> **319a3** The reason why some things are said to come to be *simpliciter*, others only to come to be something, not in virtue of the coming-to-be of one from another [in the manner we have just been describing – for all that has so far been determined is why, when every instance of perishing is the coming-to-be of something else, we do not attribute 'coming-to-be' and 'perishing' impartially to the things which change into one another; but the problem that was mentioned later was not this, but why that which learns is not said to come to be *simpliciter* but to come to be knowledgeable, whereas that which is born *is* said to come to be – *this* distinction is made in terms of the categories. For some things signify an individual, some a quality, some a quantity. So those which do not signify substance are not said to come to be *simpliciter* but to come to be something.

He has enquired in previous sections, in respect of substances, why
59,1 some are said to come to be *simpliciter*, while others <are said to come to be> with an additional qualification. Now, however, he pursues the same enquiry, not in respect of substances (for the discussion is not, he says, about things that come to be from one another), but universally about everything – < the enquiry, that is, about> how it is that we say that some things come to be *simpliciter* and some not *simpliciter*. He says, therefore, that these are distinguished by means of the categories, and that the things that come to be in respect of substance come to be *simpliciter*, while those that come to be in respect of some other category – one of the accidents – come to be something and not *simpliciter*.

> **319a14** For all that <in every category> alike [we talk of coming-to-be in connection with just one of the two columns; for

instance, in substance if it is 'fire', but not if it is 'earth', and in quality if it is 'knowledgeable', but not if it is 'ignorant'.]

In all the categories: it is something, he says, which all the categories have in common, whether we are looking at simple coming-to-be in the case of substances or at coming-to-be *something* as in the case of the other categories, namely, that change towards that which is more valuable is called coming-to-be, whereas change towards that which is less valuable and inferior <is called> perishing: thus <change towards> white is called coming-to-be, whilst when this changes towards black, it is not the coming-to-be of black, but the perishing of white.[210]

That is how Alexander interprets <the passage> in agreement with what is said in the *Physics*.[211]

319a18 [We have thus dealt with the fact that some things come to be *simpliciter* and others not,] both in general and amongst substances [themselves. We have also stated why the substratum is cause, as matter, of the continuous occurrence of coming-to-be: namely, because it is able to change from one contrary to another ...]

For he has investigated the distinction between coming-to-be *simpliciter* and the coming-to-be of something in the case of substances too, and he has also investigated it universally in the case of everything – which is what is meant by 'in general'.

319a20 ... and <because> the coming-to-be of one thing in the case of substances is always the perishing of another [and the perishing of one thing the coming-to-be of another.]

It is reasonable for him to add 'in the case of substances', because it is not the case with everything which is in actuality that the coming-to-be of one thing is a perishing of something else: for example, the case of someone who learns, i.e. comes to be knowledgeable, since being ignorant is a privation.[212]

319a22 Furthermore, neither is there any need to puzzle over the question why there is coming-to-be although things are always perishing. [For just as they say that something perishes *simpliciter* when it passes into imperceptibility and not-being, so they say that a thing comes to be from not being when it comes to be from being imperceptible.]

In the preceding <discussion>[213] he has puzzled over the reason why

60,1 coming-to-be does not give out, but there is always a continued succession <of comings-to-be>; and he has shown that there was good reason to find this puzzling, given that some of the things that are are for ever disappearing, since the things that perish go off into that which is not. So after having in the preceding <section>[214] given a concise explanation of whence <it comes about that> coming-to-be does not give out, and having said that it is on account of the fact that the perishing of one thing is the coming-to-be of another, and in this way solved all the dilemmas earlier set out, he now reminds us of the reasoning that set up the dilemma. He says that after the solution which has been given there is no longer any room for the argument which set up the dilemma, the argument which alleges that there ought not always to be coming-to-be, given that some things are perishing and going off into that which is not. He is not repeating himself by recapitulating the argument <in this way>. Immediately before he said that the majority of people judge coming-to-be and perishing *simpliciter* by whether the change occurs from what is imperceptible to what is perceptible or vice versa, because, perception being what they live by, they use it to sort out what is and what is not, and think that that which does not fall within the scope of perception, or does not do so to any great extent, does not exist[215] either. He then took this very <opinion> over as an illustration of his own thesis, namely, that the coming-to-be of one thing is the perishing of another and vice versa, and that in one sense <things> come to be from that which is and disintegrate into that which is, while in another they come to be from that which is not and disintegrate into that which is not. What is more, the majority of people, he says, judge the change from what is not perceptible to what is perceptible to be coming-to-be *simpliciter*, and perishing contrariwise, whereas that which is not perceived is not that which in every respect is not.

So there is a reason common <to all these instances for saying> without qualification that every case of coming-to-be is from that which is not, because it is from matter, which includes the privation of all things, and privation is that which is not, but also, on the other hand, from that which is, because <matter is> all things in potentiality. And that from which <a thing> immediately comes is both something which is and something which is not, e.g. if fire should come to be from air. But even if air is something which is, nevertheless it is not fire, nor does the air remain when the coming-to-be of fire <takes place>. So in this way too it <comes to be> from that which is not. But again it <comes to be> from that which is, *per se* from that which is, since <it comes to be> from the substratum which is something that is, but also *per accidens* <from that which is>, since <it comes to be> from air. For it is accidental that that from which

<the fire comes to be> is either air or wood or oil or whatever else. The same holds for perishing, only conversely.

'Furthermore, neither is there any need to puzzle over the question why there is coming-to-be although things are always perishing.' There is no need, he says, to puzzle over the question why, if something disappears when things are perishing, coming-to-be does not give out. For perishing is not <a passing away> into that which in every sense is not, nor is coming-to-be from that which in every sense is not. And he finds support for this thesis in the common usage of ordinary people's speech. They define that which is and is not in terms of the perceptible and the imperceptible. They do not call that which in no way is 'that which is not', but that which is imperceptible to them. So there is no reason to be surprised if we too speak of coming-to-be in one respect from that which is *simpliciter*, and in another respect from that which *simpliciter* is not, and of perishing <as passing away> both into what is and into what is not, in the way described.

> **319a25** So whether or not the substratum is something which is, [things come to be from not being. Thus it is equally from what is not that things come to be and into what is not that things perish. It is only natural, then, that it does not give out; for coming-to-be is the perishing of what is not and perishing the coming-to-be of what is not.]

That is to say, whether this imperceptible thing which is said to be something which is not has a certain existence or whether there is no substratum, makes no difference to the argument; for, putting it in general terms, whatever sort of thing it is into which the thing that perishes departs, that is the sort of thing from which the thing which comes to be comes to be. If, therefore, it is when that which is perishes that that which is not comes to be, clearly it is also when that which is not perishes that that which is comes to be. And notice how precisely he spoke of coming-to-be in the case of that which is not, making it quite clear that when we speak of that which perishes departing into that which is not, we do not mean <that it departs> into that which in no sense and in no way is.

'So whether or not the substratum is something which is ....' That which perishes, he says, is held by some to depart into that which is not in virtue of changing into the imperceptible, and they do not bother themselves about whether the change into the perceptible has taken place with a substratum which is something which is or not, that is, whether the imperceptible <from which it comes to be> and which is said not to be is a thing having existence or not having it. But the reason why this imperceptible thing is or is not the origin of the coming-to-be is not that they say it is or is not, but it is because it is, and is a substratum from which the perceptible comes to be.

So 'whether the substratum is something which is' means 'whether it is said by them to be or not to be'. For these people themselves did not further distinguish whether this imperceptible thing from which they said coming-to-be <takes place> was in existence and amongst the things which are, or not. For whichever of these things is the case, coming-to-be will not give out. If the imperceptible into which perishing <is a passing away> and from which coming-to-be <takes place> is one of the things which are, for this very reason it will not give out, since perishing is not <a passing away> into that which in every sense is not; but if it is one of the things which are not, since perishing is the coming-to-be of what is not <and coming-to-be>[216] the perishing of what is not, again it will not give out, given the way in which what is and what is not succeed each other.

> **319a29** However, <a doubt might be raised>[217] whether this thing which *simpliciter* is not is one of a pair of contraries [– earth, the heavy element, for instance, as what is not, and fire, the light element, as what is – or whether, on the contrary, earth too is what is, whilst what is not is the matter that belongs equally to earth and fire.]

In previous sections he was investigating the question whether there is anything which comes to be *simpliciter*, i.e. which in the proper sense of the words comes to be, and his view was that it comes to be
62,1 from that which *simpliciter* is not. So, having explained sufficiently the topics of simple coming-to-be and of that which is *simpliciter* and the number of senses in which these words are used, he now investigates what is meant by 'that which *simpliciter* is not'. Is it one of a pair of contraries, that which is characterized by the privative differentiating feature, e.g. earth or fire? Do we say that earth is that which is not and fire that which is? Or is it the case, not that the discussion is about things which are so called in the incorrect sense of the words, but that the enquiry is a general one about the things which are, in the proper sense, that which involves substance, <being concerned to ask> what sort of thing we conceive that which is not to be, when we say that they come to be from that which is not?

Here, then, he spells out more clearly what he maintained further back,[218] namely, that this thing that is not is something which in potentiality is, but in actuality is not. For it is matter, he says, which is the thing that is not – matter from which both fire and earth are generated. Should you say that matter in itself does not subsist, but exists[219] always together with some form, so that that which comes to be never comes to be from what is not, but from what is, I would say in reply, as I have already said on an earlier page, that form does indeed contribute to matter in respect of existence,[220] but contributes nothing to it in respect of the coming-to-be of that which as such is not. For it is not as being actually earth, if this is what it happens to be, that it changes into fire, but as being potentially fire, and this belongs to it *qua* matter. That which comes to be, therefore, <does so> from matter. Just so bronze, to use the example provided by the commentator Alexander, if it were impossible for it to subsist without the form of the statue, and statues changed into one another, would not on this account be deprived of its own existence, but would <all along> be something other than the statue; and the statue which came to be, even if it did not come to be from unworked bronze but from a statue, nevertheless would not be said to come to be from the statue but from the bronze of the statue. The same situation holds with respect to matter: since it always exists together with some form (because, being nothing in actuality, it is non-subsistent), that which comes to be from it does so from a matter which always exists together with something which contributes to it in respect of existence; nevertheless that which comes to be does not do so from that which the matter is actually, but from the matter, which is potentially body.

> **319a33** Again, is the matter of each of these different? Or would that mean that they did not come into being from each other or from their contraries? [(For it is to these that the contraries belong, namely, to fire, earth, water, and air.)]

He has said that that which *simpliciter* is not is other than the things which come to be. It is not that which seems to be to a lesser degree because of its differentiating features being the privative ones, but that which underlies both, both that which is to a lesser degree and that which is to a greater degree. Now he goes on immediately to enquire whether the substratum[221] is other than either of these – other, that is, than the earth and fire which he has mentioned. He refutes this summarily, saying that if the substratum were other than either and not the same they would no longer come to be from each other as from contraries. For contraries come to be from each other while the substratum is the same. But the original supposition was that the coming-to-be of one is the perishing of the other. So the substratum is not other than the contraries – I mean earth and fire. That a contrariety exists between earth and fire <is something which> he will demonstrate in the argument which follows immediately. So these <come to be> from one another as from contraries. And if this <is so>, the matter of both <will be> common <to both of them> and one.

319b2 Or <rather> there is one way in which the matter is the same and another in which it is different.

By way of putting the finishing touch to the previous discussion <he says>[222] that in one respect matter is the same as the things which come to be and in another is different. In what way the same and in what way different is what he now goes on to say.

319b3 For the substratum, whatever it is, is the same, but its being is not the same. [So much, then, for these questions.]

Matter, insofar as it is matter and according to its own nature is whatever it is, is the same for all the things which it underlies. The phrase 'whatever it is' <signifies> for Aristotle the substratum. So <*qua* substratum>[223] and, if I may speak in this way, in terms of its own nature, there is one matter for all things; for insofar as it is matter, it has a suitability for everything alike. But since being and subsistence never belong to it without some form, matter will not be the same for everything in respect of form and existence.[224] That <matter> which is thought of in relation to form is that which is proximate to it, e.g. air is the matter which underlies fire, whilst that <which underlies> air is in actuality water, to take a particular example, and that <which underlies> water is earth. So earth and air underlie fire and water, and these are the same as far as the definition of matter is concerned,[225] but in terms of form <they are> different, being thought of no longer as prime matter, but as proximate <matter>.

It is possible to speak in this way: since, as is going to be said next, matter is the same in terms of the substratum, but different in terms of the definition,[226] given that the things which need to be mentioned in its own definition[227] would also be different, in fire and earth and the rest it would be the same in terms of the substratum, but different in terms of the definition. For it is not in terms of the same definition that it receives the forms of fire and earth and the rest: in terms of
64,1 one definition it receives the form of earth, in terms of another that of fire, and in terms of other definitions the forms of the rest.

<1.4. ALTERATION>

319b6 Let us now speak about coming-to-be and alteration and how they differ from each other, [since we say that these changes are different from one another. The substratum is one thing and the affection whose nature is to be predicated of the substratum is another, and either of them can change.]

Aristotle has said already briefly what the difference is between coming-to-be and alteration. Nevertheless, he now takes up the topic again and speaks about them at the appropriate place in his order of exposition. He has listed the things which have to be investigated in connection with coming-to-be: what it is, whether it exists at all, from what and whence the things which come to be do so, why coming-to-be never gives out. So he now opportunely enquires what it is which differentiates it from the other sorts of change, and first from alteration.

He distinguishes them from each other in this way. There is one thing, he says, a sort of substratum (meaning substance), and another, affection, which is also called 'accident', and there is change in respect of both (both in respect of substance, which he calls 'substratum', and in respect of affection, i.e. accident). Accordingly, change in respect of the substratum is coming-to-be and <change> in respect of the affections while the substratum remains unchanged is alteration. This having been said, he sets up and elaborates and also solves a certain dilemma which someone without due consideration might have brought forward as an objection against his remarks.

If change in a subject which is perceptible and remains the same, i.e. [if][228] change in a substratum already possessed of form, is alteration, given that in the change from air to water transparency and wetness persist, whereas the change takes place with respect to heat and cold, change of air to water will be alteration. For the change occurs in an informed subject, I mean the transparent and wet. The same line of reasoning can produce a dilemma in the case of the other elements as well. For all those things which are next to one another[229] have one differentiating feature in common, and the other contrary: fire and air have heat in common, but differ in respect of wet and dry, whilst air and water alike have wetness and are contraries in respect of the other pair of opposites.[230] So the dilemma is one which is common to those which come next to each other.

Confronting this dilemma, Aristotle says that if hot and cold, in respect of which their change into each other takes place, belonged as affections to the persisting wet and transparent, it would be alteration, as it is in the case of water which warms up and cools down. For there, since the quality which is in the water is an affection and an accident contributing nothing to its being water, what takes place 65,1
is alteration. But in the case of the change from air to water hot and cold are not affections of the wet and transparent, unless, perhaps, in some accidental way, through both being affections of the same thing. It is like when, in the case of Socrates, we might say that accidentally the bald belonged to the pale,[231] on account of both the white and the bald belonging to the same thing; for both are affections of Socrates. So in the same way here too the hot and the cold would

not be affections of the wet, except accidentally, but these same things – I mean the hot and the cold – together with wetness exist as affections, and as species-determining[232] and perfecting affections, of the unformed matter. For if the cold is an affection and an accident of the wet, water will not have wetness and coldness as conditions of its being, but will only have wetness.

Similarly, air will be made complete not by wetness and coldness, but by wetness alone. But if the essence of each, that is, of both water and air, is made complete by wetness, they will not have differentiating features by which they are to be separated in respect of their substance, for affections do not provide substantial differentiae. Hot and cold are not, then, affections of air and water in accordance with which they also change in their coming-to-be from one another. But neither are hot and cold affections of the wet, because if they were they would not be combined to produce a single substance. And if <they are> not affections, neither <do we have a case of> alteration, as the dilemma alleges. For it was declared to be alteration, when the properties in respect of which the changing thing changes exist as affections and accidents.

Someone might wish to add this too to what has so far been said: strictly speaking, it is not *the same* wetness that is in air and in water, nor precisely the same transparency, because air is both more transparent and wetter[233] than water. So neither the wetness of the water nor its transparency remained unaffected in the change from water to air, since the warmth that is in air and <that which is in> fire are not specifically[234] identical either. And in composite things too there are many things hot in the generic sense, but specifically different; for the heat that is in wine is different from that which is in pepper or castoreum or balsam or similar things. It should be known, therefore, that the same sort of thing happens in the case of the coming-to-be of the elements from each other as happens if blood comes to be from wine, when the whole form[235] of the wine perishes and the heat that is in the blood comes to be as a specifically different heat.

And if someone wanted <to hold the view> that heat in fire and air or wetness in water and air are not specifically different, but differ only in being of greater or less intensity, they would have nevertheless to agree with this point at least, namely, that these qualities are numerically different. For when mustard or pepper is sown it produces specifically the same heat in the plants which grow from it, which are of the same species as it, but for all that, the quality that is in the seed and that which is in the fruit which comes to be from it are admittedly numerically different. In the same way, in the case of the elements too, the whole form of the air has to be understood as perishing when the water comes to be. So even if someone agrees that specifically the same wetness and transparency is produced in the water, he will still be compelled to say that it is numerically different. In that case nothing remains of the air except the matter. The change, then, is not from something already possessed of form, to something possessed of form, but from something unformed to something possessed of form, given that only that which is unformed remains. So the change from water to air is not alteration.

> **319b10** It is alteration when the substratum remains, being something perceptible, but change occurs in the affections which belong to it, [whether these are contraries or intermediates. For example, the body is well then ill, but remains the same body; the bronze is now round, now a thing with corners, but remains the same.]

He has done well to add 'the substratum being something perceptible', that is, the substratum being perceptible and remaining, insofar as it is an actually perceptible individual,[236] already possessed of form, all this being said to contrast it with matter. No doubt matter is a substratum and remains the same through comings-to-be; nevertheless we do not then have a case of alteration, but of coming-to-be. For matter is not perceptible, nor actually a particular individual.[237] So it is as if he had said, 'When the substratum is both these things, matter and form, and, while remaining the same thing, changes in respect of some affection of that which is both <matter and form> and is perceptible, then there is alteration.' For in the case of coming-to-be the substratum which remains is matter, which changes in respect of form. The words 'in the affections which belong to it' are added to indicate that which is changed in respect of the affections <it has> in itself and which replaces these affections, not in respect of <the affections it has in virtue of> its relationship with something else. For things which change in respect of some affection which comes from something outside do indeed change, but they have not altered.[238] For example, that which comes be on the right instead of on the left has exchanged its affection, but has not altered, because the change has not taken place in the affections in itself which have been received <into itself>. Another example: when the servant becomes master or the master servant.

However, the words 'in the affections which belong to it' may signify the <phenomenon> which he is going to mention next. This is something to which he has already given preliminary consideration.[239] For he says that when the elements change into one another, something perceptible common <to them both> remains, but that into which and in respect of which the change occurs is not an affection of the thing that remains. For example, when air changes into water something common <to them both> remains, namely the transparent, which is indeed perceptible, but the affection in respect of which the change of air to water occurs is not an affection of the transparent or the wet; but rather the change is in respect of the hot and the cold.[240]

The next remark is obvious. Things that change in respect of their affections do so either in respect of the contraries and the affections most opposed to each other, or in respect of intermediate <affections>. And even the intermediates, participating as they do in the contraries, effect their change in respect of the contraries; for grey, which participates in white and black, if it changes into black, effects the change into black, not *qua* something which participates in black, but *qua* something which participates in white.

> **319b14** When, however, the whole changes without anything perceptible remaining [as the same substratum, but the way the seed changes entirely into blood, water into air, or air entirely into water, then, when we have this sort of thing, it is a case of coming-to-be (and perishing of something else) ...]

He uses the expression 'the whole changes' instead of 'in respect of substance' and 'in respect of what it is'.[241] And this happens when nothing perceptible remains as substratum. The word 'entirely'[242] signifies the same thing, indicating change as a whole and in respect of substance.

> **319b18** ... most of all if the change takes place from what is imperceptible to what is perceptible either by touch [or by all the senses, as when water comes to be or perishes into air, since air is – near enough – imperceptible.]

Not that it is then most of all a case of coming-to-be, but that it seems so to the majority, who define *what is* and *what is not* in terms of the perceptible and the imperceptible, as he pointed out a little earlier. It is that which is not solid and which has no resistance that he calls 'imperceptible by touch', just as it is in fact that which possesses these properties[243] which is perceptible by touch, in the way that earth and water are in comparison with air.

> **319b21** In these cases if some affection <that is one member> of a contrariety remains the same in the thing that has come to be as it was in the thing that has perished, [e.g. when water comes from air, if both are transparent *qua* cold, this must not have the other, the terminus of the change, as an affection of itself. Otherwise it will be alteration.]

He now investigates the aforementioned problem, which he describes thus: when things change into their contraries, if some affection common <to both> remains, as in the case of water and air,[244] <this should not be considered to be an affection of one only>. For the matter changes into the contraries, coming-to-be air and water, since 68,1 it changes to hot and cold, which in fact are contraries. By a 'contrariety'[245] either he means the bodies possessed of form as a result of receiving contrary differentiating features, or it should be understood as meaning the contrary differentiating features themselves; by 'affection' he is referring to that which is one part of a contrariety, which remains the same in the thing that comes to be as <it was> in the thing that has perished. Speaking about air and water together, he says 'if both are transparent' and adds '*qua* cold',[246] not implying that air is cold by nature, but pursuing the argument by means of an example. It would be nearer the truth to say '*qua* wet', since both are wet. But it is possible to understand '*qua* cold' as being intended schematically, for use when the argument is applied to other elements, e.g. earth and water; for they are both cold. So it is the cold which remains when these two change into one another.

> **319b26** [Take the example where the musical man perishes and an unmusical man came to be, though the man remains the same thing.] If being musical [and unmusical] had not been an affection *per se* of this thing, [there would have been a coming-to-be of the one and a perishing of the other. So these are affections of the man, although there is coming-to-be and perishing of a musical man and an unmusical man. As it is, this is an affection of what remains. Such cases, then, are alteration.]

What he is saying in this passage is something like this. The change from air to water, in his view, is not alteration, because that in respect of which the change occurs, sc. hot and cold, is not an affection *per se* of the thing which is changing. The thing which is changing is the transparent. For hot and cold would not be said to be affections of the transparent, except *per accidens*, in virtue of the fact that they, I mean the hot and the cold, belong to the same matter <as the transparent>.[247] For when that in respect of which the change occurs exists as an affection *per se* of the changing thing, what takes place then is alteration, as in the case of the musical and unmusical man.[248] In this case, if musicality did not exist as a *per se* affection of the man, but was <so> *per accidens* in virtue of being an affection of that of which being a man too existed as affection, in the same way that he was saying hot and cold existed <as affections> of the transparent, the change from being musical to being unmusical would not be alteration but coming-to-be, like the change from air to water. As it is, since musicality and unmusicality are affections *per se* of man, the change between being musical and being unmusical exists as an alteration of the man, but is the coming-to-be and perishing of this whole: the musical man (and unmusical man). For alteration was said to be a <matter of> *something* coming-to-be.

The passage is put together in an inverted order, and this makes it unclear. It should be read in the following way: (1) 'If being musical and unmusical had not been affections *per se* of this thing, there would have been a coming-to-be of the one and a perishing of the other' followed immediately by (2) 'As it is, this is an affection of what remains', and then (3) 'So these are affections of the man, although there is a coming-to-be and perishing of a musical and an unmusical man'; then later (4) 'Such cases, then, are alteration'.[249] For what is
69,1 called the coming-to-be of the musical insofar as he is musical is alteration. Perhaps the words 'Such cases, then, are alteration' were inserted because of a scribal error and became a cause of obscurity, the clarity of the passage being preserved if they are removed.

319b31 So when the change is in respect of quantity, [we have growth and diminution, when it is in respect of place, locomotion, when in respect of affection and quality, alteration, and when nothing remains of which the other is an affection or any sort of accident, we have coming-to-be of one thing and perishing of another.]

In this passage Aristotle is now explaining that not every change in respect of an accident of that which is a substratum and perceptible is alteration, as, from the previous discussion, one might think one had understood him to say. For a thing's being a certain size is an accident, and the relevant contrariety here is largeness and smallness, which belong to quantity not quality. So if that which is the substratum and perceptible changes with respect to the quantitative contrariety, change of this sort will be growth and diminution. But if the change were to take place in respect of an affection or the affective <type of> quality it would be alteration, whereas if it is in respect of place and the contrariety which belongs to this, the relevant change will be locomotion. These characteristics in respect of which change can have occurred without the disappearance of the perceptible substance, whatever it may be, exist as accidents. But when, as he says, nothing perceptible remains which has as an affection or some sort of accident, that in respect of which the change has occurred (the words 'the other'[250] signify that in respect of which the change occurs), then it is coming-to-be and perishing.

320a2 What is most properly matter is the substratum [recep-

> tive of coming-to-be and perishing; but, in a way, so is that of other changes, since all substrata are receptive of contraries of one sort or another. This, then, is our way of deciding the questions about coming-to-be – whether or not it exists and how it takes place – and about alteration.]

Here you have the accurate statement of Aristotle's view about the significance of 'matter'. Properly, he says, it is that which underlies[251] substance and coming-to-be and perishing in the strict sense which is called matter, and accordingly, everything is matter of that which it underlies in the process of change. For just as all changing things participate in coming-to-be, so they participate also in matter. That which is capable of receiving contraries of any sort is matter of that <which changes>. It is in this sense then that both substance in actuality and perceptible substance is the matter of alteration, growth and locomotion,[252] as has already been said.

<1.5. GROWTH>

> **320a8** It remains to treat of growth: (a) how does it differ from coming-to-be and alteration, [and (b) how does each of the things that grow, grow and everything that gets smaller, get smaller? The first point to be considered is whether these different kinds <of change> differ from each other solely in that in respect of which <change> takes place ...] [253]

He has spoken about coming-to-be and alteration, <explaining> what each of them is and what the difference is between them. He now 70,1
proceeds to the discussion of growth, which is the third mode of change. He proposes two objects of investigation: (a) how do growth and diminution differ from the other sorts of change? and (b) how do the things that grow <in fact> grow? In the course of this he will enquire what the matter is which underlies growth, how the addition is made to the thing which grows, what it is that grows and what it is that makes it grow.

First, at this point, he proposes to explain how it differs from coming-to-be and alteration, and he then goes on to distinguish it from change in respect of place, even if this is not part of his principal argument but a sort of side-issue. For the treatise *On Coming-to-Be and Perishing* is not the proper context for the discussion of change in respect of place, and therefore he presents his complete treatment of this topic more appropriately in *On the Heavens*.

He enquires whether growth differs from coming-to-be and alteration in one respect only or in several. And in order to get to know this, we must first recognise that amongst the productive skills some differ from each other only in respect of matter and not at all in respect of form, like the skills of coppersmiths and silversmiths (for they are crafts involving different matter, copper being the substratum of the one and silver that of the other, but creative of the same form, since each makes a cup, say, or a plate and the like). Others share the same matter but differ in respect of form, like carpentering and shipbuilding (for the matter common to both is wood, but where form is concerned, the one produces that of the ship, the other that of the door or the sideboard). Yet others differ in both matter and form, those namely which are distinct in every way, like carpentry and medicine: the one has wood as its matter, the other human bodies; and the one produces the form of the door or the chair, the other the health of our bodies. So if we are trying to discover the way in which growth and coming-to-be differ, we must see <whether it is in respect of one of these alone>[254] or by both, <sc.> in respect of matter *and* in respect of form, that they differ.

In my view, then, all the <kinds of> change differ from one another in fact in respect of both. They differ in respect of matter, because one subsists in a different category from another. For growth and diminution fall under quantity, coming-to-be concerns substance, and alteration concerns quality. This is what he means by the words 'in that in respect of which'; for each of the things which change changes in respect of that under which the mode of change is subsumed. For example, that which comes to be and perishes obviously changes in respect of substance, under which coming-to-be and perishing are subsumed. And so in the case of the others.

This difference between them is manifest. And the fact that they differ also in respect of form is clear to everyone. For leading that which comes to be to substance is the form of coming-to-be; bringing about change in respect of the affective qualities, e.g. heating or cooling or making red or white or the like, <is the form> of alteration; adding to or taking away from the size <of a thing>, < the form> of change in respect of quantity; moving up or down or in one of the other dimensions, <the form> of change in respect of place.

So he passes over these points as agreed. But he enquires whether the manner also of change differs as between growth and coming-to-be and alteration. He says that the <types of> change differ from one another in this respect too, and he goes on to say what this difference is. That which alters does not necessarily change in respect of place, because in the process of altering it does not go to another place. What he proves in the *Physics*,[255] namely, that change in respect of place has in every way to precede both alteration and the other <types of> change, is something unconnected with his teaching at this point. For there he makes the point that whenever change occurs there has to be some movement in respect of place, not in every case <a move-

ment> of the thing which is altering or coming-to-be, but of something else, e.g. the cause of the alteration (for the sun has to change in respect of place so that it can alter the air around us). Now, however, his argument is that when the thing that is being altered is in process of alteration there is no necessity for *it* to exchange one place for another. In the same way there is no necessity either for that which is coming-to-be or perishing to change in respect of place; for neither does ceruse change its place when it comes to be from lead, nor does milk when it is produced from blood, nor do many things of this sort.

That which grows or diminishes, on the other hand, must necessarily go through a change in respect of place, not by exchanging its entire place for another, like that which travels, but by taking on more space over and above that which it originally had in the case of growth, and by contracting into a smaller space in the case of diminution, being similar in this respect to something which is beaten out <into a new shape>. And here you have already a difference between growth and change in respect of place; for the way in which that which is beaten out holds on to the space it already occupies and takes on extra space is the same as that in which that which grows apparently changes in respect of space. In fact, however, it is different from this <phenomenon> too. For that which is beaten out, when it increases the space <it occupies> in one dimension, necessarily decreases it in another; and again, if it occupies more space in one or two dimensions, it is bound to give up the space it previously occupied in the remaining dimension or dimensions. But that which grows or diminishes does so alike in three dimensions, either taking on extra <space> or decreasing that which it had originally.

On the other hand, he says, does not the way in which a growing thing changes in respect of place resemble the circular motion of a sphere? For as the growing thing changes in respect of its parts while remaining in its original place, so apparently does the sphere. Or is there a difference here too? For whilst the sphere continues as a whole to occupy the same amount of space despite having parts which change in respect of place, the parts of the growing thing expand into more space and those of the diminishing thing contract into less. Clearly this feature distinguishes it from coming-to-be and alteration. The thing that comes to be does not necessarily change its place, whilst that which grows occupies a different place in the way described; and whereas the thing that comes to be comes to be something else and the thing that alters <comes to be> qualitatively different,[256] the thing that grows or diminishes <becomes> neither something else nor qualitatively different, but is added to in quantity alone, as Aristotle shows in the *Categories*.[257] For when a gnomon is placed around a square the whole increases, but it does not come to be qualitatively different, since it still remains a square.

320a15 [... (that is to say, change from this to that, from a potential to an actual substance, is coming-to-be; change in respect of size is growth; change in respect of an affection is alteration] – in both cases there is change of the things mentioned from being potential to being actual) – [or whether there is a difference also in the manner of the change. For, clearly, what alters does not necessarily change its place, nor does that which comes to be; but what grows and what gets smaller does, though not in the same way as what is in local motion. For that which is in local motion changes its place as a whole, whereas what grows is like metal that is beaten out: this stays put, but its parts change their place, though not in the way the parts of a sphere do. For these change in the same amount of space, while the whole stays put. The parts of a thing which grows, however, continually occupy more space, and those of a thing which gets smaller occupy less. So it is obvious that there are differences not only in the respects but also in how change occurs in things which come to be, alter, and grow, and in which such changes occur.]

Although he has spoken of three changes, coming-to-be, alteration and growth, he goes on to use the phrase 'in both cases', either using it in the same sense as 'in every case', or using 'in both cases' to indicate (a) that which changes substantially, which means 'the thing which comes to be', and (b) that which does so accidentally, which is what that which grows and that which is altered have in common. So he says that it is a common feature of each <of the kinds of> change that it changes from being potentially such-and-such to being actually so. Coming-to-be is from being potentially a substance to being actually a substance, and similarly for the others. The phrase 'but also in how'[258] refers to the way in which the change takes place.

320a27 [How are we to understand] the respect in which the type of change which consists of growth and diminution occur [(growing and diminishing are thought to occur in respect of size)]?

Having dealt with the difference which distinguishes growth from coming-to-be and alteration, he proceeds to carry out the rest of the programme he has set for himself. This consists of three items: What is the matter of growth? What is the efficient cause and <what> the thing which comes to be[259] (i.e., What is it that causes growth and <what is it that> is caused to grow)? and What is the way in which growth takes place and the actualization itself in which it consists?[260]

First he enquires what this 'quantity' is which comes to be the matter of growth, whether it is potentially body and a thing-possessed-of-size whilst actually being incorporeal and sizeless, or is actually body (which, since it follows, he does not bother to add, as something that is bound to be understood). And he shows that it is in every way impossible for it to be potentially body but actually incorporeal, so that we are necessarily left with the other <alternative>, namely, that the matter of growth should be actually body. If, in his view, we were to say that that out of which change in respect of size comes to be is potentially body but actually incorporeal, this would have to be either something which subsists in its own right[261] and has a separate nature, or it would be something which is in some other body. If it were actually separate without being a body, it would be a point or void occupying no space, or an imperceptible body, i.e. one which lacked any perceptible differentiating feature.

Supposing <it to be> a point or void involves manifest impossibility. For a point or void would not, for one thing, subsist in its own right[262] (for it has been proved generally that there is no such thing as a void, and the point always has its being within some body or magnitude); and for another thing, it is absurd to claim that magnitude will grow from a point, since in this way we should once again be bringing in the void. For obviously, if that which grows takes on extra space, the space that it takes on when it expands will either before this have been void, and thus once again we shall have the void actually existing, or it will be body which does not exist in space. Both these alternatives are impossible. And how in any case is the addition of a point to a growing thing going to have made the whole larger? We have frequently remarked that ten thousand things without parts put together with each other will not produce a magnitude. And in general the point is not a body in potentiality but something which belongs to a body. So it is not possible for that from which growth comes to be, i.e. that which is posited as being potentially a body, to be either void or a point.

If it were a body that was not perceptible but quality-less, as is extension in three dimensions,[263] this would have to exist in a place, since every body is in a place. Furthermore, since that by which it is assimilated occupies a certain place, that which is assimilated would also have to occupy a certain place and to be devoid of qualities, and to be for this reason imperceptible; for it is not in virtue of the fact that bodies are endowed with qualities and are perceptible that they are in a place (qualities, after all, are incorporeal and sizeless), but in virtue of the fact that they are extended in three dimensions. So even if some body were not perceptible and did not participate in quality, it would still be necessary for it to be in a place. For a body's being in a place is derived from extension. It is due to quality that bodies are differentiated with respect to place (it is on account of these that some are situated above and others below), but being in place generally[264] is due to extension. For the body that is in a place must be equal to the place that encompasses it, and equal belongs to <the category of> quantity. So even if some body were quality-less and imperceptible, it would be necessary for it to be in a place.

Again, if it were in a place, it would be absolutely necessary for it to be either above or below, and <to be> one or the other <of these> either in accordance with its nature or contrary to its nature, and thus to be one of the bodies endowed with qualities. For I said <earlier> that being above or below comes to bodies from their quality, and one or the other either in accordance with its nature or contrary to its nature. If it existed above in accordance with its nature it would be either air or fire, and if contrary to its nature water or earth. Similarly, if it were below it would be existing either as earth or water in accordance with its nature or as air or fire contrary to its nature. But if this were so, it would no longer be a quality-less body, but perceptible and one of the four <elements>. Aristotle passes over these points as being obvious. So it is impossible for that which underlies growth as its matter to be quality-less body existing as something separate.

We must proceed to the other side of the dichotomy and enquire whether <the substrate> is in something as a potentially existing body and not a thing subsisting in its own right.[265] There is no need to divide this thing which is in something into that which is in the actual thing which grows and that which is in something else. It is a common point of agreement that the growing thing will grow as a result of something from outside acceding to it. So it is in something else and not in the growing thing. If, then, the matter of growth, which also underlies <growth> as body in potentiality, were to be in something else, it would have to be in it either (a) as nothing which belongs to that in which it is either as part or as affection, nor as contributing anything to the being of it, or (b) as being a part of it or *simpliciter* something of it.[266]

If one were to say that <the matter> existed in something actually existing, without being something which belonged to the substance of that in which it was, as if it were enclosed in a vessel, it would follow that that which came to be from <the matter> would come to be as a result of this <matter> being extracted from that in which it was, without that in which it was changing in any way. <It would be> as if one were to say that air came to be from water without water changing, but as a result of some matter which the water contained in itself as in a vessel being extracted from the water. According to this theory, which maintains that this is how the matter is present in something, not being actually body and not completing that in which it is,[267] nor being part of it, nor carving out for itself a certain amount of space from the whole, nothing prevents the similar supposition of a second matter in the same thing, and another, and another, and so on to infinity. But if nothing prevents an infinite number of matters being posited in the same thing, there will be an infinite number of things in actuality in the same thing, which is altogether impossible.

Moreover, this supposition leads no less inevitably to the existence of the void. For the body which is added to the thing that is to grow has clearly taken up space, given that every body is in space. So this <space> was obviously void beforehand, unless one were to suppose that, just as matter changes from being body in potentiality to being body in actuality, so also there is change from being body in actuality which is perishing to being body in potentiality. But no <such> change is seen <to take place>, either from what is not body or to what is not body. Nor, for that matter, do we see things that come to be coming-to-be from each other in such a way as to leave unaffected the thing in question, namely, that out of which the matter of the thing that comes to be is extracted; but in the case of coming-to-be and that of growth the thing in question changes as a whole. For water does not remain when air comes to be from it, but perishes as a whole; nor does bread remain when it gives rise to growth in our bodies, nor does the water which nourishes plants and causes them to grow remain when their growth takes place. So it is impossible for the cause of growth to be in something in such a way as to be nothing of it[268] in actuality. It remains for the cause of growth to be a part of that in which it is, from which it is cut off and assimilated by the thing that grows, and thus causes it to grow. If so, that which underlies the change that is growth will be a body and a thing with size in actuality, and it was this which originally needed to be demonstrated to be true.

If someone were to say that it was in something, neither as separated and belonging in no way[269] to the thing it was in, nor existing as a corporeal part, but like the formless matter of the body which is actual and informed (for this is potentially a body and a thing with size but[270] actually incorporeal, having its being in the actually existing body as its substratum and matter) – if someone were to say this, he should realise that he has discovered the matter, not of growth, but of coming-to-be and perishing. But coming-to-be differs from growth, as has already been said. For the matter of coming-to-be is the real matter – that which is formless and without magnitude – whereas the matter of growth is the body which is already subject to quantity.[271]

Because of this, in the case of coming-to-be it is possible for the same matter to be substratum for both a smaller and a larger bulk (a pint of water in perishing produces air many times larger in bulk), whilst in the case of growth the <bulk> of that which is added as a result of nourishment after replacement of that which has been dissipated is bound to correspond to the increase in size gained by the thing that is growing. For even in the case of growth, coming-to-be occurs first, as when the liver receives food which has been converted into chyle in the stomach and makes it blood; but the blood, once it has come to be, without losing its bulk, is assimilated by the parts <of the body> and adheres to them, and having become like them, brings about growth by the addition of itself.[272] So the matter of growth has already to be completely subject to quantity, even though its coming-to-be occurs previously.

> **320a29** Are we to suppose that from what is potentially possessed of size [and corporeal, but actually incorporeal and sizeless, something corporeal and possessed of size comes to be? But this can be meant in two different senses. In which sense is growth supposed to come about? Is the matter from which it comes (a) separated and existing *per se*; or does it (b) exist within another body; or are both alternatives impossible?]

Having mentioned 'what is potentially possessed of size', he does not balance it with 'or what is actually possessed of size', which would have been the <natural> sequel, but subdivides the first alternative. He does not make this explicit since it is something that can be taken for granted.

> **320b1** [For if it is separated] either it will occupy no space, [or] like a point, or it will be void [and body which is imperceptible].

The phrase '[or] like a point' has been made obscure by the insertion of 'or', which seems to signify a <further> distinction. We ought to
76,1 take it in the sense of 'but', as though the whole sentence read: 'or it will occupy no space, but will be like a point or a void'. Some of the copies have this reading: 'either it will occupy no space; for it will be a sort of point or void'. And one has the phrase 'and body which is imperceptible' instead of the disjunctive 'or' that is in front of us.[273] It should be noted that after saying 'from what is potentially possessed of size and corporeal, but actually incorporeal and sizeless', subdividing this limb <of the disjunction>,[274] he asks whether this matter it comes from is separated or exists in another body. For if it is separated, he says, it will be either a point or void or a body which is imperceptible. And yet what was to be subdivided was of the incorporeal and sizeless. How then has he accepted imperceptible body, which is in fact possessed of size, as a part of this?

320b2 And of these the first is impossible and the second necessarily involves being in something. [For that which comes to be from this matter is always going to be somewhere, so the matter too must be somewhere, either *per se* or *per accidens*.]

These categories, he says, which have just been mentioned, represent subdivisions of that which is separable and subsisting in its own right (and there are three of them; for it will be, he says, either a point or void or imperceptible body). Of these categories, then, he says, to posit on the one hand void or a point as the matter of growth is <to posit> something that cannot possibly be the case. (He amalgamates two of them into one. In what way is it impossible? Because nothing could ever come to be from a point, and it has been demonstrated in the *Physics* that there is no such thing as a void.) And on the other hand, imperceptible body must necessarily be in a place (for 'being in something' must be understood as being in a place). He goes on to explain why this is necessary; for it is impossible for any of the things which come to be to be in a place without the things from which they come to be also being in a place. But it seems that this argument does not demonstrate specifically that imperceptible body exists in a place, but is intended to apply generally to anything whatever that might be posited as being the substratum of change by way of growth. For if that which grows takes on more space[275] and is in a place, and everything that has come to be in a place has come to be from some substratum which itself[276] is in a place either in its own right or *per accidens*, the substratum from which the thing that grows has grown must necessarily be in a place either in its own right or *per accidens*. But if it is in a place in its own right, it is body in actuality and perceptible: if *per accidens*, it is body in potentiality and formless matter. For it is on account of matter that he has added the words '*per accidens*', since body existing in a place comes to be from this, which itself is in a place, not in its own right but *per accidens*, in virtue of the fact that the body in which it is is in a place. But we must not say that the substratum of growth is formless matter; for this is what underlies coming-to-be and perishing and not growth, as we have indicated. It remains to say that what underlies growth is body in actuality.

The argument that has been described, therefore, constitutes an overall refutation of the whole of one side of the dichotomy, that which claims that the matter of growth is body and magnitude in potentiality, and is not addressed specifically to the <suggestion that it is> 'imperceptible body'. For this reason, the alternative interpretation, that set out by Alexander of Aphrodisias, is perhaps better. What is meant, according to him, may be this: Of these two ways – two ways were spoken of, one which posits the matter as existing separately in its own right, and one which <takes it> to exist in something – of these two ways, according to the one which posits the matter as separated, it is not possible for it to be in a place. For neither a point nor void will be in a place; but the imperceptible body will not be either, if by the imperceptible body is meant the mathematical <body>. For this exists only in thought.

If it is understood in the way that has been described it cannot be in a place, but the necessity for it to be in a place is expressed here: 'It is altogether necessary that the matter of the thing that is growing should be in a place either *per se* or *per accidens*', on account of the reasoning set out <above> which includes the remark 'for that which comes to be from it will always be somewhere'. Clearly, therefore, the matter which is postulated according to the one way <of interpreting it>, which claims that it is potentially possessed of size and existing separately in its own right, would not be the matter of the growing thing, since it could not on this hypothesis be in a place, whereas the matter of the growing thing must necessarily be in a place.

320b5 But if it is in something, if separate in such a way as not to be of the thing it is in [either *per se* or *per accidens* …]

He now pursues the other side of the dichotomy, enquiring whether the matter of the growing thing subsists *in* something. It is necessary, he says, if it is in something, for it either to be nothing of[277] that thing in which it is, whether as a part of it or as contributing something *simpliciter* to the composition of it, or else to be a corporeal part of it[278] – and for the moment he postpones submitting this alternative to further subdivision. And he shows that absurdities follow from the statement that it is in something, but is nothing of the thing in which it is.

78,1 **320b7** … many impossible things will follow.

It may be that by 'many impossible things' he means, not that many things that are impossible follow from the hypothesis (for he does not say 'many things <that are impossible>'; and he employed only one argument), but that many, and <indeed> infinitely many, such kinds of matter could be supposed to exist, which is impossible.

320b11 [I mean, as would be the case if, when air came to be from water, it were to happen without water changing, but because its matter was in the water as if in a vessel. In this case there would be nothing to prevent there being an infinite number of matters, which might accordingly actually come to be.]

Moreover it is clear that air does not come to be from water in this way, [as though emerging from something which itself remains].

He has established that the matter of the growing thing cannot be *in* something in such a way as to be nothing of that in which it is by means of one argument, to the effect that an infinite number of things could come to be from the same thing, resting this argument on an example of coming-to-be, namely the change from water into air. Now once more he makes a second attempt to demonstrate the same thesis, relying for support on common observation. For, he says, when water changes into air the air is not seen being extruded, as it were, from the water with the water remaining unchanged, but the water as a whole, from which the air is being generated, <is seen> perishing. Observe, however, once again that whilst his enquiry concerns the matter of the growing thing, he presents the argument as though it concerned coming-to-be and perishing, showing that the matter of what comes to be does not exist in something in such a way as to be nothing of the thing in which it is.

320b12 So it is better in every case to make the matter inseparable, [by way of being one and the same numerically though not one in definition.]

Having refuted the view that the matter exists in something without being anything belonging to that in which it is and the view that it can be separated from that in which it exists, he immediately adds a corollary, saying that it is better in every case to posit that the matter cannot be separated, given the absurdities which will face those who maintain that it is separated without any change in that from which it was separated. So this is why he says 'it is better in every case',[279] i.e. that it is better for everyone to speak thus, or that it is in every way better. So if the topic of his present thesis is the matter of the growing thing, his claim is that it is 'inseparable',[280] in the sense of not being separated from that in which it is, but <it> exists as something belonging to it and has become what that in which it is said to be is. So that <one must> say, not that the water surrounds the matter of the air, but that the water itself is the matter of the air. For it has been said that the matter of the thing that grows is body, not in potentiality, but in actuality, and that the way in which it is in something is by existing as a part of the thing in which it is.

If, however, the topic of his thesis is not the matter of the growing 79,1
thing, but about the matter of that which is coming-to-be, i.e. about prime matter, that which is formless,[281] on this interpretation too his thesis would be correct. For this[282] too is inseparable, being unable to

be separated from that in which it is. The words which follow are in keeping with this understanding; for he adds, 'by way of being one and the same numerically though not one in definition'. For the incorporeal matter is one and the same in number with the water, but <it is> not the same in definition, since it is one thing for it to be matter, another <for it to be> water.[283] And the same statement <holds> also for the matter of the thing that grows: being water is one thing and being the matter in a plant is another.

'So it is better in every case to make the matter inseparable.' The intention was from the beginning to refute the view that the matter of the thing that grows is body in potentiality and not in actuality. Pursuing his enquiry by means of a series of divisions, he showed first that it was not possible for this <matter>, if it were body in potentiality, to subsist in its own right. Then next his intention was to investigate whether it exist *in* something, either by way of being nothing which belongs to that in which it is, or by way of being something <which does so belong>. And since he has shown that it is impossible for it to be in something by way of being nothing which belongs to that in which it is – it will result, he says, in its being separated without that in which it is in any way changing, and many impossible consequences will follow from this – he has left unrefuted the other arm <of the division>, I mean existing in something whilst being something which belongs to that in which it is, as though it were something true which could be understood as being tacitly implied. But if the matter of the growing thing is *in* something and contributes something to the composition of that in which it is, it will be <so> either as a part in a whole or as formless matter in the composite thing.[284]

However, formless matter, as has already been said, is the matter, not of growth, but of coming-to-be and perishing, whereas the object of the present enquiry is the matter of growth. It remains therefore for it to be as a part in a whole. But if this <is what it is>, the matter of the growing thing is in actuality body and something possessed of size, which was what had to be proved originally. If someone were to say 'What part in a whole, in that case, is the matter of the thing that grows? Why is it said to be a part rather than a whole?', he should recognise that the aim was to show that the matter of the thing that grows is in actuality body and a thing possessed of size, and not in potentiality. We made a full and exhaustive division of that which is in something, and we found one segment of the division, being in something as a part, which, we admitted, remains unrefuted, not because the matter of the thing which grows is said to be a part of a whole (for it was not the aim to determine this – whether it is part or whole), but introducing the matter of the thing that grows as body in actuality, not in potentiality; for this was the aim, since it made no difference whether it was a whole or a part.

The overall structure of the things that are being proved is of this sort. However, we need to find out what it is that is now being inferred. He first shows that it is impossible to suppose <that there is> matter in something which is able to be separated from that in which it is without that in which it exists in any way changing, using as an example coming-to-be and the change of water into air. He then draws an inference, saying 'So it is better in every case to make the matter inseparable'. If you take this to be said with a view to the original aim <of the discussion>, his statement concerns the matter of the growing thing, and he is claiming that it is necessary to posit the matter of the growing thing as not being able to be separated from that in which it is, since it exists as that very thing which the thing in which it is is said to be. An example would be, if the matter of air turned out, not to be contained in water, but to be the water itself, being, that is, body in actuality, which is in fact the case.

There is no difference in number, he says, between the matter of the growing thing, that is, the body which exists actually, e.g. the water, from the prime matter of the water which is changing into being water. It is the same in number and in substratum, as will be demonstrated more fully in what follows, but it is not one in definition; for the definition of the matter in so far as it is matter is one thing and <the definition of it> in so far as it has become water <is> another thing. What he is now saying is compatible with what he will be saying a little further on, when he says that the matter of the growing thing is not different in number from that of the thing that is coming-to-be, but only in definition.[285]

It is possible to take <the words> 'it is better in every case to make the matter inseparable' as relating, not to the original aim <of the discussion>, but to what has just been said. Having at the start stated the thesis which alleges that the matter of the growing thing is in something without belonging in any way to that in which it is, he clarifies his remark, taking coming-to-be as a model, saying: 'I mean, as would be the case if, when air came to be from water, it were to happen without water changing, but because its matter was in the water as if in a vessel'. Then, after this, while sketching the refutation of this sort of thesis, namely, that matter cannot be supposed to be in something and be capable of being separated from it without that in which it exists changing in any way, he again focuses the argument on the change from water to air, which is a case of coming-to-be, so that it is in relation to what has just been said, which, as we have said, was inserted by way of providing a model, that he adds the remark 'So it is better in every case to make the matter inseparable', intending his words to apply to the primary, formless matter of things which come to be. For it is better in every case, he says, for the matter of the air, which is in the water from which the air comes to be, to be 81,1 inseparable from the water in which it is. For it is not numerically different from the water, but one and the same <as it>, and the difference is only in the definition. For being water is one thing and being matter is another.

320b14 But points cannot be posited as the body's matter either; nor [for the same reasons] can lines: [the matter is that of which these are the limit, and it is impossible for it ever to exist without affections and without shape.]

On the subject of points he has said earlier that they are not the matter of the growing thing, regarding this[286] as a consequence of the theories which make the matter of the growing thing potentially body and separate in its own right. Now he seems to be attacking those who make bodies come to be from surfaces. They treat the fact that they do not produce bodies from things without size as a point in their favour from this point of view (since surfaces are things possessed of size); but for all that they do not escape the <charge of maintaining something which is> impossible. For even if surfaces are things possessed of size, they are not in space. It was proved at the start that whenever the thing which comes to be is *somewhere,* it has to be the case that that from which it comes to be is also in space either *per se* or *per accidens.* But it is not possible to suppose that surfaces are in space even *per accidens* on account of the fact that they preexist bodies, whether, as in Plato's view, because bodies are composed by way of synthesis out of surfaces, or because it is by their being made to flow that bodies are produced in thought.[287]

Whilst it is his intention to attack those who produce bodies out of surfaces, he brings in points as well, since it would follow from their view that what is possessed of size is also produced from points too. For, as he says in *On the Heavens,*[288] 'The same thought that makes bodies out of surfaces makes them out of points too', although this latter seem more ridiculous – to make something possessed of size out of that which is altogether without size.

Alexander understood 'But points cannot be posited' as 'For points cannot be posited', so that there should be no break in the whole thought of the passage: 'For it is better in every case to make the matter inseparable, for points cannot be posited as the body's matter either, nor can lines.' For neither[289] can any of these subsist in its own right, nor can extension come to be from unextended points. Alexander, then, interprets the words 'nor can lines be posited as the body's matter' in this way, as though the argument was directed at those who produce body from surfaces, since, as he says himself, it belongs to the same thought to produce body out of surfaces and surface out of lines and lines out of points. However, this does violence to the text; for it is lines that were mentioned, not surfaces. This is why it has to be said that earlier on he had proved that it was impossible to suppose 82,1 points to be the matter of the growing thing, and now his teaching is that the same holds for lines, repeating the argument he used about points. The reason why it is not possible to suppose lines either <to play this rôle> is something which he goes on to state himself: 'for the same reasons', <i.e.> because none of these things will be able to subsist by itself, nor to occupy any space in its[290] own right.

But points cannot be posited as the body's matter; nor can lines. We insisted earlier that Aristotle seems to have moved over to the discussion of prime matter, despite having intended from the beginning to present his teaching about the matter of the growing thing. Half way through, in order to illustrate the point, he brings back[291] the discussion about coming-to-be, and seems to follow the thread of the argument and treat of prime matter which is what underlies coming-to-be, moving away from what was originally intended. So now too the commentator Alexander understands the matter of body to be formless prime matter, and interprets in the light of this the way in which the connection is made with the whole passage which follows: the matter is that of which these are the limits. He says that after telling us that it is impossible for lines or points to be supposed to be matter, he proceeds now to say what the matter of body is, claiming that the matter is that of which points and lines are the limits and boundaries, i.e. he says, actual body; for this is what has lines and points as its limits. But since matter existing on its own is neither actual body nor bounded by lines, he goes on to say in what state it has to be if lines are to be its boundaries and limits, so that you may grasp his reason for saying that lines are the limits of matter.

This is the reason why lines are its limits, namely, because it is at no time without some affection or form, for its being is bound up with these. So it is in virtue of the fact that it is inseparable from affection and form that the matter is actual body, and not in so far as it is formless and prime <matter>. What is said here is the same as what was originally said earlier,[292] that that which comes to be comes to be from something actually existing and possessed of form. This is the sort of interpretation Alexander gives, and what he says makes it clear that he regards the present discussion as being concerned with the matter of things that come to be, matter which for its existence requires form and in this way attains actual subsistence, but considered as matter and as capable of becoming a this something and a this,[293] is formless and incorporeal.

But now suppose then that Aristotle's discussion does not have as its subject the matter of things that come to be, but that of the growing thing, which in reality and considered as matter of a growing thing is body in actuality. In that case, when he says, 'But lines cannot be posited as the body's matter either; nor can points',[294] <the expression> 'of the growing thing' should also be understood, in order to make him speak of the matter of the growing body * * * to teach, when he says 'Since there is a matter of corporeal substance also'.[295] The immediately succeeding words, 'matter is that of which these are the limit', follow more appropriately on this interpretation, his meaning being that actual body and not that which is <only> potential is the matter of the growing body, which can never exist without affection and form. You will be able to connect this remark with the interpretation which has just been given if you maintain that what is said by Aristotle is that the actual body, which is considered as being in three dimensions, never subsists without affection and form. 'Form' would refer to the natural kind,[296] and 'affection', here, would indicate the accidents.[297]

320b17 One thing comes to be *simpliciter* from another thing, as has been determined elsewhere ...

'*Simpliciter*' is to be taken as meaning either 'properly speaking' or 'generally', and 'from another thing' represents 'from something actually existing', since it has been established[298] that one thing's coming-to-be is another thing's perishing. As for the words 'as has been determined elsewhere', he dealt with these matters also in the *Physics*.[299] He enquired how contraries come from one another and said that the explanation was that there was some underlying thing common to them which was receptive of both turn by turn.

320b19 ... being caused to do so by something actually existing either of the same species or of the same genus [(fire, e.g., by fire, or a human being by a human being), or by an actuality (for a hard thing is not caused to come to be by a hard thing).[300]]

Since everything that comes to be comes to be from something and <is caused to do so> by something, after saying what it is that growing comes from, namely, that it is from something possessed of size in actuality, he now says what it is that causes it to do so, i.e. the efficient cause; for it is impossible, as Plato says, for anything[301] to have coming-to-be without a cause. This is why Aristotle, having spoken about the material cause of growth, speaks now also about the efficient cause, in so far as is helpful to him for present purposes. For he does not now give us the efficient cause that is specific to growth, but only that which applies without qualification to all coming-to-be, both that which concerns substance and that which concerns alteration. He says, therefore, that that which comes to be is caused to do so by something actually existing either of the same genus or of the same species as that which comes to be. He himself supplies examples of causes of the same species, as when fire is produced by fire or a human being by a human being; but as for causes of the same genus, he makes clear himself what it is that he is maintaining <things are caused by in this case> by saying 'or by an actuality'. For even if the agent were not of the same species as the thing that is coming-to-be, it <would> definitely <have to be> of the same genus, at least in this very respect, namely, that it exists in actuality in the same way as the thing that is coming-to-be.

'A hard thing,' he says, 'is not caused to come to be by a hard thing', which makes it clear that what causes it is not something of the same species, but a cold thing[302] – if this is in fact how it comes about – by solidifying it; and that is something of the same genus as the thing which is coming-to-be, in that it is cold in actuality in the same way as that <sc. the hard thing> is hard in actuality. So in this way it is caused to come to be by something of the same genus, since <it is caused to come to be> by that which exists in actuality. For the efficient cause, whatever it may be, in every way actually is. Those plants which grow spontaneously[303] do not owe their coming-to-be to[304] an efficient cause of the same species, but to something which exists in actuality and which in this way is of the same genus. The creative rational principles,[305] which exist in actuality, are the causes of the things which grow spontaneously. And white is not caused to come to be from white (as in thousands of similar cases), but from something which exists in actuality. What he is saying now will be something he can use in his account of growth, enabling him to show that there is some efficient cause of growth which assimilates and aggregates the matter of the growing thing to the thing which causes it to grow.

> **320b22** Since there is a matter of corporeal substance, and this is already the matter of a particular kind of body, [for there is no kind of body common <to everything>, the matter of size and affection will be one and the same as this, separable in definition but not separable in place, unless the affections too are separable.]

After enquiring about the matter of the growing thing and showing that it is body in actuality, so that no one should think that this was prime matter, he now sets out his view that there is a matter of body itself, which is primary and formless and necessarily incorporeal. For matter is different from that of which it is the matter. So the matter of body will not be body, but <will be> incorporeal. And if it is that which underlies all forms, then it will be formless. The matter of corporeal substance is one thing, that of growth another. For it will seem to be the case that, if the one is incorporeal, formless and primary, the other, <the matter> of growth, <will be> body in actuality.

He says then that the matter of substance is the same as that of growth and that of alteration; for he explains growth by means of size and accidents by means of affection. For if the matter of substance were one thing and that of quantity and quality and the rest another, accidents would be separable from body, which is impossible. So the matter of coming-to-be and growth and alteration will be the same, though not the same in every respect, but in one respect. And he goes on to say how it is the same, claiming that the one matter can be
85,1 separated from the other in definition, but not in place. For the actual body which underlies growth and alteration is different in definition from primary and formless matter (for there is one definition of prime matter and another of body), but numerically and in substratum both are one and the same and occupying the same place. For were you to say that the matter of substance existed in one place and that of growth and the affections in another, the corporeal substance would be in one place and the affections in another, which is something impossible, namely supposing affections <to be> outside bodies subsisting in their own right.

'And this is already the matter of a particular kind of body,' for there is no kind of body common <to everything>. <This is> because, he says, coming-to-be is of individual bodies, of a 'this something'. For there is neither coming-to-be *simpliciter* nor subsistence of that which is common and predicated of the rest. The universal subsists only in the creative rational principles. So the matter too is of a particular body, not of that which is common. For if it were of the common body, it would no longer be actually existing matter, since that which is common does not exist in actuality. So, just as the universal body is existent in the creative rational principles, so the universal matter must be thought to be; for nothing universal is in subsistence, whether body or matter of body.

> **320b25** The difficulties already examined have made clear [that growth is not a change from something which potentially has size, but actually has no size: the void this implies would be separated, and the impossibility of this has been stated in earlier works.]

Having investigated the matter of growth, and shown that many absurd consequences follow from the view that growth comes to be from that which has size and <is body> in potentiality but lacks in

size in actuality, he now draws together his conclusions <by saying> that the thing which grows does not grow from that which has size potentially, but from some natural object[306] actually possessed of size. For if it were from something not possessed of size that a thing which has size increased and grew, there would be something common or something void which was separated. Both these words are in the manuscripts and both make good sense.[307] If 'that which is common would be separated' was what was written 'that which is common' would signify matter, since it is the common substratum for everything. What was being said would be that if growth and size came to be from what lacks size and is potentially body, it would be what potentially has size, which is the separable matter of size and of actual body subsisting in its own right. But if what were there is 'the void would be separated', he would be saying that if growth comes to be from what has size potentially but actually has no size, the void 86,1
will be separated and something subsisting in its own right. For if the thing that has grown takes on a larger amount of space not occupied by that which approaches it and produces the growth (for *ex hypothesi* that is without size), this amount of space which the thing which has grown took on would previously have been void – something which was shown to be impossible in the fourth book of the *Physics*.[308] And that matter cannot be separated either from all form is something we have said on many occasions.

Given that none of the things that perish depart into what in no sense and in no way is, the reductio ad absurdum which introduces the void should be recognised as correct. Should it be said that <things> pass away into what is not and are generated from what is not, this supposition does not immediately entail that the void exists in actuality. For the place which is left by the thing that is perishing is filled up by the thing which comes to be. In the same way, in the case of growth too, if someone were to say that not only does growth come to be from that which is possessed of size in potentiality, but that which decreases also changes into that which is possessed of size in potentiality, it still does not make room for the void. So since it is agreed that that which decreases does not change into that which is possessed of size in potentiality, the argument succeeds along these lines.[309]

Should anyone enquire what he means by the addition of 'separated' (for it would have been enough to say that there would be a void), it should be realised that it is said by way of contrast with the plenum; for his teaching in the *Physics*[310] was that the plenum differs from the void only relatively, and that a plenum is nothing else but a void filled with body, and in return a void is a plenum deprived of body. So 'separable void' signifies nothing else but 'void subsisting in its own right'.

> **320b28** Again, change of this sort would be characteristic not of growth but of coming-to-be [*simpliciter*; for growth is the increase of something already possessed of size and diminution is its getting smaller (and this is why what grows is bound to have some size).]

From this point on the reading[311] 'for that which is common (i.e. the matter) would be separate' will seem appropriate. For in addition to this absurdity,[312] he says, this sort of matter belongs more to coming-to-be than to growth. He says, therefore, that the coming-to-be of something possessed of size from what is sizeless is not a special feature of change by way of growth, but of change in respect of substance, i.e. of coming-to-be. For growth is not the coming-to-be but the increase, and getting smaller the decrease, of size. 'This is why,' he says, 'what grows is bound to have some size'. But there is also the reading 'what comes to be' <in place of 'what grows'>,[313] and Alexander mentions this reading, saying that 'larger or smaller' ought to be understood from the context, so that what was said would be 'This is why what comes to be is bound to have some size, not, he says, what comes to be *simpliciter*, but what comes to be larger or smaller'.

87,1 **320b32** So [growth can]not [be a change] from sizeless matter [to actualized size];[314] for this would be the coming-to-be of body rather than growth.

The common notion of growth gives support to the view that in the case of growth it is not from a thing possessed of size not previously existing that something possessed of size comes to be, but that increase or decrease takes place in a previously existing thing. However, it has not yet been established that growth being change to something larger of a pre-existing thing already possessed of size of itself necessarily implies that the matter of growth is not possessed of size in potentiality but in actuality. This has not yet been established. For what, as far as the present argument goes, prevents growth being increase in something preexisting already possessed of size, whilst the increase comes to be from something possessed of size <only> in potentiality, which would be matter of the growth? I say 'as far as the present argument goes', because earlier he used other means of establishing that growth does not come to be from what is possessed of size <only> in potentiality, the principal point being that what is possessed of size cannot come to be from what is sizeless, or for that matter increase towards something larger; for this, it seems, would carry an implication of the void. We must, however, recognise this: none of the things which come to be comes to be from things that are not or from incorporeal things, but all the things which come to be do so from bodies which exist in actuality, but which have in potentiality that which the thing which comes to be is. Yet for all that we do not call the body which subsists in actuality the primary matter, but the common substratum which is considered to be the subject of the change, which is everything in potentiality, but in actuality is always considered together with a single form.

In exactly the same way in the case of growth too, even if someone were to suppose that what the growing thing grows from is a body, nevertheless, nothing prevents the matter of growth being that which is body in potentiality, as also in the case of coming-to-be.[315] And in terms of the enumeration of the possibilities which was made earlier, even if the other possibilities are shown to be impossible – those which involve the matter of the growing thing being body in potentiality and not in actuality – still the arguments provided by Aristotle cannot in any way rule out the possibility that allows for the matter of the growing thing to be possessed of size in potentiality, existing in something, not as a part of that in which it is, nor as being nothing in any way belonging to that in which it is, but as matter is in a composite thing – unless, that is, one makes the gratuitous assertion that this sort of matter is not that which belongs to growth but to coming-to-be.

> **320b34** It will be better at this point to take up as though we were meeting it for the first time the question [what sort of thing growth or diminution is, whose causes we are seeking. It appears that when a thing grows, every part of it has grown, and similarly when a thing diminishes, every part has become smaller; also that it is by something's acceding to it that it grows and by something's leaving it that it diminishes. Now that by which a thing grows is necessarily either incorporeal or body.] 88,1

With the object of finding out what the matter of growth is, he began the argument with a distinction: either the matter of growth is body in potentiality but incorporeal in actuality, or it is body in actuality. By means of the preceding arguments he has proved that it is not body in potentiality, whether as separable and subsisting in its own right or as existing in something else. So now he intends to examine also the remaining arm of the distinction, I mean whether the matter of growth is perceptible body in actuality. He reconstructs the whole argument, making the division more universal and pursuing the argument in both directions by developing further paradoxes. But before he does this, he sets out the properties that belong to growth according to the commonsense notion <that we have of it>. He says that we must, as it were, come closer to the investigation of growth, and coming to grips with it, so to speak, get an initial hold of the kind of thing it is whose causes we are seeking; and we would achieve this if we enquired what properties belong to growing according to our commonsense notion <of it>. The theory of it that we produce has to be accountable to these; for anything that failed to accord with what is said about it by common sense would not be said about it appropriately. The commonsense notions are the starting-point for all demonstration.[316]

He does this too in the *Physics* in his teaching about place. Intending to treat of this, he investigates first the properties that common sense attributes to it, so that we can accept the conclusions about it if they accord with these, and throw them out if they do not, and <so that> he may show the solutions of the paradoxes which present themselves about place to be correct by their chiming in with the commonsense view of the properties <of place>. <Now he sets out> the features of the growing thing <according to the commonsense view>,[317] which are three: first, the fact that there is growth in every single part of the growing thing; secondly, the fact that growth takes place as the result of something acceding from outside; and thirdly, in addition to these, although he does not bring this out here but adds it in the following section, the fact that the growing thing remains and is preserved in the form it took previously.

After mentioning these, it remains for him to raise doubts about the matter of growing things, pursuing the argument by means of a distinction. That by which the growing thing grows must necessarily be either body or something incorporeal, taking 'incorporeal' now in a more universal sense, since it includes also body in potentiality. But absurdities follow from supposing <what it grows by to be something> incorporeal; for we shall become involved in a separable void subsisting in its own right, as was said earlier. And if that by which growth comes to be is body, body will pass through body, since that by which it grows is assimilated by the whole of the growing thing, since if there were any part to which it was not assimilated, that <part> would obviously not grow either. <So>[318] it would follow necessarily that body would pass through body, which has been shown in the *Physics*[319] to be impossible. Once these claims have been made, accounts of growth have to be produced of a kind which will be in accordance with the features of the growing thing recognised by common sense and will escape the paradoxes and the absurdities that follow from them.

321a6 If it is incorporeal there will be a separable void.

Assuming that it is by something acceding to it that the growing thing grows, he enquires what this thing is that accedes to it, whether body or <something> incorporeal, and he finds a puzzle in each of the alternatives. If, he says, it is incorporeal, there will be a separable void, which is just what he also said previously. For the growing thing takes on additional space, whereas that by which it grows is supposed not to be in space, being incorporeal. It is clear, therefore, that that space which the growing thing takes on, before it was occupied by the growing thing, was separated from body and empty.

> **321a6** But it is impossible for the matter of size to be separable, [as has been said earlier].

He brings this forward as the second absurdity which follows from saying that that by which growth occurs is incorporeal. It should not be thought that the passage depends on what has gone before. It is as if he had said, 'Again, it is impossible for the matter of size to be separable'.[320] But there are two ways of understanding the remark, either <i> as saying that it is impossible for the matter of size to be separable (for he showed earlier that it was impossible for the matter of size, i.e. the primary matter which is incorporeal, to be separable without being body in actuality, since it cannot subsist in its own right) or <ii> as saying that it is impossible for the matter to be separable from size, not in the sense that matter has size in virtue of its own definition, but that when it is and subsists it is inseparable from size. For it is required for the existence of size, though it is itself sizeless according to its own definition. If, therefore, he says, you maintain that that which accedes and produces growth (for this is taken as given) is incorporeal, since this is the matter of growth, you are supposing that incorporeal matter is self-subsistent and separable. So if the reading 'there will be a separable void' is correct,[321] we shall understand 'and it is impossible for the matter to be separable 90,1
from size'[322] as <setting out> a further difficulty. If, on the other hand, 'common' is right, i.e. matter, there will be no break in the argument. By saying 'and it is impossible for the matter of size to be separable' he has added that that which is common, i.e. the matter, cannot be separable.

> **321a7** If, on the other hand, it is body, there will be two bodies in the same place, [that which is growing and that which is making it grow; and this too is impossible.]

He now moves on to the alternative, and raises problems for the view that it is by body that growth comes to be. There will be, he says, two bodies in the same place, and body will pass through body. The absurdity comes into the open when it is agreed that every part of the growing thing grows. For if the growing thing grows in every part <of itself>, that which accedes <to it> will be juxtaposed everywhere to the pre-existing growing thing. And if this is so, it will pass through all of it, in order to make it grow everywhere. But if it were said that that which accedes passed through the whole of the growing thing, it would be necessary either to suppose the whole growing thing to be a through-way or for body to pass through body, which is the same as to say that two bodies are in the same place. This has been proved to be amongst the things that are impossible; for the greatest of things will be in the smallest, e.g. the sea in a vase or the earth in a shell.[323] So the same mistake is made by saying that that by which a body grows is body as by saying that it is incorporeal. Both views imply a vacuum. For if body goes through body, the place which has been vacated by the body of that which accedes will be empty, and if, on the other hand, that by which the body grows is incorporeal, there will be a separable void, as has previously been said.

> **321a9** Nor, for that matter, is it possible to say [that growth or diminution takes place in the same way as the change from water into air, despite the fact that there too the size becomes greater. For this will be, not growth, but coming-to-be of that which is the terminus of the change and perishing of its opposite.]

After raising objections against each alternative, and showing that if we say that that by which growth comes to be is body it will follow that two bodies will be in the same <place>, and if <we say that it is> incorporeal there will be a separable void, he returns to the attack, as it were, against both objections. He asks whether it is not the case that these consequences follow necessarily for those who say that growth occurs in the same way as coming-to-be. For when water changes to air, a larger quantity of air comes to be from a smaller quantity of water; nevertheless, it is not possible to say either that
91,1 two bodies will be in the same place or that there will be a separable void. But this reply would fit better the argument against the other member of the disjunction, which supposes that that by which growth comes to be is incorporeal. Just as when water changes to air, a larger quantity of substance comes to be from a smaller without any body approaching, and nevertheless nothing absurd follows, <so it is possible> to suppose the same way <of changing occurs> in the case of growth also.

In a further argument against this Aristotle shows that it is impossible to suppose that this is the way in which growth <occurs>. Generally speaking, he says, the change of water into air is not growth, and this will be clear from what is said in accordance with the commonsense conception of growth. What sort of thing is it which we should in fact say has grown? For the air has not grown, because it did not even exist beforehand, nor has it, while remaining air and taking something to itself, come to be larger, because there is no room on this hypothesis for saying that body acceding to it made it grow. But neither for that matter has the water grown – something that has perished and no longer subsists. So if neither the water nor the air can be said to have grown, the change from water to air has been different in every respect from growth.

Someone might reasonably reply to this, claiming that while it is true that the change from water to air differs from growth, the same difficulty arises for both growth and coming-to-be. <For>[324] just as in the case of growth the view that the growing thing takes to itself more space without any actual body joining it implies a vacuum, so in the case of coming-to-be, where a larger quantity of air comes to be from a smaller quantity of water without anything acceding to it, the same argument requires either that we posit empty space which the air that has come to be from water takes over, or that body passes through body. And it might be said that, whilst, on the one hand, air coming-to-be from water demands more space, so conversely water <coming-to-be> somewhere else from air takes up less space, so that there never comes to be a vacuum (for the space that the contracting body vacates at this point is taken over by the body which is somewhere else expanding, as the parts of the air continuously exchange places with each other and fill up the space vacated by the contracting body, and give up in turn their own place to the body that is coming-to-be) – <if so>, then these same things could be understood also concerning growth. For someone might say that the place that has here been taken up by the thing that has grown has been vacated by the thing that is diminishing elsewhere, and not by the thing that accedes to the growth; for it is from body in potentiality that the growing thing grows and into this that the diminishing thing changes.

But against this it will be said that it is far-fetched to postulate that when something grows here somewhere else something is bound to be shrinking. This, however, is what is in fact maintained in the case of coming-to-be. For it is necessary in this case too, if there is not to be a vacuum, to suppose that, if water is turning into air here, somewhere else air is turning in the opposite direction into water. So this difficulty would be a shared one: either there will be a vacuum; or we shall have to assume without proof that to the same extent that water is changing here, air is changing elsewhere. And not only <do we have to say this> when change of the elements is brought about by nature, but also when it is brought about by art; for example, when I cause water to evaporate, somewhere else either art or nature is causing the same amount of air to change into water, and it is clear that the same amount of water must be supposed to come to be elsewhere as I have caused to evaporate here.

But this would seem to be altogether laughable, first the fact that one is making such a gratuitous assumption to the effect that, if someone here decides to make water evaporate or to set fire to wood or something else, elsewhere the same amount of body will be changing from a finer type of substance to a coarser, in order that it may not happen either that a vacuum should come to be or that body should pass through body.[325] Secondly, an even greater absurdity results: it is absolutely necessary, if a small change occurs like a little water here evaporating, that a large quantity of air should be moved instantaneously over great stretches of the world so that a mutual filling up of places may occur, as the parts of the air give up in turn their places to each other without leaving any gaps.

Let us take a large scale example to make the argument clearer. Now if in winter in this part of the world or in this city, wherever it happens to be, air condenses and changes into water, the place vacated here by the air that has become water is filled up by the air which has been generated from water in the antipodes (the reason being that when it is winter with us it is summer with them) – in that case it necessarily follows that, immediately the water is generated here, in an instant the water there is changed conversely into air in equal quantity to the amount that has perished here, and all the air in between has been moved, pushed out by the air that has come to be in the antipodes, in order that the void that has come to be here may be filled by the particles of air in between giving up their places in turn to each other. The same would have to happen if even a cup of water were to evaporate.

But this is not only absurd, but far-fetched and impossible. It is an impossibility for so much air to be moved instantaneously, and in general instantaneous movement is impossible. Actually, we see, even when in some place a very strong wind passes over a wide area, a complete calm often reigns in the places surrounding it at no great distance from it, which do not feel this violent motion of the air in their neighbourhood. And often in a short part of an hour the air is observed to be greatly condensed and suddenly to become rarefied, and undergoing this many times over. Shall we then imagine the converse of these phenomena occurring also in the antipodes, or simply in another place?[326] I mean by 'the converse', for example, what happens when air here condenses and elsewhere becomes rarefied, and when here it becomes rarefied and elsewhere condenses, and this often many times in the same hour.

So since the conclusions we have reached are not true, but it is true that body does not pass through body and that there is no void, how do we solve the puzzle? We say then that it is the nature of air to settle down on itself and condense and from having had a larger bulk to become smaller, and again to rarefy and from having been smaller to become larger, and that it is natural for it to condense and settle down on itself, not only when it is being chilled, but when it is being pushed or compressed. This, in fact, is how Aristotle showed that rains occur in summertime in Ethiopia; for the mist that is thrust down from the North by the monsoon winds comes up against the Arabian mountains, which are of a great size, and being crushed always by what comes behind is condensed by the compression and changes into water.[327] It is possible at the time of the summer winds in Ethiopia to see the rain pouring down like a stream continuously without any coldness <being present>.

And the same <phenomenon> occurs also in the baths. The steam goes upwards and reaches the ceiling, and having nowhere to get out is compressed into itself, and in its condensed state it comes to be water and is caused to flow downwards by the heaviness that is part of its nature. But just as it is condensed by being compressed, so we observe it to be rarefied by being extended; for it is possible with one's mouth to suck out a large quantity of tightly packed air from a bottle with a narrow mouth without any other air entering from elsewhere. Obviously neither the whole of the interior space nor a part of it has become void, for this is impossible. So the rarefied air that is left behind has occupied the entire space. If, therefore, it is possible for the air both to be compressed and settle into itself, and again to be rarefied, we should realise that when water evaporates here, either by being boiled or in some other way, the air which has come to be pushes aside <the air> which lies alongside it, and that <the air> that is next to it, until some air condensed by compression relinquishes the amount of space that the air that comes to be has occupied.

And it is not in the least necessary for the same amount of air somewhere else to have changed into water or for movement to have taken place of all the air <there is> (this is far-fetched and unreasonable), but only for enough air to have been compacted by the thrust of <the air> that has come to be to leave an equivalent amount of space for <the air> that has come to be. The same <is true> also if it is condensed and changes into water. <The air> which lies alongside that which has condensed is compelled by the force of the void[328] to follow <the air> which has contracted, and again that which lies alongside *it* <is compelled to follow> that which is next to it, until some other air has rarefied over enough space to fill up the amount of space left by <the air> which has condensed. There is certainly no need for the same amount of air to come to be from water somewhere else as air has changed here into water.

> **321a14** [It is not growth of either of these:] but either of nothing at all or of whatever there may be that both have in common (both that which has come to be and that which has perished)

[as, for example, body. The water has not grown, neither has the air: rather, the one has perished and the other come into existence: it is the body, if such there be, which has grown. But this too is impossible. For the features which belong to a thing which grows or gets smaller must be kept in its definition, and these are three: (a) each part of the growing object possessed of size is larger – of flesh if it is flesh; (b) something accedes to the thing which grows; and (c) the thing which grows is preserved and remains. For, whereas in the case of something's coming-to-be *simpliciter* or perishing nothing remains, in those of alteration and of growth or diminution that which grows or alters does remain the same, although in the former case the affection and in the latter case the size does not remain the same.]

After saying that neither has grown, neither what there has been change *into* nor what <there has been change> *from*, he now says that it remains either that the thing which has changed in cases like that of the change from water to air is nothing or that there is something which has changed – something which is a substratum common to what has come to be and what has perished, and that this is body. Then immediately he sets up an argument to show that this too cannot be said to have grown, because in this case the features that belong in general to the growing thing are not safeguarded – I mean the fact that every part of the growing thing has become larger, the fact that something accedes, and in addition to these the fact that the growing thing remains. Of these <requirements that of> remaining is not present so far as body is concerned: it does not remain, but something comes to be from something else, something rarer from something denser, something larger from something smaller.

It is not reasonable to say that that which remains is the universal, for the universal neither is generated nor does it perish, nor does it subsist at all having its own existence, but the body which comes to be and perishes is always that which is particular and individual, and it is this which actually subsists. So if the individual body perishes, and one body comes to be from another, manifestly they have no common body which remains, except prime matter, which, being one and the same, is regarded as the subject of change. For this is how coming-to-be has differed from growth and alteration, by the fact that in the case of coming-to-be that which changes does not remain, whereas in the case of growth and alteration it remains the same as far as the substance is concerned, but changes in respect of the accidents, in the case of growth in respect of size, and in the case of alteration in respect of affection. If it were to be said that in the change from water to air three-dimensional extension, in so far as it is that, remains, and only becomes larger from being smaller, it should be recognised that, even if this were so, it would still not have changed in virtue of something acceding from outside.

Furthermore, if the three-dimensional extension existing in its own right without any form came to be greater, it would perhaps be 95,1
possible, though implausible, to concede that this sort of thing was growth; but now, given that the growing thing has to keep its previous form, as in the case of flesh and bone and things like this, whereas the three-dimensional extension, having been informed by the form of water, does not in the change to a greater bulk (I mean the <coming-to-be>[329] of air) keep its previous form (I mean that of water), it is obvious that this sort of thing would not be growth. Nor is the three-dimensional extension remaining a special feature of the change from water to air, but it occurs generally in all coming-to-be and in all change. For it has been frequently shown that the primary substratum must be unchanged in the case of all changing things. But in the case of growth the same form which the growing thing had even before it grew has to remain, whereas this does not happen in the case of the change from water to air. So this sort of thing is no longer growth.

> **321a26** If, then, what has been spoken of is to be growth, [it would be possible for something to grow without anything acceding to it or anything remaining, or for something to get smaller without anything leaving it, and for the growing object not to remain. But this must be kept; for it was laid down that growth is like this.]

If, he says, what has been spoken of, that is, the change of water into air, were to be said by us to be growth, because of the fact that its bulk has come to be larger, we should be compelled to say that the growing thing failed to remain <through the change> and that the growth occurred without anything acceding <to the growing thing>, and we should be rejecting the things that are said about growth in accordance with the common conception. But if it is necessary to keep these things, as indeed it is, the change from water to air would not be <a case of> growth.

> **321a29** The question might also be raised, which is it that grows, the thing to which something is added – [as, for example, if there is growth in a man's calf, this becomes larger, whilst the thing by which it grows, the nourishment, does not. So why is it not the case that both have grown? The thing added and the thing to which it is added are both larger, just as when you mix wine with water – each increases in the same way. Is it because

the substance of the one persists, but not that of the other, namely the nourishment? For in the other example too it is the ingredient which prevails in the mixing which the result is said to be, that is, wine, since the mixture as a whole does the work of the wine, not that of the water.]

He sets out all the puzzles and problems that have been raised about growth and arbitrates between them before producing the appropriate teaching on the subject. For when the puzzles have been presented first and have obtained the solutions they require the account of the matter is more easily set right. At this point he begins an enquiry relevant to the definition of growth, asking whether both, that which is added and that to which addition is made, are things that grow, or only that to which addition is made. Both that which is added and that to which addition is made seem to have come to be bigger, as is the case with wine and water; for when you mix water with wine, each seems to have come to be more, both the water and the wine. His decision about this puzzle is that we have to say that it is only that
96,1 to which addition is made that has grown, e.g. if a calf were that to which addition is made, and nourishment were what is added, * * *[330] would not be said to grow. And he gives the explanation. Since it has already been accepted that the growing thing must remain, and the calf remains, not the thing that accedes (for this changes in respect of its substance), it would be reasonable only for the calf to be said to grow, not the thing which accedes.

But in the case of the mixture of water and wine too, when someone mixes a little water with a larger quantity of wine, it is only the wine that we say has grown, because it remains exhibiting the power of wine. In the same way also, if you mix a little wine with a larger quantity of water so that the wine is overcome by the water, we do not say that the wine has grown because it does not preserve its characteristic power, but the water, which does preserve its characteristic power and the specific features of water. For in general it is not the one that perishes nor the one which is beaten that we say has grown, but the one which wins and which remains. If the mixture were equally balanced, not in terms of quantity but in terms of power, so that each <contributor> is affected in the same way by the other, you would say that in this way each one had grown – or perhaps it would be more true to say that <each one> had perished; for the power and the pure functioning[331] of both is no longer preserved. Obviously in the case of mixtures his use of the word 'growth' is rather stretched; for neither does the same form survive in a pure state, nor does every part of it[332] increase, but all that is the case is that by the addition the whole has come to be greater.

321b2 Similarly in the case of alteration too, if something continues to be flesh ...

His object being to prove that what grows is that to which the addition is made, not that which is added, his first argument rested on the fact that that to which addition is made survives while that which is added changes. He now, however, adduces the case of alteration in order to make the things he is saying about growth more clear. As in the case of growth there is the growing thing and there is also the thing by which it grows, and there is also the power of growing which has its existence in the growing thing, so also in the case of alteration there is the substratum, that is, the thing that is being altered, and there is the thing by which it is altered, and there is also the power by which the alteration is accomplished.

As in the case of growth, therefore, it is only the substratum which we say has grown (for the power of growing and receiving nourishment is in it), so in the case of alteration too it is the subject which we say has been altered, e.g. the flesh, when it changes in respect of some affection without losing its form. And there are occasions when that by which a thing is altered is in no way affected and does not change, as when our bodies are warmed by a fire beside which we are <sitting> without the fire being affected in any way by us in return. The thing which produces the alteration remains unaffected in a similar way to the thing which is added, when this too does not grow. But there are occasions when it too is itself affected in some way and suffers alteration, like the air in the baths which warms us and which is affected by us in return. In this respect the thing that produces the alteration differs from the thing that is added and produces growth, because the latter never grows, whereas the thing that produces alteration is sometimes altered itself too and sometimes not.

However, that which is added will seem on occasion perhaps to grow, when, <that is,> the nourishment which accedes is turned to wind and comes to be greater in quantity. But truth is not like this. For this is not growth but perishing: we would not say that the food that has been turned to wind has grown, nor that the power of growth is in it, but rather in the growing thing. But, even though that by which it has been altered is affected in some way and is often also altered itself, still it does not have in itself, he says, the power by which the alteration is accomplished; for this, he says, is in the thing which underlies <the change> and is altered, which both survives and is preserved, just as also the power of growth is in the growing thing.

A question worth puzzling about is how, according to Aristotle, the origin of the change by way of alteration is in the thing that is being altered, and not in the thing that produces the alteration. In the case of the thing that is growing it is clear that the origin of the change is in it. For the power to grow and be nourished, which changes the nourishment and assimilates it, is in the thing that grows. This is obvious too from the fact that the nourishment perishes, whereas the thing that is nourished and grows survives, keeping always the power to grow and be nourished. If, therefore, it is necessary for the nourishment to be destroyed, in order that it may in this way nourish and cause growth, and with the destruction of the substrata the power which is in them is also destroyed, manifestly neither the power of nourishing nor the power of causing growth resides in the nourishment, unless it is being considered as matter.

So the efficient[333] cause of the growth and nourishment is in the thing that grows and is nourished, for this remains and changes the nourishment into itself. In the case of alteration, though, it seems unreasonable to place the 'origin of change', which in Aristotle always signifies the efficient cause, not in the thing which does the altering,[334] but in the thing that is being altered. If then we were to say that the efficient cause exists in the thing that is being altered, we will be making it be altered by itself, which is absurd. The theory and the evident facts are at loggerheads with each other. For we are warmed by fire and we are chilled by snow, and no one who made use of perception would say that the efficient cause of the warmth or the chill was in our body, the thing that is being altered, and not in the fire and the snow. Wax too is altered, coming-to-be a sphere, say, from being a cube, and it is obvious to everyone that the power of alteration is not in the wax but in the person who is moulding it. So how is it that in these cases Aristotle says that the cause of the alteration is
98,1 not in the thing that is doing the altering, but in the thing that is being altered?

Alexander's reply to this objection is that the topic of the discussion is not the efficient cause. For, he says, it is not the origin and power of *altering* which is in the thing that is being altered, but <the origin and power> of *being altered*, which, in a way, comes to be the cause of the altering for the thing which produces the altering.[335] For the things which produce alteration only alter things which have the power to be altered. So in this way Alexander maintains that the phrase 'the origin of change' should not be understood as a reference to the efficient cause. But in some cases of alteration it is possible to find the origin of change, the efficient cause as it were, existing in the thing that is being altered – as in the case, for example, of the alterations which take place in connection with the bodies of animals owing to drugs not actually in possession of observable coldness or heat, but potentially warming or cooling. All things of this sort, pepper, pellitory, hemlock and the like, when applied to inanimate bodies evince no power and do not alter them, but when they approach the bodies of animals, these they do alter by being changed in turn by the nature and life that is in the body, and when they are changed give proof of their own power. So in all such cases the origin of change is plausibly said to exist in the body that is altered.

It is possible, then, to think up a solution of this sort to the puzzles contained in the passage which is before us, a passage whose meaning remains doubtful and not settled definitively by the commentators. But perhaps this <solution> too may be rejected by someone. For it is not true, in the cases of alteration we have been considering, that the origin of change is in the thing that is altered. Rather, the power that is in the drugs is brought into actuality by our bodies, and once it is brought into actuality it eventually reacts in this way on our bodies and alters them. So the cause of the power[336] of the drugs being brought into actuality is in our bodies, but the efficient cause of our bodies' being altered by the drugs is in the drugs, having eventually, that is, become hot or cold. For that which has not become actually hot will not be able to heat anything else and make it actually hot. For as he said himself a little further back, the agent has to be of the same species or genus in a completely actualised manner. So what happens in the case of these drugs is like what happens if a large number of people are in a room and the air in the room, after being 99,1
warmed by them, in turn warms them. In this case too the bodies' contact is the cause of the air's being warmed and the air once warmed itself in turn warms the warming agents. So in this case too the proximate cause is in the thing that does the altering and not in the thing that is altered.

It is worth asking why it is that, given that all changes belong to one or other of four kinds, as is often said – change of substance, change of quantity, change of quality and change of place – in the case of change of substance, I mean perishing and coming-to-be, and in that of change of quality, i.e. alteration, the cause of the change is in the agent[337] and not in the thing which comes to be or is affected, whereas in the two remaining cases, that of quantity and that of place, the efficient cause[338] is in the patient. For the thing that comes to be does not have itself as its own efficient cause, but rather that which fashions it,[339] e.g. the builder or the father or whatever else might be the maker,[340] and it is from outside that the thing that perishes in turn gets the explanation of its perishing; for nothing is by itself destructive of itself, since all things by nature are desirous of being.[341] And we have shown that the cause of alteration too does not exist in the things that are altered, but in the things that do the altering. It has also been agreed that the efficient cause of growth is in the things that grow, for the natural power that is in each part <of a growing thing> unites the nourishment that has been joined to that part and assimilates it to the substratum.[342] The things that change place too are themselves causes for themselves of this sort of change. For if movement[343] comes to be the cause of change of place and their own internal nature is the cause of the movement of bodies (because nature is the cause of movement and rest), the things that change are themselves the causes for themselves of the change of place.

When these facts have been established it is worth asking for an explanation of them. Why is it that the causes of change of substance and change of quality are not in the things that change but come from outside, whereas the things that change are themselves the causes of their own changes of quantity and of place? I say, then, that if the thing that is coming-to-be does not yet exist, how is it possible for that which does not yet exist to be itself a cause of its own existence? For the cause of anything, as has often been said, must exist in actuality, whereas that which does not yet exist does not exist in actuality. And it has been said already that nothing is naturally itself a cause of its own destruction, since all things are naturally desirous of being. But alteration too is an affection of the subject and when it comes to be intensified destroys the body; for when intensified heat or cold and dryness and wetness destroy bodies.[344] But we say that in itself nothing is destructive of itself. But becoming white and becoming
100,1 black and all those alterations which neither harm nor benefit the substratum for this very reason are likely to be externally caused. For the things that are brought about by the natural powers of each thing are certainly to the advantage of the substratum in respect of its being. For nature has no operation which is either harmful or in vain or excessive, unless something occurs as a consequence of things in nature coming together,[345] as for example having woolly hair results from the coming together of hot and dry. If, however, this were to come about as the result of the original composition, this sort of thing would clearly not be alteration at all but coming-to-be. If, on the other hand, there was a change from a dry mixture, say, to a wet one, and this brought about an alteration either in the colour or in the curliness of the hair, which came to be straightened, it is clear that the cause of the change in the mixture would have come to be the cause also of the alteration of the colour or of the hair, whether this was the environment or the things that approach it or whatever else.

So much, then, for coming-to-be and alteration. But the reason why the growing thing has in itself the efficient cause of its growth is evident from what has already been said. For if that which nourishes it and causes it to grow is going to be assimilated to that which is nourished and which grows, obviously it is in potentiality like the growing thing, and since it is <so only> in potentiality, it could not be the cause of it itself changing <into>[346] that. It has already been said that the agent is of the same species or genus as the thing that comes to be, so it is ever likely that the thing that grows and is nourished is the cause of the assimilation to itself of the thing that nourishes it and causes it to grow. And if movement is the cause of change of place, and each thing's internal nature is the cause of its movement, given that its nature is the origin of movement and rest <for that> in which it exists primarily, *per se* and not *per accidens*,[347] it is reasonable that the things which change should themselves be the cause of their change of place.

> **321b3** … if something continues to be flesh, i.e. to be what it is, but possesses some affection of those belonging to it *per se* [which it did not possess before, it is this which has altered.]

When, he says, without losing the 'what it is' and remaining flesh[348] something changes in respect of some affection of those which belong to it *per se*, then in his view it is said to have changed. He uses the 101,1 phrase 'affections belonging *per se*' here, not in the sense of '*per se*' which he expounds in the *Analytics*, (namely, belonging to something primarily, exclusively and always, as having three angles equal to two right angles <belongs> to the triangle, <the sense> according to which, when that which has <the affection> is destroyed, <the affection> is destroyed with it), but he means by '*per se*' here 'that which comes to be in the body itself', e.g. whiteness and heat, and not something external and attaching to it in virtue of a relation with something else, as if something were to become right from <having been> left or above from <having been> below, and in similar cases.

> **321b8** For that which enters <the body> could on occasion become larger as well as the body which benefits from it, [e.g. if, having entered, it became wind; but immediately on being thus affected it is destroyed, and the mover is not in this.]

He told us that the efficient cause is not in what makes a thing grow, but in the thing that grows and is altered, and that 'sometimes that by which a thing is altered is unaffected and its substance unaltered, but sometimes it too <is affected and altered'>. And it seems that, just as on occasion that which does the altering is also altered, sometimes the nourishment also grows, <namely,> when it turns into wind; and in this case it will seem as though it has in itself the power of growth, which, as has been said, is held to be in the growing thing. This is why he now sets out the reason for the mistake and refutes the view that the nourishment grows and therefore has the power of growth in itself. For when it changes to wind, the nourishment is destroyed and does not remain what it was. So plainly it does not grow, given that what grows must acquire increase in size while remaining in its previous form. And if the nourishment does not grow, it will not have the power of growth in itself either.

> **321a29** The question might also be raised, which is it that grows?[349]

We have a list of three things, the thing which grows, that by which it grows and the power of growth. Aristotle has dealt with the problem of how things grow, whether by something corporeal or by something incorporeal, and he now turns to the problem about that by which a thing grows. For since the nourishment in the thing it is nourishing seems to become larger and would seem in this way itself to have grown, he accordingly rectifies the account of this too <by saying> that even if it does become larger, it will not grow. For commonly accepted characteristics of growth are not preserved, and first of all the view that the thing that grows must remain; for the acceding thing perishes and does not remain. The points he introduces about alteration, assimilating the phenomena of growth to those of alteration, are brought in as a model, since the power of growth cannot be actualised independently of the power of alteration.

> **321b5** That by which it is altered is sometimes unaffected and its substance unaltered, but sometimes is affected itself. [But that which makes it alter, the principle of movement, is in the thing which grows and the thing which is altered, because the mover is in these.]

Here, finally, he discusses the efficient cause of growth, using the power of alteration as a model. For what belongs to this presumably belongs also to the power of growth. Just as,[350] therefore, in the case of the power of alteration, if the cause of alteration is proportionate to the thing altered, the former acts upon the latter without itself being affected – as, if the incoming nourishment were proportionate to the natural digestive power, the nourishment would be affected by the power which would remain unaffected – if, however, the incoming <food>[351] were disproportionate quantitatively or qualitatively, the power of alteration is affected by them and becomes weaker, rather than <itself> affecting them … [352] The same must be said also in the case of the power of growth, because so long as the power of growth is proportionate to the matter of growth it acts upon it and makes the growing thing grow, but when it is disproportionate it is, rather, acted upon by it. But lack of proportion comes about for many reasons: because of quantity, because of quality, or because of duration. For since the operations of nature have limitations, when bodies reach the size proportionate <to them>, the matter[353] being then unsuitable, the power of growth will be weakened and is affected by the matter rather than acting upon it, owing to dryness, perhaps, or coldness or simply the lack of proportion in the mixture. It should be recognised that if he says that the cause of alteration sometimes is not at all affected and sometimes *is* affected he does not contradict what he says elsewhere,[354] that agents which belong to the same genus are themselves also affected. What he is saying now is that they act or are acted upon according to the balance of power between them: sometimes they act more than they are acted upon, sometimes the opposite.

> **321b10** Since the problems have now been sufficiently aired, [we must try actually to find a soluton to the difficulty, while safeguarding the fact that in growing the growing body remains and something accedes to it, and in getting smaller something departs from it.]

He has listed the features that belong to growth according to common sense and has thrashed out all the problems that bear upon the theory 103,1
of it. Now, finally, his wish is to set out his own view about growth, his job being to frame it in such a way that it both accords with the features given it by common sense and avoids the objections which are thought to tell against growth itself. The features that belong to growth according to common sense consist of three items: the fact that something remains, the fact that growth occurs as a result of something acceding <to the growing object>, and the fact that every single part of the growing object becomes larger, and <every part> of the diminishing object smaller.

The objections which were thought to tell against what is said about growth were these: implying the subsistence of the void, and body's being said to pass through body. For the view that that by which growth takes place is something incorporeal entails that there is a matter separable from size and a subsistent void, and the supposition that growth takes place <by something passing> through body, given that every part becomes larger from the addition of something which accedes <to it>, entails either that the whole of the growing thing affords[355] passage and is void, if that which accedes to each part of the growing object has to pass through the whole before being added to it, or that body passes through body and two bodies exist in the same place.

Such were the preliminaries, and he needs to make his teaching about growth accord with them, so as both to preserve the features that belong to growth according to common sense and to avoid the objections that are raised against it. At the beginning of his account of growth he selects two points which will be useful to him in what is to come. One is the fact that it is not the anhomoeomers which are the things which grow primarily, but the homoeomers, and it is in virtue of their growth that the anhomoeomers which are composed of them are said to grow (for nourishment is not added to the growing object by coming-to-be face or hand, but either flesh or bone or one of the other homoeomers; so these are what grow primarily).

The other point is that each of the things that are enmattered are spoken of in two ways, sometimes in respect of their matter and sometimes in respect of their form. For sometimes we call the form of flesh 'flesh', and sometimes the matter, and sometimes the two together (which is left on one side as familiar and contributing nothing to the present <discussion>). For when we say that flesh is in a state of flux and that its being consists in influx and efflux, or that it is composed of the four elements, we mean by 'flesh' the matter of flesh; but when <we say that> flesh is in top condition or is a bad mixture, or soft or hard, we mean by 'flesh' the form; and when <we say that> it is divisible or extended in three-dimensions or large or small in quantity, we are talking about the two together.

104,1 What we have to investigate is which of these is the sense in which the homoeomers are said to grow, whether in terms of the matter or in terms of the form. For if someone were to say that it was the matter which grew, he would neither save the features that belong to growth according to common sense nor solve the puzzles that are involved. He will not save the permanence <of the subject of growth> on this interpretation (since the matter does not remain the same, but <all the time> one lot is flowing in and another flowing out), nor can the ability of every part to become larger be ascribed to the matter, first of all because it does not remain (for how could it become larger in every part when it is flowing out and when one lot of matter is always coming-to-be from another?), and secondly, we shall also fall into the previously mentioned absurdities. For if, when the acceding nourishment meets a body, it is added to every part of the matter, it will have to pass through the whole of it. For how <else> would it be added to every part of it? Any part to which it is not added will not grow, since everything which grows has to grow through the accession of something <to it>. So that which is added will pass through the whole of the matter of the growing object. But what a thing goes through has to be void or penetrable.[356] So, if <the nourishment> is to pass through the whole of it, the whole growing body must be void or penetrable. Otherwise, body will pass through body and two bodies will be in the same place. So it is evident that there is no way in which the matter can be said to be the thing that grows. And if so, neither is it the combination of the two[357] which grows, for if the combination of the two grew, the matter too would certainly grow.

It remains, therefore, for the form to be the thing which grows, since this is the only thing which remains, as we have shown, not without matter (for this is impossible), but always being kept the same with matter which comes to be larger and smaller and different at different times, some flowing away and some being assimilated. But when we say that the form is that which grows, do not think that the form itself undergoes change in respect of its eternal and substantial[358] definition (for in its own definition form is incorporeal and sizeless), but in respect of quantity; for it is this which also signifies growth. Form is said to change in respect of quantity in that it comes to be in more or less matter.[359] This is the way in which a hand or a face is seen to grow, not by the form of the face or the hand changing, but by the part coming-to-be larger while the form remains the same but comes to be, now in a smaller, now in a larger <quantity of> matter.

How, if this is what we say is the thing which grows, we shall preserve the features that according to common sense belong to growth and <how> solve the puzzles: that is what we have next to consider. First, when the growing object is said to be the form, it is 105,1
true that it remains, as has already been said. Given that the matter manifestly does not stay the same, if someone were to suppose that the form too did not stay numerically the same, the combination of the two would surely not be the same either. So Socrates was not always numerically the same. So if composite things, as long as they exist, are numerically the same, but the matter of these does not always stay the same, it remains then that the form stays the same. It is in respect of this that each of the things that are has being and is said <to be what it is>, and from this they are also said to be numerically the same, seeing that the form, in respect of which they have being, is the same. And only if it is said of this is it feasible that the thing which accedes should make every part grow. For if we said of the matter that the nourishment is added to every part <of it>, the aforesaid absurdities would follow: either the whole would be penetrable or void, or body would pass through body.

But neither does the matter remain, nor is it one and numerically the same: rather, it comes to be different at different times, having its being in a state of flux. Form, on the other hand, remains always one and the same, both the substantial[360] form and the form in the sense of the figure and the shape. For the form both of Socrates and of the flesh and of the bone is always the same in both a larger and a smaller <quantity of> matter.[361] The same applies to the form in the sense of the figure and the shape. It is as though there were a sack, and the things which were thrown into it were different at different times, but the sack, constituting a boundary[362] for the things that were thrown into it and being as it were their form, remained always the same despite the fact that the things that were bounded by it were different at different times. And to allow the model to approach more closely to what we wish it to illustrate, if water were to pass through a tube made of skin in smaller or larger quantity at different times, the shape of the tube would remain one and the same although now contracted, now expanded, whilst the water over which it is stretched like the shape in matter would not be one and the same (since some of it would always be flowing out and some coming in in its place).

That is how we ought to think also about the things that grow, namely, that their matter is never the same, yet the form which exists in it, while remaining one and the same, increases in bulk, growing, not *qua* form but *qua* something which participates in quantity. For if some addition, either of genus or differentia, were made to the defining formula,[363] clearly the form would grow *qua* form. Now, however, this is not what happens. So it is not *qua* form that growth belongs to it, but *qua* something endowed with quantity.[364] Otherwise, if it was in so far as it was form that it grew, the separable form would have grown much earlier; for if that had not grown, the enmattered form would not have grown either. So it is not *qua* animal that it grows, nor *qua* circle, nor *qua* flesh, but *qua* half a metre of flesh or half a metre of bone, or generally as some form endowed with quantity. For it is in virtue of being stretched over a larger <quantity of> matter[365] that it is said to grow.

The following objection might be raised: perhaps it is not only the matter of things that grow that is not always the same, because it is in a state of flux inwards and outwards, but also the form itself. For if the form has being in the matter as substratum, and it is impossible, when the substratum perishes, for that which has its being in that <substratum> to be preserved (for in that case it would be separate, and *not* inseparable from matter), then the form of the growing thing cannot be preserved <and remain> the same either.

In reply, we say that if all the matter were to perish together at the same time the point just made would be correct, but, as it is, it seeps away bit by bit, a new replacement is immediately found for it, and thus form remains one and the same numerically.

Let us use a model to make this account clear to ourselves. If someone noticed a shadow cast by some body on a river flowing past, the shadow, being in the water as in a substratum would be one and the same numerically, but the water would not remain the same, but bit by bit some would flow away and more would replace it. The form must be thought of in just the same way, the matter being replaced bit by bit, but itself[366] always remaining one and the same numerically. Because even the colours often remain the same without the matter remaining. For the replacement of matter bit by bit does not take place in such a way that something of the form is removed as well, as when a statue has, now its foot, now its hand, now its head replaced. What happens in that case is that in time the whole statue comes to be numerically different, not only in respect of its matter, the bronze, but also in respect of its individual figure and shape. So it is not in this way that the matter is emptied out in the case of growth (if it were like this the whole would be going to become mutilated,[367] which is not what we see happen), but it is in the way that in the case of the example that we have described, that of the river, sometimes the amount of incoming water is greater than the outgoing and sometimes that which comes in is less than that which flows away, but the whole river itself as a whole is continuous with itself. The parts of the water succeed each other continuously and fill up again without a break the place of that which has flowed away, leaving no gap between them. The same thing happens in the case of our body with a dissipation[368] of matter taking place everywhere at the level of minute particles, and if from any place it becomes greater the balance is immediately restored from the surrounding things which close in on it without a gap occurring.[369] This is because there is, according to the Hippocratic saying, 'a single flowing together, a single breathing together, all things affected together'.[370]

So the form is in no way affected as the influx and efflux of the matter takes place. For if, as well as the matter not remaining, the form did not remain but became numerically different things at different times, neither would the thing that is composed of the two of them remain numerically the same. So given that, as long as this man, e.g. Socrates, exists, he is numerically the same although his matter is not the same, in that case his form has to be the same. But it must not be thought that the whole of the matter as a whole replaces itself over time, seeping away bit by bit, so that there is no <bit of> body in us when we have grown old <which was part> of the matter[371] that was in us at the time of our original framing. For if that were so, it would be possible for animals to be immortal, their matter always being at its peak. As it is, however, the matter is not able to keep its form throughout its whole extent, since it becomes weary with time, the parts that have been fitted together being incapable of preserving throughout the harmony and correct mixture as a result of their being affected by the contrary powers. So it must be supposed that not all the matter is dissipated, but that the more solid parts of it particularly remain always numerically the same. This is why we also see the scars of wounds which may chance to have been received in youth remain in flesh and bones until death. So for this reason too the form also must remain numerically the same.

These considerations make it clear that the growing thing is preserved, not in respect of its matter, but in respect of its form. And in respect of the matter it is impossible to preserve either <the accepted fact> that every part of the growing object has grown, but it is possible in respect of the form. For it is impossible for addition to be made to every part of the matter, since it is also impossible for body to pass through body. But every part of the form does become larger.

For every one of the parts equally becomes larger as a complete whole.[372] The face grows as a complete whole to the same extent as each of its parts, namely the eye and the nose and the rest; for each part of the eye and of the rest of the parts has an equivalent increase in size. And (A) he avoids all the absurdities, (B) it is manifest that it is not by anything incorporeal that things grow, but also (C), although growth takes place by body, neither is there going to be void nor will body pass through body. For that which accedes does not have to travel in its entirety through the whole <of the growing thing>, but the matter that comes in[373] is merely placed alongside the earlier matter.

And when an addition of water is made to a tube made of skin and what is added is merely placed alongside the existing <water>, and when this has propelled forward what is in front of it, in this way the expansion of the water takes place equally at all points, and thus every part whatsoever of the tube is stretched to the same degree. This is just like what happens in the case of growth. The nourishment is converted into blood and is drawn along and made to flow everywhere through the veins in each of the homoeomers, and the natural power[374] in each of the parts digests this and changes it into the substance of the substratum,[375] so that this is the way it comes about that growth occurs. For in the substance of the bones and in that of the flesh and of the rest there is a moistness which is distributed throughout, and particularly that in the <parts> that grow, for these contain more moisture. So the blood, circulating around each of the parts outside, is juxtaposed to this moisture and propels it forward, or rather, drawn all the way round by the parts, makes it larger in every dimension. It then is digested by the nutritive power and changes into the substance of the substratum.[376]

So since nature concerns itself also with the shape of the parts, when the underlying matter has increased in quantity, it deploys each of the forms over this to the same extent, and in this way we say that every part has grown in that the same degree of expansion of the shapes has taken place. Just as, when the quantity of water inside it has increased, the outside of the tube gets the same degree of expansion in every part of itself, so in the case of things that grow when their matter increases in quantity it comes about that their forms are stretched over it in equal measure. And since the juxtaposition of the blood takes place in the three dimensions, for this reason the growth also occurs in every dimension.

What the thing is that grows and how, in Aristotle's view, growth takes place has now been stated. Against this statement it would be possible to raise these objections. In the first place, how does this take account of the need for the thing that grows to achieve its growth by the accession of something <to it>. For if that by which it grows, i.e.

the blood, does not pass through the whole of the growing thing, but is merely juxtaposed to what was there before, and every single part <of the thing> grows, it will not after all accede to the whole of the growing thing. For the blood was not juxtaposed to every part. Secondly, if it is not the matter which grows but the form, the access does not after all come about to that which grows, but the nourishment accedes to one thing and what grows is another thing.

In reply I say that these points are in no way contrary to what Aristotle says. For when he speaks in this way, he says simply that it is necessary for the thing that grows to grow through the accession of something, not that it has to accede to the form; so what accedes accedes to the matter, but what grows is the form. So when the matter has been added to and a forward thrust has been made, what results is an increase in the quantity of the matter underlying[377] every part of the form.

But this very point prompts an objection: How does the propulsion or traction come about, and what in any case is it that is pushed or pulled? For it is not feasible for the flesh itself to be pulled or pushed, i.e. the compound.[378] If this were so, the result would be that the flesh of the chest came to be that of the arm or the thigh or some other <part>. And if they say that the same moisture that is dispersed in the flesh or the bones is propelled by the blood juxtaposed to it, I shall ask what sort of thing this moisture is to be. If the moisture which is an essential component of the flesh is one of the elements of which it is made,[379] how then is it possible for its elementary moisture,[380] which is an integral part of its substance, to have been propelled without the whole flesh submitting to propulsion or having previously been destroyed? But if this moisture is not of its substance,[381] but is like that which nourishes it and which accedes to it from its nourishment, it cannot be that it exists throughout the whole of the flesh. Since this is body and not a quality, it cannot pass through the whole flesh, for in this case a body would be passing through a body. This would result in not every part <of it> growing. For if the blood were juxtaposed to certain parts <of it> and then, when it had been changed in this way, the form was deployed over it, it would come to be larger as a whole, not each perceptible point of it, as he says himself.

For if wood has been added externally to a door or a box, the whole has become larger but each of the parts of the box has not received enlargement. And when the *gnomon* was placed around a square it increased the size of the square as a whole. However, it did not enlarge each of the parts of the previously existing object, but its place remained unchanged. In just the same way manifestly in the case of things which grow, if there is juxtaposition of matter with certain parts, it would result in a manner of growth for the growing things similar to that which has just been described. But this is contrary to the evidence; for in reality we see each part of the growing thing becoming larger.

Perhaps it is possible to preserve growth in the other dimensions, but not in that of length. For the sake of example, let us consider just one part, say bone. If the blood not only circulates outside this, but is also diffused through it and penetrates deep into it, its nature, receiving a larger amount of matter, expands the shape of the bone and keeps it the same in a greater bulk. As an illustration, imagine wax in the shape of a flute, and then wax being poured over this, or into the inside of it as well, wherever it can reach. Next imagine some technique using breath or some other method to enlarge the flute and make it wider. Clearly in this case the addition has not been made to every part. Nevertheless, the growth of the shape has not been accomplished as it was in the case of the square around which a gnomon was placed, but the flute has increased its bulk throughout its whole extent in every part <of itself>.

110,1 Something like this, then, is what we must think of in the natural case, namely, that a larger quantity of matter has circulated around the bone and nature has expanded the whole shape through the whole of this, rather than fashioning an addition to it. So growth in terms of width might be able to be conceived of in this way, but it is not possible <to conceive> in this sort of way of growth in terms of length. For since the flute-shaped bones have solid endings, and this is where the junctions of the parts of the body are found, how does the flute-shaped variety of bone increase in size? If the addition of blood took place at the final extremities of the length, obviously there would be a change to something of the same form as the substratum.[382] So the solid parts of the bones would grow, but not the flute-shaped parts. But if the addition took place in the inside of the bones and this was the way in which they increased lengthwise, the blood would pass into the inside either around the whole surface of the bone or not around the whole of it.

If along the whole of it the bone would be divided through and through, and once again the growth would not be <growth> lengthwise of every part, but what would happen in the case of the bones would be like what would happen when, if someone had placed another square alongside a square, it had made the whole oblong, since that which underlay it previously[383] would not have grown lengthwise, but a sort of growing together of two things of the same kind would have taken place. And how will the solid parts of the bones at their extremities manage to increase? If the addition were to take place, not to the whole surface of the bone on the inside, but only at certain parts, the length would not grow throughout the whole, but only certain parts; and this is impossible. For the whole will be broken up if certain parts of the bone grow lengthwise and some do not. For nature will not be able to extend lengthwise the flute-like shape of the bone unless the matter which is extended with it has previously been underlying <the change>. Otherwise how is it at all possible to say that every single part of the bone grows lengthwise? For every part might grow equally in breadth as a result of the fact that the flute-like shape of the bone becomes less convex from being more convex; but in terms of length, how would <the accepted fact> that every single part grows be saved? Let us grant that the blood is circulated around the whole lengthwise and changes into the nature of the bone: it is manifest that this changed <material> has been added to and united with what was there originally and has made the whole greater in length, but there has not been an increase of length for every single part.

I could say the same things in terms of depth. For if the addition of blood is not made throughout the depth but is juxtaposed to certain parts only, how could every part grow in terms of depth? Let there be a some flesh having the depth of a finger, and let some blood accede to this and circulate around it and be dispersed in it. It is obvious that it will not be juxtaposed to every part of it, but only to some. When
the blood has been changed into the substance of flesh, obviously the 111,1
whole will have become larger. If I take some parts of the flesh like those from the deeper levels, to which blood has not been juxtaposed, will I say that this too has become larger? Clearly not. For no matter has been added to that over which the form has been deployed, but the same <matter> has remained which was there originally. In the same way in the case of length too, if some parts were taken which have not had blood juxtaposed to them, there would be the same result. For nothing would grow if no addition had been made to it. But whereas those things whose shapes are spherical or curved generally and are raised to a larger bulk are said to grow or to be diminished in every part in virtue of being more or less convex, as has already been said, since there is no part which has not become more or less convex, in the case of those whose shape is not curved I do not know how it is possible to say that every part grows since the addition is not made to every single part.

> **321b14** Again, that every perceptible point has become larger or smaller, [and that the body is not void, nor do two objects possessed of size occupy the same place, nor does a thing grow by anything incorporeal.]

Since he has said 'point', it is as well that he has added 'perceptible', instead of <saying that> there is no part so small as to have the proportion of a point to the body which has not become larger. It becomes larger by growing, smaller by being diminished.

> **321b16** Before getting hold of the explanation we must settle <some points> first.

'Explanation', i.e. of the solution of the puzzles about growth. For after saying what it the thing that grows and how it grows he has solved the puzzles about growth. The explanation of growth, he says, is what will solve the puzzles about it. But before he says what it is, he tells us, it is necessary first to determine certain things which will be useful to us for giving an account of growth.

> **321b17** One is that the anhomoeomers grow in virtue of the homoeomers growing, for they are composed of them.

The face does not grow from having a face added to it, nor does a hand from <having> a hand <added to it>, but it is from the growth of flesh and blood and sinew, and in general all the homoeomers, that the
112,1 growth of the anhomoeomers results. For the homoeomers are, as it were, the matter of the anhomoeomers; for it is such and such a composition of the homoeomers that makes the anhomoeomers. So it is no surprise that the growth of the homoeomers results in the growth of the things of which they are the components. And he does well to determine this point in advance. For since the thing that grows has to remain, it needs to be known first of all what sort of things, properly speaking, grow, so that we can enquire about them whether they do, in reality, remain, and in what way they remain. For if the thing that causes growth is absorbed into the growing thing by becoming like it, as he says, and the growing thing were a face, the nourishment too would be absorbed by becoming a face. This is absurd, but there is nothing absurd about saying that the nourishment becomes bone or flesh.

> **321b19** Next, that flesh, bone, and [all such parts are twofold, as are the other things that have a form in matter. Both the matter and the form are called flesh and bone. The thesis that every single part grows and that in growth something accedes to the growing object is a possible one in terms of the form, but in terms of the matter it is not.]

The second of the points that he determines in advance is that every enmattered <substance> is spoken of in two ways, sometimes in respect of its matter and sometimes in respect of its form. For we call

<something> flesh sometimes in respect of the substratum[384] and sometimes in respect of the form.

Sometimes we call both together[385] flesh and bone, e.g. when we say that the flesh is affected <in some way> or the bone is broken we are manifestly talking about the composite of matter and form; but he passes over this as something well known and contributing nothing to his present purpose. This is what solves every difficulty for him. For if, when we say that the flesh has grown, we understand what sort of flesh we are speaking of, namely that which <is flesh> in respect of the form and not that which <is flesh> in respect of the matter, we will find that all the difficulties are resolved. For if, he says, we were to say that the matter grows, we would not avoid the difficulties, nor would we save the features that belong to growth. For neither does the same matter remain, nor does every <part> of it come larger. But if we say that the form grows, we save everything: the same form remains, because it is not the essence[386] of flesh considered as form to be a determinate quantity but to be of a determinate sort. And we were speaking also about the rest. But he does not mean that the form is preserved in separation from matter (for this would be impossible), but <he says what he does> because the form is kept <the same> whether the matter is more or less, whereas the matter does not still remain <the same> if it is at one time more and at another time less.

> **321b24** We should think of it as though someone were measuring out water in the same measure: [that which comes to be is all the time different.]

He draws an analogy between the measure and the form and between the matter and that which is being measured. He does not use the illustration to make a point about growth but in order to show what it is that is permanent and what it is that is in flux. In the case of 113,1
things that are being measured, they are the same in respect of the measure, but in respect of the substratum and the matter they are not the same: it is just so in the case of things that are being nourished and are growing. In respect of that which measures and defines them, i.e. their form, they are the same, but in respect of their matter they are different at different times. If you think of the measure as expanding and sometimes receiving more and sometimes less of that which is being measured, the model will fit the case of growth.[387]

> **321b25** It is in this way that the matter of flesh grows: an addition is not made to each and every part, but some flows away and some comes in new.

'This way' means 'not remaining the same', just as the water in the measure is not the same, but some of it is flowing away and some coming in new. And not all the pre-existing matter has matter that comes in assimilated to it (for it does not <all> remain), but a part of it has <new matter> juxtaposed to it. So when that which comes in is more than that which flows away, then, he says, the matter of the flesh is said to have grown. But clearly he is misusing the word 'growth', because this sort of thing is addition, not growth, since it does not preserve the features proper to growth.

> **321b27** <What is added to is> each and every part of the shape and the form.

There is not, he says, an accretion to every part of the matter, but there is to every part of the shape and the form. For the flesh increases in bulk throughout. He speaks of 'the shape' either because of the measure (he uses this model and image of growth in respect of the measure, and the measure is given its shape by that which is measured so that it is expanded in a similar way when a larger quantity of matter passes through it), or else he says 'the shape' because each of the things that grow, being homoeomers, has by nature a shape appropriate to it. For this is how with them too they have their essence.[388] For one shape belongs to a knuckle, another to a knee. So just as it comes to be originally with its own shape, so also when it grows it does so while maintaining its shape. It would not be able otherwise to keep its own shape in the course of growth, unless it grew everywhere in the same way.

114,1 > **321b28** This is clearer in the case of the anhomoeomers: a hand, for instance, grows proportionately; [for here the difference between the matter and the form is clearer than in the case of flesh and the homoeomers. This is why we would be more inclined to think of a dead man's flesh and bone as still existing than his hand and arm.]

Clearer confirmation of the fact that there is growth in every part of the form of the things that grow comes from the case of the anhomoeomers. For the anhomoeomers seem to display the difference between matter and form more clearly (for the actualisations of their forms are more evident), whereas the distinction between the matter and the form of the homoeomers is not so obvious. This is confirmed by considering the dead. For no one would say that the hand of a dead person was, in the proper sense of the word, a hand, unless in the sense in which a <hand carved> in stone or one drawn <in a picture is> also <said to be a hand> (for it does not do the work of a hand), but we think that the flesh and the bone are still the same as those of the living person were, since their actualisations are not so evident.[389] So since the forms are more evident in the case of the anhomoeomers, it is easier in their case to see that the form is the thing that grows and that every part of it grows equally. For when we say that the hand has grown or the face, we do not mean the matter of the hand but the form, since the hand and the rest manifest the form more than the matter. And when we say that the face has grown, we are not saying that the nose has grown rather than the eye, but each of the parts grows equally. But the parts of each part also grow equally; for the whole nose grows the same amount. Similarly, each finger of the hand <grows>, and each joint of each finger.

> **321b32** So there is a way in which each part of the flesh grows and a way in which it does not; [for there is an accession to every part in terms of form, but not in terms of matter.]

For since flesh is spoken of in two ways, both in respect of its matter and in respect of its form, it is not the case that every part of the flesh has grown in respect of its matter, but every part has grown in respect of its form.

> **321b35** Nevertheless the whole becomes larger through the accession of something which is called nourishment, and is contrary, [but which changes into the same form. For example, wet could accede to dry, and having arrived could change and become dry. For in one way like grows by like, in another way unlike by unlike.]

He had said what the thing that grows is, namely that it is not the matter but the form, and he now intends to say what it is that causes it to grow. And this has to be either body or incorporeal. He has 115,1
already shown that it is not incorporeal, but body: he now enquires what sort of body it is, whether similar to the thing that grows or dissimilar and contrary <to it>. And he says that in one respect the thing that causes growth is similar to the thing that grows, but that in another respect it is dissimilar and contrary. For in potentiality it is similar, but in actuality it is contrary.

Since that which grows does so by the addition of something similar (for flesh has to grow by <the addition of> flesh and bone by <the addition of> bone), for this reason it is necessary that the thing which makes it grow should be similar to the thing that grows. But again, since the nourishment has to be affected by the thing that is nourished and caused to grow, and like is not affected by like but contrary by contrary, for this reason again[390] the thing which nourishes and which causes growth has to be contrary to the thing which is nourished and which grows. So if the thing which causes growth has to be affected by the thing which grows and thus change into the substance of the latter, it must needs be similar <to it> in potentiality, but contrary <to it> in actuality.

The nourishment, then, being in potentiality similar to the thing which is nourished and which grows, when incorporated in it and acted upon by it, after becoming actually what it was potentially (sc. similar) and being assimilated <to it>, nourishes the flesh and the bone and each of the other things and causes them to grow. The nourishment itself does not change of itself,[391] nor in separation from the thing that is nourished and caused to grow. For it is not a case of flesh acceding to flesh and in this way nourishing it and causing it to grow. For if the nourishment changed into the substance of that which it nourishes before it was incorporated into the latter, this sort of thing would be a case rather of coming-to-be, not of growth; but the nourishment has first to be mixed with what it nourishes and then, after being affected by the latter, to change into its substance. If wood is put under a burning fire and then, being acted upon <by it> makes the flame grow, we say in that case that growth of fire has occurred; but if outside <the fire> we were to kindle the wood and then, when it had caught, place it so as to rest on another flame, we would say that a coming-to-be of fire and an addition of it had occurred, not growth. What happens in the case of things that grow in the full sense is the same: if the nourishment changed into flesh and in this state was added to flesh it would be coming-to-be of flesh and addition, not growth; as it is, what happens is not this, but the nourishment is first joined to the substratum and then the nature that is in this makes it change into its <own> substance.

> **322a4** And a question arises also what sort of thing that by which a thing grows has to be. [It is obvious that it is potentially that sort of thing the growing thing itself is, e.g. flesh if it is flesh. So actually something else.]

'And' here has to be understood as 'for'. For it is as someone who has already solved the puzzle that he introduces this new point. For after saying that that which causes growth is in one way similar to that which grows and in another way dissimilar, similar in potentiality and dissimilar in actuality, and solving the problem raised, he brings the difficulty forward in this way, as though he had said 'A question might also be raised what sort of thing that which causes growth must be, whether similar to the thing that grows or dissimilar'. Then, as one who has already given the solution to the problem in what he has already said, he continues 'It is obvious that it is potentially that', i.e.

it is clear from what has already been said. And if it is potentially that, evidently it will be actually something else,[392] but not just *anything* else, because it is not the case that anything whatsoever is affected by anything whatsoever, but <rather> that contrary <is affected> by contrary; for it is in so far as the nourishment partakes in the contrary to the substratum that it is affected by it.

322a6 When it has been destroyed this has come to be flesh ...

What is potentially similar to something, if it is to become actually similar to it, has to perish and get rid of what it previously was actually and become actually what it then was potentially.

322a7 ... although not this itself *per se*; for that would be coming-to-be, not growth.

If it has to be by perishing that the cause of growth comes to be like the growing thing, this must not be itself perishing *per se*,[393] for that sort of thing is coming-to-be, not growth. And at the same time by these means he teaches us the difference between coming-to-be and growth, namely, that coming-to-be is change of the matter itself *per se*, whereas growth is change of the matter[394] of the growing thing, not of itself *per se*, but changing in the growing thing.

322a8 But rather the thing that grows because of this.

That is to say, 'But the thing that grows changes because of this'. For in the case of coming-to-be the matter itself changes *per se* from not being to being, whereas in the case of growth the growing thing changes through the matter which is incorporated in it, which has evidently been affected by its natural power and has become what it is. So at the same time the matter has been affected by <the growing thing> and has changed into it and it also has changed because of this <matter> to a larger size. So growth too <does> not <take place> without coming-to-be. But since the matter does not itself change *per se* but having come to be in the growing thing is assimilated to it, this is called increase rather of the form and growth, not coming-to-be; for 117,1
this is not a case of that which *was not* coming-to-be, but of that which *is* taking on a larger size.

322a8 How, being affected by this <growing thing>, has it grown?[395] Mixed with it, as if one were to pour water into wine, and it (the latter) were able to make what is mixed with it into wine?[396] [Again, as fire does when it gets hold of combustible material, so the power of growth which resides in the growing thing which is actually flesh gets hold of the thing which is potentially flesh when it accedes and makes it into actual flesh. So it must happen when the two are together: if it were when they were apart it would be generation. For fire can be made in this way by placing wood on top of an existing fire, and in this instance what we have is growth; but when the wood catches fire by itself what we have is generation.]

Having explained what it is that grows and dealt similarly with what causes it to grow, he states too the manner in which growth takes place. That which causes growth is mixed with that which grows and is caused to change into the substance of the thing that grows by the natural power that is in the latter, and this is the way in which it produces growth. It is as though one were to pour water into a jar of wine, which had the power to change into itself everything that is poured into it and to assimilate it. The water, when mixed and turned by the power of the wine into its own substance, increases the quantity of the wine and changes it into a larger mass. And as fire sets light to fuel and changes it into its own substance and is in this way made larger by it, so it is too with things which grow.

At the same time by this means he has given us his teaching about the efficient cause of growth, I mean, the power of the soul to nourish and to produce growth. It is clear that the fact that every single part of the growing thing grows does not mean that that which makes it grow has to be mixed with every <part> and pass through it (for <that way> either the whole would have to be void or body would have to pass through body), but it is enough that, while the assimilation takes place in certain places <only>, growth takes place everywhere. In the same way something that is being emptied is seen to be everywhere wrinkled, although the neighbouring parts are not all emptied at the same time, as happens in the case of patients who are bled, because the blood from the whole body is drawn away together with <the blood in> the part that is being emptied.

So, no doubt, in the case of things that grow also, the incorporation <of nourishment> takes place <only> in certain parts, but the addition takes place everywhere, that which is being added always propelling forward what is in front of it, not slipping through it, as is the case with the tube which is extended together with the greater quantity of water. For all through the body there is dispersed a certain liquid which has the power of nourishing the substratum and whose nature is to change into the substance of the subject. Since the nourishment is liquid and is mixed with the pre-existing liquid in the body, it comes about that this increases everywhere proportionately, not because the former passes through it everywhere, but because it propels forward that which is in front of it, and that in turn what is in front of it. And thus with the quantity of matter increasing the form advances to greater bulk on all sides; for each of the parts has its own 118,1 being with its appropriate shape which advances to greater bulk as the matter everywhere increases. Just as nature originally gave subsistence to each of the parts together with its own shape, so after this[397] it also exercises care and keeps guard over them.

So <in saying> that the form associated with shape[398] produces nourishment and growth equally in every part, where nourishment is a matter of the persistence of the form and growth its advance to a larger quantity – thus far the argument goes forward well. But where the substantial form is concerned, e.g. that of flesh as flesh or <that> of bone <as bone>,[399] how could <the thesis> that these forms are nourished or that they grow be saved? For if every single part of flesh is endowed with a form[400] and it is by body that that which is nourished and grows is nourished and grows, how can it be maintained that the whole of the flesh is nourished throughout? For if that which nourishes has to be incorporated with that which is nourished, in that case the parts with which nothing is incorporated will not be nourished. But it is impossible for every <part> to have something incorporated with it. So neither will every part be nourished or grow. And how will every part of the form of the flesh grow? For whilst the whole as a whole has become larger, it is no longer true of each part; for the addition of matter has not been made to each part of the flesh.[401] But where no addition of matter has been made, there is no change <of what is like> to what is like either. So neither is there any advance to a greater mass.

Perhaps it should[402] not be said at all that a form of this type[403] is nourished or grows, but only that it has become greater. For if, while it is nourished and grows by body when it changes into the substance of the former,[404] body is unable to pass through body, that which becomes like it and is knitted together with it will surely be different, and it will not be something pre-existing which something acquires from that which comes into it, whether form or thing possessed of size. And if each of the parts of the flesh is composed of matter and form, the form having its being in the matter, manifestly when the matter of the flesh flows out, the form which has its being in it will accompany it. For it is not the case that the matter is separated and the individual form remains – <the individual form> which in fact subsists in the matter. If the form departs with the matter and each of the parts of the flesh and the other <homoeomers> is like this, that which in that case does not <even> remain would neither be nourished nor grow, but to that which does remain would be added what comes to be, unless it were to be said that flesh and the others were nourished in terms of quality, the nourishment by being juxtaposed acting upon the qualities <of the thing> and moistening and heating the juxtaposed bodies.

But in this way, whilst nourishing of flesh and the others might be 119,1 preserved, the same is no longer true for growth. For that which moistens or heats a thing with nothing but its quality does not make that which is affected by it larger in size, but only alters it in terms of quality. So as far as the substantial <form>[405] is concerned, the fact that every single part has grown would not be preserved. For the whole would have become larger, but not, according to this account, every part. For not everything would have had something added to it and changed – or rather, this would not have been true of any, but all that would have happened would be juxtaposition and unification, as if water had been united to water.

Perhaps then it is not true to say that every part comes to be larger and is nourished, if this is asserted in the sense that every smallest part itself *per se* is nourished and increases. But just as the addition of nourishment is not made to every part, but on account of the continuity of the whole it is said as a whole to have something added to it; and with the whole becoming larger in this way because the whole is that which is composed of all the parts, it is reasonable to say that each part also is expanded along with the whole. In the same way, since the whole is also nourished and preserves its own character,[406] any part too[407] of flesh and the rest is said to be nourished, being kept together with the whole.

> **322a16** A quantity, understood universally, does not come into existence, any more than does an animal which is neither a man nor any particular animal [(quantity here corresponds to the universal there).]

Growth is the coming-to-be of a quantity, and he has said that growth is <produced> by something corporeal, not something incorporeal. That being so, he wishes to prevent anyone saying that, if everything that comes to be comes to be from what is not of this sort, that which has quantity must come to be from that which lacks quantity. In fact our present position is that something having quantity comes to be from something having quantity (for the matter of the growing thing is that which actually has quantity). It is with this in mind, therefore, that he says that if coming-to-be were from universals, the thing having quantity that came to be would have to have come to be from something lacking quantity.

But since there is coming-to-be neither of universal quantity nor of any of the other universals, there is nothing absurd in something having quantity which comes to be having come to be from something else having quantity. For a particular thing having quantity comes to be from a particular thing having quantity, just as a particular animal comes to be from a particular animal. For being belongs *per se* to none of the universals, but they have being in the things that are particular. So the thing having quantity is a particular thing having quantity, e.g. a certain quantity of flesh or a certain quantity of bone. So there is nothing surprising about a certain quantity of flesh coming-to-be from a certain quantity of blood and something else from something else.

And it is obvious that none of the universals comes to be, since neither does any of the universals subsist *per se*. But as it is, this is not the reason why nothing having quantity comes to be from something lacking quantity. For despite the fact that the universal human being and the universal animal do not come to be, nevertheless a human being comes to be from what is not a human being and an animal from what is not an animal, for the seed is not an animal, nor yet a human being. Not, that is, from what is not a particular human being but is <another> particular human being,[408] but from what is 120,1
not a human being *simpliciter* and from what is not an animal *simpliciter*. But this is not how it is in the case of that which has quantity; for a thing having quantity does not come to be from a thing not having quantity *simpliciter*, but a thing having a particular quantity from a thing having a particular quantity. So there is a difference between this and the rest. For the seed, not being an animal, comes to be an animal, and not being a human being, comes to be a human being; but it is not the case that something not having a particular quantity comes to be something having a quantity, but always something having a particular quantity comes to be something having another quantity. The reason for this is that what is an animal is not, as an animal, incapable of change, nor is anything else of this sort, but that which has quantity is incapable of change, since that which is body too, as body, is incapable of change. For it is not as body that it changes, but as air or fire or something else of that sort. And the reason, once again, for this is that the three-dimensionally extended[409] underlies all the forms as their proximate matter.

> **322a19** What comes into existence is flesh or a hand or bone or the homoeomers that compose these. And what accedes to the growing thing is a given quantity, but not a quantity of flesh.

i.e. a given quantity of flesh comes to be, and a given quantity of bone, not a given quantity *simpliciter*. And a given quantity of flesh comes to be when a given quantity of something which is potentially flesh, but not a given quantity of flesh, accedes to it. For it is not the case that it comes to be flesh outside and is then joined to it, but it is joined to it first and in this way comes to be flesh.

> **322a20** In so far as it is potentially both these things, i.e. a quantity of flesh, it will produce growth (for it has to come to be both a thing having quantity and flesh): in so far as it is potentially just flesh, it will nourish.

He has explained how growth takes place and what it is that grows and what that thing is by which something grows. Now he intends to give his view about the difference between nourishment and growth, and why it is that we are always being nourished as long as we exist, even if we are becoming smaller, but are not always growing. So he says that the nourishment which accedes, whether bread or meat or whatever else, is potentially that to which it accedes, e.g. flesh perhaps, and also has a certain quantity. So it is potentially flesh and potentially a certain quantity of flesh. Since it is potentially both these things, when it changes into something actual, in so far as it is actualised as flesh, to that extent it has just nourished but not caused growth. For nourishment is the preservation of the form, but growth is the progress of this to a larger size. So nourishment and growth are the same in subject (for that which nourishes and that which causes growth are one in subject), but different in definition; for it is one thing for it to be potentially flesh and another to be <potentially> of such and such a size.

121,1 **322a23** For nourishment and growth differ in definition. [Accordingly, a thing is nourished as long as it is maintained in existence even if it gets smaller but is not always in process of growing.]

By 'nourishment' and 'growth' he means that which nourishes and that which causes growth. So this, being one in subject, has both these powers, and when it is actualised in accordance with both it both nourishes and causes growth, but when in accordance with just one it nourishes but does not cause growth. This is why, he says, a thing is nourished as long as it exists, even when it is getting smaller, but does not always grow, because then the nourishment as what is potentially flesh is being actualised, but as a thing having quantity it is not actualised. For when that which flows out is more than what flows in, it is no longer actualised in quantity. I do not mean to deny that the nourishment always makes a certain addition in respect of quantity to the thing it is nourishing (for it is not by a quality that it gives nourishment but by its substance; so the nourishment always contributes something having quantity to the thing it nourishes together with the form), but what he means is that it is not actualised as far as quantity is concerned, that it is not able to make any addition to the size <of the thing> as a whole whilst the outflow is copious or equal <to the inflow>. For when what flows away is equal to what comes in, only nourishment occurs and neither growth not diminution, and when what flows in is more than what flows out, nourishment and growth occur, but when it is less, nourishment and diminution. For though the quantity is diminished the form is preserved, since the form of flesh does not consist in being something of such and such a size, but in being something of such and such a sort.

322a25 And nourishment is the same as growth, but its being is different.

Being one in subject, it has a certain form and also has quantity; for in potentiality it is flesh. *Qua* potentially flesh it nourishes: *qua* having quantity it causes growth.

322a26 *Qua* potentially a quantity of flesh, that which accedes [is what makes flesh grow; but *qua* potentially just flesh, it is nourishment.]

In saying this he does not mean that it has quantity potentially, but where being a quantity of flesh is concerned it is this potentially.

322a28 This form without matter is, as it were, an immaterial[410] power in matter.[411]

Since he has said that the nourishment, when it is nourishing but not causing growth, is actualised only in respect of the form, not in respect 122,1
of quantity, so long as it has being (for the extension[412] is the substratum as matter for the forms), to prevent you getting the idea that it is actualised in this way when separated in reality from the matter, which is impossible, he spells out this particular point, namely, that although in terms of its own definition it is an immaterial power, it has its being in matter. So, whilst it exists with matter, it is not actualised in respect of the matter when it is nourishing but not causing growth. Alternatively, as Alexander says, the phrase 'This form without matter' is equivalent to 'The nourishment, when it is nourishing but not causing growth, preserves the form without any addition of matter.'[413]

322a29 If some matter accedes to it …

A comma is needed at this point.

322a29 … being potentially immaterial, having potentially quantity as well, these will be larger immaterial <things>.

In turn he means when that which accedes causes growth. He says that if some matter accedes, i.e. some nourishment existing potentially without matter, i.e. having potentially the form of flesh or that of bone or simply of that which is being nourished, and having potentially also quantity, i.e. being capable of adding something in terms of quantity to that which is being nourished, for that space of time the things to which such matter is acceding will be larger immaterial <things>,[414] i.e. they will grow in respect of the form and progress to a larger size – which is to say they will be both nourished and caused to grow at the same time. For instead of saying that they will be greater in respect of the form (for this is what grows), he says 'they will be greater immaterial <things>'. And he says 'having potentially quantity' instead of 'being potentially of such and such size and capable of causing growth, because in every case the acceding nourishment has actual quantity, as he has shown, but it is not in every case of a size to possess the power to cause growth.

> **322a31** If, however, it is no longer able to produce this, but is like water in increasing quantities continually mixed with wine, which ends up by making it watery, and indeed water, then produces diminution of the quantity. The form nevertheless persists.

Having said what growth is, he accordingly says also what diminution is. So his account is this: When the nourishment that accedes is too much for the growth-causing power, and the latter is diminished, 123,1 being overwhelmed by the incoming matter, as happens with people who suffer from indigestion, then there will be diminution of the thing having quantity in virtue of the fact that while matter is by nature in a state of flux, the incoming nourishment does not add an amount equal to the outgoing on account of the weakness of the power, the nourishment becoming too dominating to allow it to be affected as much as it should be by the power of alteration and assimilation in the subjects. For this reason nourishment occurs (for the form remains), but because that which is flowing out is more than that which is being added, the result is that diminution takes place. He uses an illuminating model, namely, that of what happens when water is poured into wine, and whereas at the start it is acted upon by the wine rather than acting upon it, eventually, as the amount of water increases, the power of the wine is weakened and is affected by the water rather than acting upon it. But the analogy does not hold in every respect. In respect of the lessening of the power it would fit the case of diminution; for there too, when the power of nourishment is diminished and assimilates less than is flowing away, diminution occurs. However, in so far as the quantity is increased as water is poured into the wine, in this respect the model does not resemble the case of diminution; for there the quantity is lessened together with the power. So let what is modelled be merely the weakness of the power. Continual exercise wearies it (for the actualisation of the power involves the body in which it also has its being), and being weary it can no longer make quantitative additions to the thing which is being nourished, there being only a small amount of alteration, but nourishing is all it does. So because the outflow is becoming greater, diminution occurs, and particularly of that which is the primary seat of this power, I mean the hot-wet. For that which first takes advantage of the growth during the <period of> increase, owing to the fact that the cause of nourishment is in it, is also the first to take advantage of its weakness and, being diminished by the smaller amount of assimilation, is overcome by the contrary powers, the cold and the dry, and it is in their superiority that senility consists.

Notes

1. The term rendered 'accompany' here and in the ensuing discussion is *parakolouthein*. Aristotle himself only uses this term once in the *Physics*, in a passage that may be the inspiration for Philoponus' usage: at *Phys*. 4.12, 221a24 he describes time as a necessary concomitant of natural things (SB).

2. The term translated 'aim', *skopos*, is a technical term in Neoplatonist exegesis. One of the tasks of a commentator is to elucidate the *skopos* of a work. See, e.g., Simplicius *in Cat*. 8,10-15, (forthcoming in this series); Philoponus *in Cat*. 7,2-8; H.J. Blumenthal, *Aristotle and Neoplatonism in Late Antiquity: Interpretations of the De Anima*, London 1996, pp. 29-30 (SB).

3. *caelo* here is the Latin translation of *ouranou*, the Greek word which is normally translated 'heaven' or 'heavens', but which also has the sense of 'the world'. Hence Philoponus' feeling that an explanation is called for of why this book of Aristotle's contains a discussion of the four elements, which exist in the sublunary or terrestrial sphere, the innermost of the concentric spheres which constitute the world, in contradistinction to which the remaining, outer spheres are described as 'heavenly' or 'celestial'.

4. 28B.

5. 269D.

6. The word here translated 'physical', *phusikos*, has on previous pages been rendered 'natural'. It seemed appropriate here to keep the connection with the *Physics*. The noun from which it is derived is the Greek for 'nature'. The realm of the physical, or natural, is identified by Aristotle with the realm of natural change.

7. In the ancient Greek catalogues of Aristotle's works, a title *Peri phutôn* is listed by Diogenes Laertius and by Hesychius, but neither mention a *Peri metallôn*: see Ingmar Düring, *Aristotle in the Ancient Biographical Tradition*, Göteborg 1957, pp. 47, 86 (SB).

8. Some modern scholars have doubted that *Meteorology* Book 4 is by Aristotle, following an argument by I. Hammer-Jensen, 'Das sogenannte IV. Buch der *Meteorologie* des Aristoteles', *Hermes* 50, 1915, 113-36. More recently, others have questioned her arguments: see H.B. Gottschalk, 'The authorship of *Meteorologica*, Book IV', *Classical Quarterly* 11, 1961, 67-79; Ingemar Düring, *Aristotle's Chemical Treatise: Meteorologica Book IV*, New York 1980, 18-26; David Furley, 'The mechanics of *Meteorologica* IV', in *Cosmic Problems: Essays on Greek and Roman Philosophy of Nature*, Cambridge 1989, 132-48; Eric Lewis, introduction to *Alexander of Aphrodisias: On Aristotle Meteorology 4*, London and Ithaca N.Y. 1996 in this series (SB).

9. The Greek particles *men* and *de* correspond to the translations 'on the one hand' and 'on the other hand'. Joachim agrees with Philoponus that the *de* in the first sentence of the present treatise indicates that it should be read as a continuation of *On the Heavens*: see *Aristotle On Coming-to-be and Passing-away: a revised text with introduction and commentary*, Oxford 1922, p. 62 (SB).

10. The word translated 'place' here and in the last sentence, *topos*, sometimes needs to be translated as 'space'. It can be either a mass term, like 'space', or a count-noun, like 'place'. In Aristotle's view the place of an object is the inner surface of the body which contains it – the place of a fish swimming underwater at any given moment is the inner surface of the water surrounding it at that moment. Since the universe is finite for Aristotle, there is nothing surrounding it, so it is not contained by anything and cannot have a place, i.e. cannot be 'in a place'. One may well wonder how this sentence is compatible with the remark at 3.4 that the only change which the celestial body can undergo is change of place.

11. Reading *kath' hên*, as Vitelli suggests, rather than the MSS' *kath' has*. The latter reading would be possible only if the preceding *tês tôn tessarôn stoikheiôn holotêtos* were emended to *tôn tessarôn stoikheiôn holotêtôn*. We would then need to translate 'the four elements taken as wholes'. These would have to be thought of as four zones occupying the sublunary region: the outermost is composed of fire, the next of air, the next of water, and the innermost, which is the sphere at the centre of the universe, is the earth itself. Of course, things are not as tidy as this, because quantities of earth, water, air and fire escape from their natural places and become mixed with particles of other elements. But a good proportion of each element will always be found in its natural place, and no element will cease to exist altogether. So globally, 'taken as wholes', the elements are as imperishable as the celestial spheres which surround them.

12. Reading *esti* with a paroxytone accent.

13. For instance, rabbits die and are replaced by other rabbits, so that the form of *rabbit* never perishes, although all rabbitty individuals do so. Aristotle and his followers were not worried about endangered species, believing each species to be, as such, imperishable. See *GC* Book 2.11.

14. This word translates the Greek *kenon*, which it is sometimes convenient to translate 'void', sometimes 'empty', as it is translated later in this sentence, and sometimes as here 'vacuum'. This is because it sometimes functions as an adjective, sometimes as a mass term, and sometimes as a count-noun.

15. *Cael.* 3.3, 302a15.

16. Vitelli gives as reference *On the Nature of Man* p. 350K (VI p. 34,17 (Littr.) (SB).

17. This translates the Greek *hupokeimenon*, which is a participle from a verb meaning 'to underlie'. The *hupokeimenon* or substratum is, therefore, that which underlies qualities, etc., the subject of which expressions signifying qualities, etc., are predicated. It is also spoken of by Aristotle as 'that out of which (or from which)' something comes to be. I shall translate the word as 'substratum' unless its participial status is crucial, in which case 'underlying' will be more appropriate. In both cases it will be necessary to appreciate that it is a technical term of Aristotelian metaphysics. (See also below, n. 353.)

18. Aristotle's doctrine of natural places is being appealed to (see above, n. 11): if fire or air is in the upper regions (the two outermost zones), it is in its natural place and is where it is 'naturally'. If it is in either of the lower regions (the two inner zones), it is where it is unnaturally. Again, there seems to be an inconsistency between the implication here that whatever is a body must necessarily exist in a place and the statement at 3,12 above, that it is not in the nature of celestial bodies to be in a place. Celestial bodies are, after all, bodies. (See above, n. 10.)

19. sc. being without quality or form.

20. He is speaking of prime matter, which, when it is subjected to a form, constitutes body. In reality it is never separated from form, but it can be so separated in thought, and considered in this way by itself is something less than body, and thus incorporeal.

21. The word 'wet' is used here to translate *hugron* in the Greek. This is ambiguous as between 'wet' and 'liquid' (or 'fluid'), as Aristotle himself was aware (see 2.2, 330a12ff., and the note in my Clarendon Aristotle Series commentary on *De Generatione et Corruptione*, p. 160). As 'liquid' it is opposed to 'solid', and it cannot have this sense here, since it is opposed to 'dry', which is a specifying feature of fire. Fire can be supposed to be dry, but scarcely solid.

22. Something is homoeomerous if all its parts are the same as itself and as each other. This is how a lump of pure gold appears to be. However small the parts into which you divide it, they will appear as gold. A hand, which is divisible into skin, bone, muscle, etc., is anhomoeomerous. See below, 11,24ff.

23. Philoponus has fallen into anacoluthon. He omits to provide an 'or'-clause to correspond to the 'either' earlier in the sentence.

24. Williams translates *paskhein*, 'to be affected' or 'to suffer change', as 'passion,' as a complement for 'action' and to align with the adjectives 'active' and 'passive'; it has a broader sense than the modern idea of emotional affect (SB).

25. See Proem, n. 17.

26. sc. the formal and final causes.

27. The Greek word translated here as 'moist' is *hugron*, for which see Proem, n. 21. [For the role of 'exhalation', *anathumiasis*, see *Meteor.* 1.3, 340b28ff. There, Aristotle uses the term *atmis* for the cold and wet vapour, *anathumiasis* for the hot and dry. Philoponus says in his commentary on this passage that Aristotle had previously called both *anathumiasis* (*in Meteor.* 36,12). See H.P.D. Lee's notes to the Loeb edition, Aristotle *Meteorology*, London 1978, pp. 26-7 (SB).]

28. The MSS here have *hupokeimenois*, which would require the translation 'which lie beneath it'. This, however, is difficult to make sense of in the context, and I propose, following a suggestion of one of the team of vetters, emending the text to *huperkeimenois*.

29. *Meteorology* 2.9, 369a10ff. (SB).

30. In his distinction between 'causes' and 'accounts' (*logoi*), Philoponus is, in effect, distinguishing the question 'What is the cause of this effect?' from the question 'What is the mechanism by which the cause produces the effect?'

31. The word translated 'alteration' is *alloiôsis*, which Aristotle uses to signify qualitative change, change in what is thing *is like* as opposed to what it *is*. The word is connected with the word *alloios*, which occurs in the line from Homer at 9,1 below, which I have there translated 'altered'. The contrast between 'other' and 'altered', which Philoponus makes at 9,3 is in Greek a contrast between *allos* and *alloios* ('other' and 'of a different kind'). The word *poion*, which Aristotle uses in the *Categories* to signify quality, is formed in the same way, and the difference between alteration and coming-to-be is related to the difference between quality and substance. (One is reminded of the distinction between *homoousios* and *homoiousios* which played such a large part in the Arian controversies and the Council of Nicaea, and of Gibbon's sarcasm about the importance accorded to an iota). In 9,4, however, I have translated *alloion* as 'qualitatively different' rather than as 'altered'. While it would have brought out the etymological connection to say tautologically 'whereas alteration makes it altered', it would not have drawn attention sufficiently to the relation between the concept of alteration and the category of quality.

32. 'Telemachus ... Athena' is deleted by Vitelli, presumably because he regards it as an intrusive gloss. The quotation is from *Odyssey* 16, 181.

33. I am going later to translate this phrase, *tis genesis*, by 'coming-to-be *something*' or '*something* coming-to-be'. but more of Aristotle's theory will have to be taken on board before the point of this can be appreciated (see below, n. 193; cf. also the note on 318a25 in my Clarendon Aristotle Series volume).

34. The word, *ousia*, here translated, traditionally, 'substance', is connected with the Greek equivalent of the verb 'to be'. If something remains the same in substance, what it *is* remains the same, although what it *is like* may have changed. Coming-to-be is change in what a thing *is*, alteration change in what a thing *is like*. (See above, n. 31.)

35. By 'we' here Philoponus means himself and his fellow Aristotelians. They, like many scholars of the present time, interpreted Aristotle as teaching that in substantial change there is a subject of change, 'prime matter', which in itself has no characteristics, i.e. is 'formless'. That which persists through substantial change ('coming-to-be *simpliciter*') is in itself formless, but at any given moment it is 'possessed of form', to use a word which occurs in the next sentence. The Greek word which I translate 'possessed of form' is *eidopepoiêmenos*, the past participle of a verb whose Latin equivalent would seem to be *specificere*, whence, presumably, our own word 'specify'. I was tempted to use 'specify' to translate *eidopoiein* in the rest of this translation, but unfortunately I have no evidence that the English word was ever used in this sense.

36. See above, 8,29.

37. The point is that one of Aristotle's predecessors who claimed that everything is composed of one underlying substance, say, water or air, would be unable to claim that real coming-to-be ever occurred, but would have to say that the underlying substrate simply took on different forms. Aristotle, conversely, wants to say it is possible for genuine coming-to-be to occur: what comes to be is a compound of two principles, form and matter, not an alteration of a single substrate (SB).

38. Vitelli prints a lacuna here. It is not easy to see how the sentence, which has already become intolerably cumbersome, could be completed. [The missing thought seems to be that they can admit only alteration and not coming-to-be (SB).]

39. The text printed by Vitelli here makes the following words a separate sentence. In the apparatus, however, he suggests inserting *hoti* at this point, and this alone seems to permit us to construe the passage.

40. See Proem, n. 22. Things which are homoeomerous are themselves called 'homoeomers'.

41. The Greek word which I have translated 'natural stuff' is *phusin*, the accusative of *phusis* which is usually translated 'nature'.

42. Literally 'is ignorant of his own voice'.

43. i.e. what Anaxagoras called 'coming-to-be'.

44. sc. Aristotle.

45. The phrase 'the same in name and definition' represents a form of the Greek word *sunônumos*, which Aristotle gives this sense in the first chapter of the *Categories*, in contradistinction to *homônuma*, which is used to describe things which are the same in name but not in definition.

46. The name for things which are not homoeomers.

47. This technical term of the school of Democritus and Leucippus means 'incapable of being split'.

48. The Greek word this represents, namely, *stoikheia*, whose Latin and English equivalents are *elementa* and 'elements', is the regular word for letters of the alphabet. The contrast between letters and the syllables made up of them is regularly used to illustrate the relationship between the physical elements and the composite bodies which they combine to produce.

49. In this sentence the original of the word I have translated 'other' is *alla*, the word I have translated 'different things' is *hetera*, and the phrase I have rendered 'have different qualities' is *heteroia*. The contrast between *hetera* and *heteroia* is the same as that between *allos* and *alloios* explained above in n. 31.

50. *panspermia*, a technical term of Anaxagoras'. Williams leaves this untranslated in the Clarendon text (SB).

51. The MSS here read *phaskon*, the participle, thus leaving the sentence without a main verb. I follow Vitelli, who suggests reading *ephasken*.

52. The Greek word here, *homomereias*, is different from that commented on above in nn. 22 and 40. It is not used by Aristotle himself. There is controversy amongst scholars over whether it was actually used by Anaxagoras, or whether, as seems more likely, it derives from Aristotle's use of his own term *homoiomerê* to describe the things, flesh, bone, sinew, etc., of which Anaxagoras is talking. See W.K.C. Guthrie, *A History of Greek Philosophy*, vol. 2, Cambridge 1965, pp. 325ff.

53. The word translated 'this' (*touto*) here and in the next sentence is accompanied in the MSS by another word *auto*. At the second occurrence I have translated the phrase 'just this'. It seems best to follow Vitelli's suggestion and delete the word *auto* at its first occurrence.

54. Vitelli's comma between *menontos* and *tou hupokeimenou* interferes with the sense of the sentence.

55. The word translated 'being' here is the word elsewhere mostly translated 'substance'. It is the verbal noun from the verb 'be'.

56. Philoponus may have been trading on the fact that the word properly translated 'birth' here (*phusis*) is the same as that properly translated 'nature' two lines back.

57. sc. the followers of Empedocles.

58. Again, he shifts to talking about the followers of Empedocles.

59. For the argument to go through, this must be taken to mean 'all the qualities'. Aristotle has an argument to support this claim (which I discuss in the note on 314b26 in my Clarendon Aristotle Series edition of *De Generatione et Corruptione*); but Philoponus does not rehearse that argument in this passage.

60. The followers of Empedocles.

61. The word I have here translated 'the same', *akinêton*, would more literally be translated 'unchanged' or 'unmoved'.

62. Again the word used by Aristotle, *êremousês*, would more literally be translated 'unmoved' in the sense of not being subject to locomotion.

63. Literally 'forms' (*eidê*). Since this word is also used in the sense of 'species', it is not difficult to make it bear the sense of 'specifying characteristic' (*differentia specifica*). Aristotle indeed uses *diaphora* at this point.

64. I have translated the word *eidopoiountai* here by the phrase 'have as their specifying characteristics'. See above, nn. 35 and 63.

65. Literally 'by nature' (*phusei*).

66. See above, n. 61.

67. I have printed a translation of the word which appears here in Aristotle's MSS, *hêi*, rather than that given by Philoponus, *ê*, which would require 'Or it is clear' to be substituted for 'This shows' with a loss of appropriateness to the argument. The difference between *hêi* and *ê*, as written in Greek, is not a difference in letters but in accents, breathings and an iota subscript.

68. See above, *CAG* pp. 23-4, commenting on 314a13ff.

69. The phrase 'the differentiae which are the specifying characteristics of the elements' represents *tas eidopoious diaphoras tôn stoikheiôn*, whereas 'specifying characteristic' in the previous line represented *eidos*. See above, nn. 35 and 63.

70. The word translated 'and these' (*haistisin*) is feminine, agreeing with the word translated 'differentiae' and ignoring the neuter word translated 'affections'. This suggests that *kai pathôn* ('and affections') should be deleted from the text.

71. The phrase 'the differentiae which are the specifying characteristics' again translates *eidopoious diaphoras*. See above, n. 69.

72. The phrase 'specifically identical' translates *homoeides*.

73. The phrase 'receiving their specifying characteristics' translates *eidopoioumena*. See above, n. 69.

74. Plato, *Timaeus* 73E.

75. This translates *oude*, which is the undisputed reading of Aristotle' text at this point and which is printed by Vitelli, rather than *ouden* which he says is the reading of the Philoponus MSS.

76. At 316a4.

77. This word is not found in extant works of Plato, but Aristotle, at *Topics* 6.2, 140a5, says that it, together with a number of other unusual words, is used by Plato.

78. Philoponus' lemma reads *kai peri tas allas kinêseis* (accusative), as do several of the MSS of Aristotle at this point, although they are unanimous in representing him as using the genitive with *peri* in the preceding phrases.

79. The Greek words are *kinêseis* and *metabolas*, respectively. The former word is often used to refer to events which it would be unnatural to call 'movements' in English, but if we were to translate it 'changes' here, as it is often reasonable to do elsewhere, we should deprive ourselves of the possibility of expressing a contrast with *metabolai*.

80. See Book 5, 225a20ff.

81. In Greek, *peri tôn allôn kinêseôn*. Philoponus, despite his title of *ho grammatikos*, seems to be mistaken about Aristotle's usage in this matter, vide Bonitz 519b20ff. (I am grateful to the scholar who commented on my translation in draft for this observation and for those made in the two following notes.)

82. *Iliad* 24, 721. It is not obvious how this, or the following quotation from Aristophanes, provides a parallel with Aristotle's use of the accusative with *peri*, since neither of them actually uses the word *peri*. The word translated 'in mourning' is the accusative plural of the word for 'mourning': *thrênous*. However, some MSS of Homer have the genitive, *thrênôn*, at this point. The word translated 'sound' is given in the MSS of Philoponus as *autên*, but the word in the text of the Iliad here is *aoidên*, which alone makes sense, and which my translation assumes is the correct reading. There is a word *aütên*, which occurs in a very similar context in *Odyssey* 11, 383, which may have given rise to the misquotation.

83. Vitelli points out that the quotation is actually from the *Lysistrata* (408-10).

84. i.e. Aristophanes has the accusative *ton hormon* instead of the genitive *tou hormou*, which we would have expected. The scholion at this point suggests that Aristophanes' phrase *ton hormon hon eskeuasas* is an abbreviation of *tou hormou, hon hormon eskeuasas* ('of the bottle, which bottle you made').

85. sc. Aristotelians.

86. Democritus is not mentioned by Aristotle in his chapter about growth (*GC* 1.5).

87. Aristotle has already used the word *panspermia* at 314a29, but Philoponus has nothing to say about it in his note *ad loc.* It is a technical Atomist term meaning the stock of atoms which form the whole (*pan*) seed-bed (*spermia*) of the Universe.

88. The phrase 'other colours' here translates *alloios*, for which see n. 31.

89. This is what Philoponus says, but it seems impossible to understand why he says it.

90. The equivalent in Greek of the negative prefix 'im-' is a single letter *a*- (alpha privative), so that the illustration is more apt in Greek than in English.

91. This word translates *stoikheia*: see n. 48. The illustration is not particularly apt. A suggestion has been made by M.L. West in *Philologus* 113, 1969, 150-1, that the word translated 'comedy' here, *kômôidia*, is a mistake for *trugôidia*, a word found in Aristophanes and glossed by *kômôidia*.

92. Book 3.1; Book 4.2, etc.

93. I have used 'scientific', rather than 'natural', to translate *phusikôtera*, because the contemporary sense of 'scientific', implying connection with the natural sciences, although historically associated with *epistêmê* rather than *phusis*, captures the sense of the word in this context.

94. See previous note; and cf. *Metaphysics* 1, 985b15-19.

95. At 316a6-7 of the modern text, Aristotle contrasts inexperience to 'being more at home in physical investigations' (*en tois phusikois*), not 'being at home with nature' (*têi phusei*). The point seems the same, but Philoponus feels called upon to explain the phrase here translated 'with nature'. Two MSS of Philoponus have an article in the genitive, not the dative (SB).

96. See chapters 1 and 7; and cf. Book 4.2.

97. The MSS both of Aristotle and of Philoponus have variant readings here, and in the following lines, some having *diathigêi* and some *diathêgê* instead of *diathêkêi*.

98. i.e. Ionic. Abdera was the native city of Democritus.

99. 315b9.

100. The Greek *hais* is the dative of a relative pronoun the antecedent of which in the text is 'principles'. Omitting the *s* would convert it to the nominative, *hai*, and thus allow it to be the subject of the verb translated 'are able to', which would otherwise have to take 'the followers of Democritus', understood from the context, as its subject. Aristotle's MSS are divided between the reading *hais* and the reading *hai*, and Philoponus knows both variants.

101. *logoi* in the Greek. It is impossible to find a single translation for this word which will fit all the uses to which it is put in the next few paragraphs.

102. By 'subsistence' he means the property of being a substance.

103. sc. objects in the natural world, animals, plants, heavenly bodies, etc.

104. Vitelli prints *dioti* ('because'): one MS and Aristotle's text have *hoti*, which could have the same meaning as *dioti*, but could also be translated 'that' to introduce an oratio obliqua statement of what 'the latter' say.

105. There was a tradition that Plato bequeathed some 'unwritten doctrines' to his followers. It is not clear from the present remarks whether Philoponus accepted this tradition, although it was accepted by Porphyry and Simplicius. (See H. Cherniss, *The Riddle of the Academy*, p. 90.)

106. Frege asserts the converse of this: The reference of the name 'the centre of gravity of the Solar System' is something simple, i.e. without parts; but the sense of the name is complex, dependent on the sense of each of the separately meaningful expressions of which it is composed.

107. This translates *moriôn*, which Vitelli suggests here as an emendation for *monadôn* (units), the reading of the MSS.

108. Philoponus understands 'is in potentiality' as implying 'is not in actuality', for which there is good Aristotelian precedent.

109. The word translated 'thing possessed of size' is *megethos*, which sometimes needs to be translated 'magnitude'. In the present passage, however, it is intended to have its concrete, not its abstract, sense.

110. Philoponus' text actually has 'atoms' here, not 'points', whereas the argument demands 'points'. We should perhaps conjecture that the MSS' *atoma* is a mistake for the word for 'points', *stigmas*.

111. i.e. since points are understood as partless, if they are in contact it can't be the case that part of one point – the left edge, say – touches part of the next; points that touch will exactly coincide (*epharmozein*), whereas it is always possible to place another point between any two points on a line (*Phys.* 5.3) (SB).

112. On this distinction between exposition and detail commentary on the text, see Introduction, n. 4 (SB).

113. The word which Philoponus uses here and which I translate as 'increase' is his and Aristotle's standard word for 'grow'. We should have expected a word meaning 'proceed'. Presumably for a process to increase is for it to go on for a longer time. [See below, 51,18 (SB).]

114. text here (quoting Aristotle) reads: *kai holôs, ei pantêi diaireton, ean diairethêi, ouden estai adunaton gegonos*. The MSS of Aristotle have *de* after *holôs*, *pephuke* after *pantêi* and *an* in place of *ean*, except for two MSS which at this point read *kan*.

115. It is Aristotle's doctrine, e.g. in *Cael.* 1.12, that if it is possible that something should happen, over an infinitely long period it will happen. Conversely, what never happens, could not possibly happen. To the extent that this doctrine rests on the commonsense view that it would be ridiculous, for example, to ascribe a capacity for generosity to a person who over many years acted with consistent meanness, it seems reasonable to substitute 'long' for 'infinitely long' as Philoponus does here.

116. Instead of Philoponus' 'is composed' (*sunkeitai*) Aristotle's text has simply 'is' (*êi*).

117. Reading, with the Aldine editor, *ouk an eiê*, rather than *hama*, which is what Vitelli prints.

118. There seems to be only one piece of MS evidence for *ou khôriston*, which gives quite the wrong sense. The received reading is *ti khôriston*. The *ou* in Philoponus' lemma seems to have taken the place of the *ti*.

119. I cannot see the justification for this remark by Philoponus.

120. Philoponus draws a comparison here between the problem about the composition of a divisible body and the controversy among Neoplatonists about the status of prime matter. Aristotle thinks there is a matter underlying every change, and that things are composed of form and matter. Many took him to mean that there must be a most basic 'prime matter' that lacks all qualities so as to be receptive of all possible forms. But if matter lacks all qualities, including those which are definitive of body, it seems to be incorporeal. The problem then is how corporeal entities come to be composed from incorporeal form and incorporeal matter. Philoponus' eventual solution, which he develops elsewhere, is to take the substrate to be three-dimensional extensionality, distinguishing between being extended and having a definite extension. See Sorabji, *Matter, Space and Motion*, ch. 2, and de Haas, *John Philoponus' New Definition of Prime Matter* (SB).

121. The Greek word *pou* can mean either 'where' or 'somewhere', although in the latter case it is unaccented. Hence the possibility of treating the sentence either as statement or as a question. (Vitelli prints the word in capitals, which would not take accents even on the interrogative interpretation, presumably to avoid printing the text itself in a way that would commit him at this stage to one or other interpretation.)

122. Philoponus is thinking of 'natural' places. See above, n. 10.

123. The difficulty, presumably, is that there is no reason to assign to points either of the natural motions, upwards or downwards.

124. Aristotle merely gestures towards the claim that points can't possibly exhibit the characteristics of body, whereas Philoponus teases out the absurdities.

Philoponus agrees with Aristotle that void can't exist in actuality, although he elsewhere disagrees with Aristotle's arguments on this and distinguishes between the logical and physical impossibility of void: see David Sedley, 'Philoponus' conception of space', in Sorabji (ed.), *Philoponus and the Rejection of Aristotelian Science*, London and Ithaca N.Y. 1987, 140-53 (SB).

125. See above, 28,12.

126. This translates *dia perinoian*.

127. I follow the Aldine editor in omitting the repetition of 'he says' at this point.

128. *Cael.* 3.4, 303a3ff.

129. *Phys.* 4.1, 231a21ff.

130. 969b29ff.

131. This is Williams' translation of the modern text of Aristotle, which has *to d'einai hama pantê diaireton dunamei*. Philoponus later discusses a slightly different phrase, *pantê diaireton einai to sunekhes*, 'the continuum to be everywhere divisible' (34,19), in a passage that appears to be a literal quotation, but also *pantê diaireton to sôma* (34,27), *to hama pantê diaireton einai to megethos* (35,2) and *to hama pantê diaireton einai to sôma* (35,3-4), i.e. that it is impossible for 'magnitude' or 'body' 'to be everywhere divisible' (SB).

132. Aristotle has two words for 'point': *stigmê* and *semeion*. There seems to be no difference of meaning, but here, as in my Clarendon Aristotle volume, I have marked the verbal difference by translating *stigmê* as 'point' and *sêmeion* as 'position'. Where only one of these terms occur in a passage I have translated the two Greek words indiscriminately as 'point'. The Greek word here, *sêmeia*, does not differ in meaning from the word translated 'points', but it is necessary to use 'positions' to indicate that we have two different words.

133. The connection is not as obvious as that to everyone.

134. See above, 28,15ff.

135. *Phys.* 3.6, 206a21ff.

136. The word translated 'infinite' (*apeirou*) is what Philoponus wrote here (according to the MSS). But it is impossible to make sense of it. The point surely is that there is an infinite number of parts which can be taken from a finite whole. Perhaps *apeirou* is a slip of the pen for a word like *holou* ('whole').

137. The Greek here has *eis apeira*.

138. The Greek here has *ep' apeiron*.

139. Here and in the next sentence 'into an infinite number' or 'into infinity' represents the Greek *eis apeira*.

140. *Phys.* 3.6, 207a17.

141. The Greek for 'complete' is *teleion* and for 'end' *telos*.

142. Again, *eis apeira*.

143. sc. Aristotelians.

144. The phrase that I have translated 'part that results from the division' would, if literally translated, read 'divided part'.

145. Vitelli's insertion.

146. In Greek, *ep' apeiron*.

147. The reference seems to be to *mekhri tou* ('up to a certain point') in 316b32, which Philoponus has wrongly cited as *mekhri toutou* ('up to this point'). [In his Clarendon translation, Williams' renders *mekhri tou* somewhat more freely as 'there must be a limit' (SB).]

148. Philoponus' lemma reads *huparkhein* here, but the MSS of Aristotle have *enuparkhein*.

149. Philoponus here omits the words *allôs te kai* which are in the MSS of

Aristotle. Together with the following word *eiper* they could be translated 'not least if'.

150. The Greek word here is the present-tensed *esti*. The MSS of Aristotle have the future-tensed *estai*. I translate this word here as 'exist', although I usually reserve 'exist' for the translation of *huparkhein* (as in the case of the fourth word of this lemma), because it allows one of the interpretations which Philoponus proceeds to give in his commentary on the passage to run smoothly.

151. Here and in the next two sentences only the words in angle brackets are the translations of words inserted by Philoponus to eke out the text in ways that make his various interpretations more plausible. Thereafter angle brackets will return to their normal function to indicate an insertion by the translator.

152. sc. from the thesis that a thing possessed of size is everywhere divisible.

153. Philoponus' words here literally mean 'to be next to each other by an infinite distance'. But it is fairly clear that he is rehearsing the distinctions Aristotle provides in Book 5 of the *Physics*, where 'next to' (*ephexês*) is the term for the relation which orders the number series, where there is no finite distance between, say, 4 and 5, although we should hardly wish to say that they were infinitely distant from each other.

154. i.e. to overlap.

155. Vitelli indicates a lacuna in the MSS, while noting that one MS inserts *kai houtôs* ('and in this way') at this point.

156. There could not, of course, be *one* consecutive point. Presumably what is being denied is that there is a point, A, and another one next to it, B (and another one next to that, C, etc.). You cannot get beyond A.

157. This, i.e. position, is merely a dividing point, or point of juncture (RRKS). For the word translated 'position' see above n. 132. Before the words translated 'and this' in this sentence the text of *De Generatione et Corruptione* has *ê stigmê stigmês*, which would need to be translated 'or point to point'.

158. i.e. if a thing possessed of size could be divided at contiguous positions, it would itself be no more than a point of division or junction and would not be divided into things possessed of size or composed out of things possessed of size (RRKS).

159. He is talking about the remark 'This is division and junction'.

160. The term Williams translates 'corresponding affection' is *sumpatheia*, an important concept in Epicurus' theory of perception: cf. *Letter to Herodotus*, 43-65. There, Epicurus uses the term to explain the susceptibility of soul atoms to the affections of the aggregate, as well as the ability of the sense organs to be stimulated by the motion of particles in such a way as to produce sense impressions. The term has other uses in Stoicism, where it describes the ability of distant bodies to act on one another by the tension of the *pneuma*. See also Philoponus' citation of Hippocrates at 106,34, n. 370 (SB).

161. See above, n. 17.

162. Philoponus means that genus of which all other genera and species in a given category are species, e.g. *quality* in the category of quality, *relation* in the category of relation, etc. Aristotle's Greek has been interpreted by some as 'that which is first *amongst* the categories', i.e. substance, which gives the result which Philoponus wishes without the complicated argument he provides to obtain it. (See my notes on *De Generatione et Corruptione* ad loc.)

163. Literally, 'So there will be nothing from which the coming-to-be of substance'. The same words appear, and are similarly translated, at the end of the following sentence.

164. 260Cff.

165. The Greek is *tôn physikôn* [This term is often used to refer to the Presocratics writing on natural philosophy. See A.P.D. Mourelatos, 'Pre-Socratic origins of the principle that there are no origins from nothing', *Journal of Philosophy* 11, 1981, 649-65, for the principle that nothing comes from nothing (SB).]

166. The Greek is *autê kath' hautên* – 'itself by itself' or 'itself *per se*'.

167. Book 3.5ff.

168. 'Continuing sequence' represents *heirmou*, which literally means 'chain' or 'concatenation'.

169. The phrase 'existent in reality' translates *en huparxei on*.

170. See above, n. 35.

171. Above, 43,7-8.

172. Philoponus' lemma here reads *hôs hoti* where the MSS of Aristotle read *hoti*. (The Aldine editor omits *hôs*, presumably by way of correction.) Other examples of *hôs hoti* where we should expect *hoti* by itself occur in this work at 100,18; 106,8.

173. The Greek word translated 'belongs' is *huparkhei*, which is regularly used by Aristotle, as here, to means 'is truly predicated of', but which by Philoponus' time had also acquired the sense of our word 'exist'. No doubt Philoponus intends the air of oxymoron which would attend the statement 'Not being exists'.

174. Is Philoponus here anticipating the final conclusion of Aristotle's discussion of the matter, whereby 'to be *simpliciter*' for a substance signifies having the appropriate essence: to be for a man is to be a rational animal?

175. Philoponus' construction is somewhat ragged at this point. This 'either' (*êtoi*) lacks a following 'or', and it is not true that that which comes to be from that which *simpliciter* is not is itself said *simpliciter* not to be.

176. The word translated 'quality' here is the abstract noun *poiotêti*, and the word translated 'such-and-such' is the cognate concrete adjective *poion*, which I translated 'quality' two lines above. Cf. above Chapter 1, n. 31.

177. The sense requires that 'that which *simpliciter* is not in substance' at the beginning of the sentence is balanced here by 'that which comes to be out of that which *simpliciter* is not'; but whereas the word *to*, which I have translated 'that which', occurs at the beginning of the phrase translated 'that which *simpliciter* is not in substance', it is absent here. (It is, however, present in the parallel passage at 46,17.) This seems to be an error either in the transmission or in what Philoponus originally wrote.

178. sc. the first of the *summa genera*, i.e. the categories,

179. This seems odd, for whiteness is not substance, but it does not follow that it is not one of the other categories. What Aristotle actually says is that that of which substance cannot be predicated cannot have any of the others, quality, quantity, etc., predicated of it either. What is not a man or anything else in the category of substance isn't pale or dark or tall or short, i.e. cannot have any predicate in any of the other categories predicated of it.

180. Perhaps he is referring back to 317a33.

181. The word I have translated 'occurs', *huphistatai*, is the ancestor of the word 'subsists', but it seemed impossible English to talk of coming-to-be subsisting.

182. The Greek word *huparxis* translated twice in this sentence as 'reality' is more usually translated as 'existence'.

183. 317b29.

184. sc. things in other categories than that of substance.

185. The story is that 'metaphysics' got its name when Andronicus of Rhodes, editing Aristotle's manuscripts, grouped together a series of treatises and, cataloguing them after the books on physics, called the collection 'after the physics'. For a recent critical assessment of Andronicus' importance, see Jonathan Barnes,

'Roman Aristotle,' 1-69 in Jonathan Barnes and Miriam Griffin (eds) *Philosophia Togata II: Plato and Aristotle at Rome*, Oxford 1997 (SB).

186. In *De Generatione et Corruptione* 2.10.

187. Again, he means beings in categories other than substance.

188. Vitelli follows the Aldine editor in supplying *ti* at this point.

189. Book 3, chapter 5.

190. See Chapter 1, n. 35.

191. This interpretation of *homoiôs*, which I have translated here as 'equally', is implausible. In my Clarendon translation I found it more appropriate to translate *homoios* as 'alike'.

192. Williams translates *kata meros* as 'partial' here: it refers to accidents (SB).

193. The original contrast is that between to coming-to-be (and being) something or other, e.g. fat (sc. copulative coming-to-be), and coming-to-be period, *tout court* (sc. existential coming-to-be). The Greek for 'period' or *tout court* is *haplôs*, which I have normally rendered by its standard Latin translation *simpliciter*. Aristotle, however, introduces a technical use of the adjective *haplê* to which the adverb *haplôs* corresponds, which he attaches to the noun *genesis*, translated 'coming-to-be', and this adjective I have translated 'simple'. But to provide a contrast with this he also uses the adjective *tis* (meaning 'some') which he attaches to the noun *genesis* ('generation', or 'coming-to-be') to form a nominalisation of the phrase 'to come to be something'. The literal translation of this phrase, *genesis tis*, would be 'some coming-to-be' (but see below n. 196). This would be impossible English, so I have had to resort to paraphrase. But there is a further complication. The Greek sentence *ti ginetai*, of which the phrase *genesis tis* is the nominalisation, is ambiguous as between 'comes to be something' and 'something comes to be'. The noun phrase inherits the ambiguity of the sentence. At this point what Aristotle is contrasting with coming-to-be *simpliciter* is no longer *coming-to-be something*, but has become *something coming-to-be*.

194. See above, n. 193.

195. One might wonder what else it might come from. (I am grateful to a commentator on my translation for this comment.)

196. A possible way of understanding *genesis tis* is as 'a sort of coming-to-be' (cf. my translation at 9,9 with my note *ad loc.*) or 'qualified coming-to-be' or 'a marginal case of coming-to-be' – one might almost say ' "coming-to-be" in a Pickwickian sense'. It is perhaps in this way that a Parmenidean might be prepared to recognise the coming-to-be of what is not as a case of *tis genesis*.

197. This phrase is regularly used by Aristotle to indicate what are often called the elements; earth, air, fire and water.

198. In Aristotle's view fire is hot and dry, air hot and wet, water cold and wet and earth cold and dry.

199. This phrase, which is added by the Aldine editor but not printed by Vitelli, is not in the MSS of Philoponus, but is in most of those of Aristotle.

200. The phrase 'that which contributes form' translates the Greek *eidopoion*. See above, n. 35.

201. I follow Vitelli's suggestion of reading *prostetheike* instead of *prostitheika*.

202. Literally 'being in subsistence' – *einai en hupostasei*.

203. Philoponus' text is a little different from the modern, but as it is unclear how precisely the sentence of Philoponus' would be completed, Williams translates with the modern text (SB).

204. This is more or less the transliteration of *katêgoria*, the ancestor of our word 'predicate', amongst others. In my Clarendon translation I rendered the word 'positive characteristic', but here it seems necessary to reserve this phrase to render *hexis*, which signifies the possession of a property, as opposed to 'privation' which signifies lack of a property. See my commentary on Aristotle's text for a discussion of his use of the word *katêgoria*.

205. The phrase 'things which have it as their form' translates *eidopoioumena*. See above, n. 35.

206. The phrase 'absence of perception' represents *anaisthêsia*, which would properly mean 'insensibility'. The point, however, is not so much the inability of perceivers to perceive, but the inability of the objects to be perceived. Philoponus' remarks in the following paragraph show that he is not insensible of this awkwardness.

207. On the suggestion of the scholar who commented on my translation I follow the MSS G and T here and read *to* in line 23 rather than *tôi*.

208. It is impossible not to be reminded here of Berkeley's *Esse est percipi vel percipere*.

209. Reading with Z *to hou heneka tou heneka tou*.

210. Perhaps the thinking behind this valuation of black and white is something like this: black is what we (seem to) see in the complete absence of light, whereas we need light to see white. To see black is, as it were, to see nothing.

211. cf. Book 3.1, 201a3ff.

212. The missing premiss seems to be that a privation is not the sort of thing that could perish.

213. 318a13-23.

214. 318a23-5.

215. The words I have translated 'does not exist' could be rendered more literally 'is not'.

216. These last bracketed words represent Greek words which Vitelli follows the Aldine editor in inserting in the text.

217. The Greek words which these bracketed English words represent are disputed, variant readings being found both in the MSS of Philoponus and in those of Aristotle.

218. viz. 317b16.

219. The Greek word I have translated here as 'exists' is the word which corresponds to the English verb 'to be', but it is not here functioning as the copula.

220. This word translates *huparxin*, for which I have normally reserved 'existence' as the translation.

221. The word translated 'substratum' is the participle of the verb translated 'underlies' in the previous sentence.

222. The Greek word I have translated by 'he says' is an addition of Vitelli's.

223. There seems to be a lacuna in the text at this point. The words I have placed in brackets in this sentence and the next translate the suggestion made by Vitelli on how this lacuna is to be filled.

224. Matter as such exists only in potentiality. It does not exist in actuality until it has received form. [The 'suitability,' *epitêdeiotês*, of matter is important for Philoponus in delimiting the potential specific to different kinds of things. Hence he needs to clarify that, while matter is in one sense suitable to everything, it always occurs with a form and specific potential. The child, unlike a stone, has the potential to be a geometer: Philoponus calls this 'suitability'. See *in GC* 1.10, in the companion volume. Todd discusses Sambursky's claim that Philoponus uses the term in a technical sense in '*Epitedeiotes* in philosophical literature: towards an analysis', *Acta Classica* 15, 1972, 25-35 (SB).]

225. The word which is translated 'definition' here and in the following sentences is '*logos*'.

226. sc. the definition of 'air', *qua* proximate matter, is 'the matter of fire' and that of 'earth' is 'the matter of water'.

227. A literal translation of the Greek here would be 'given that the things whose definitions it would have in itself', but it seems clear that what Philoponus means to say is something like what I have written.

228. The word translated 'if' is omitted from one of the MSS, and the sense is much improved if we go along with this omission.

229. There is an order in which the elements change most easily into one another: fire, air, water, earth, fire, and the same in reverse. Those which are *not* next to each other in this order, fire and water, air and earth, change into each other with difficulty. See below, Book 2.4.

230. sc. heat and cold.

231. Saying that the bald belongs to the pale is, in the jargon of Aristotle's logic, a description of what someone does who says 'The pale <one> is bald'. Such a statement does not predicate anything *per se* of a subject: if it predicates anything of it at all, it does so only *per accidens*, in that paleness and baldness are both predicable of something else. I have argued that Aristotle's reluctance to give a subject-predicate analysis of such propositions (cf. *Posterior Analytics*, 1.22, 83a4-17) anticipates Russell's Theory of Descriptions. See my 'Aristotle's theory of descriptions', *Philosophical Review* 94, 1985, 63-80.

232. The expression 'species-determining' is intended to translate *eidopoia*. Cf. above, n. 35.

233. The word *hugros*, translated 'wet' in this paragraph, often has the meaning 'fluid' or 'liquid' see Proem, n. 21); and 'wetter' here might be replaced by the phrase 'having greater fluidity'.

234. The Greek translated 'specifically' here and in other places in this paragraph (*kat' eidos* or *eidêi*) is the origin of our use of 'specific' as opposed to 'numerical identity'. It could also be translated 'in kind', since *species* in Latin represents the Greek *eidos* in its various uses as equivalent to 'form', 'kind' and 'species' as opposed to 'genus'.

235. The Greek word here is *idea*.

236. The phrase I have translated 'individual' would be rendered literally, 'a this something'.

237. See previous note.

238. The phrase 'which comes from something outside' represent the single word *exôthen* in the Greek. For the idea of change without alteration, cf. recent discussions of 'merely Cambridge Change', e.g. my 'Aristotle on Cambridge Change', *Oxford Studies in Ancient Philosophy* 7, 1990, 41-57.

239. See above, 65,2-6.

240. If we were to describe the change as the transparent (or the wet) being first hot and then, later, cold, we would be predicating 'hot' and 'cold' of the transparent (the wet) only *per accidens*. Hot and cold are not here affections of anything perceptible which persists through the change, as having hair and being bald are (at different times) of Socrates if he changes from having hair to being bald.

241. Vitelli follows the Aldine Editor in deleting *de* (represented in my translation by 'and'), but it is difficult to see how to construe the sentence without a connective. One might have expected *te* rather than *de*.

242. In my Clarendon Series translation I used 'entirely' to render *pasês* and *pantos*, which correspond in editions of Aristotle's text to *ex hapasês* and *ex hapantos* in Philoponus's text at this point.

243. sc. solidity and impenetrability.

244. Vitelli indicates a lacuna at this point. The bracketed words which follow translate words used by the Aldine editor to fill the gap.

245. The Greek is *enantiôsin*.

246. Aristotle's MSS at this point read, not *hêi psukhra* ('*qua* cold'), as in Philoponus' text, but *ê psukhra* ('or cold'). My own translation of *De Generatione et Corruptione* reads 'if both are transparent or <wet, but not> cold' at this point, supposing '*hugra, all' ou*' to have fallen out of the text between *ê* and *psukhra*. I suggested this emendation of the text in a note in the *Classical Review* n.s. 22, 1972, 301-3. It is not clear how *ê* ('or') became corrupted to *hêi* ('*qua*'), nor how *qua* is to be understood here.

247. cf. above, n. 232, above.

248. Philoponus has in mind the case where a musical man becomes unmusical.

249. The MSS give the following order: 1, 3, 2, 4. The Loeb editor follows the MSS ordering here, and I do the same in my Clarendon Series translation; but Joachim in his edition of the text adopts, with acknowledgement, the reordering suggested here by Philoponus.

250. 320a1.

251. i.e. is substratum to.

252. Reading, with the Aldine Editor, *phoras* rather than *phthoras*. It would be easier if the Greek could be translated 'It is in this sense then that the matter of alteration, growth and locomotion is both substance in actuality and perceptible substance'.

253. In his Clarendon translation, Williams renders *en tôi peri ho* as 'in the respect in which', but here, as Philoponus shortly interprets this phrase as referring to a substantive describing the respect of change, not to the various respects of change, the latter reading is followed here (SB).

254. Vitelli prints a lacuna here, but indicates that the words printed as an insertion in my translation were suggested by the Aldine editor.

255. Book 8.7.

256. Here and in the following lines I use the phrase 'qualitatively different' to translate the single Greek word *alloion*, for which see Chapter 1, n. 31.

257. Chapter 8, 11a5ff.

258. 320a26.

259. sc. larger or smaller.

260. For an analysis of Philoponus' commentary on Aristotle's treatment of growth, cf. De Haas, *John Philoponus' New Definition of Prime Matter*, pp. 132-64.

261. Literally 'itself by itself'.

262. See previous note.

263. What Philoponus seems to have in mind here is bare extension, as envisaged by the theories described by Richard Sorabji in *Matter, Space and Motion*, London and Ithaca N.Y. 1987, ch. 1-3.

264. i.e. the fact that it is in some place or other, as opposed to the fact that it is in this place rather than that.

265. See above, n. 261

266. The meaning of this phrase is to be gathered from looking back to the phrase 'either as part or as affection' earlier in the sentence. It is as though Philoponus had said 'as being a part of it or an affection of it or, for any X, an X of it'.

267. Frans de Haas suggests that this should be understood: 'how the matter <of growth> is present in something, not being actually body and not completing <the essence of> that in which it is' and discusses the phrase *sumplêrôtika tês ousias* in his *John Philoponus' New Definition of Prime Matter*, pp. 201-9 (SB).

268. See above, n. 266 for the sense of 'of' here.

269. The phrase translated here *mêden ousan ekeinou* is much the same as that translated 'to be nothing of it' (*mêden autou einai*) to which the last footnote refers.

270. I have translated the text printed by the Aldine editor (supported by one MS), which omits *kai* before the word translated 'actually'.

271. The words 'already subject to quantity' represent a single word in the Greek: *peposômenon*.

272. The term translated 'assimilated' here, *proskrithen*, is relatively rare, but widely used by Alexander of Aphrodisias. The other term used both here and in the subsequent discussion, *exhomoiôsis*, is Galen's term for the process (SB).

273. Joachim records one MS as reading *ê* (or) instead of the *kai* (and) which is what he himself prints. The text Philoponus is using seems to have this reading and he is reporting *kai* as a variant.

274. There appears to be a lacuna in the text here. The Aldine editor supplies words which I have translated as 'he asks whether'.

275. The word translated 'space' here is the same as that translated 'place' later in this sentence and in the following sentences. See above, n. 10.

276. Reading, in accordance with Vitelli's suggestion, *autou* for the MSS' *toutou*.

277. See above, n. 266

278. The word I have translated 'composition' – *sustasis* – can mean something more specific, namely the degree of density of a body. Thus it might be thought that a heavier metal mixed with a lighter contributed something to the *sustasis* of the resultant alloy.

279. The word I have translated 'in every case' could either be masculine or neuter. It is impossible to preserve this ambiguity in English, but it is what Philoponus is spelling out when he gives the alternative interpretations: 'it is better for everyone to speak thus' and 'in every way better'.

280. This represents the Greek *akhôristou*, which is ambiguous as between 'inseparable' and 'unseparated'.

281. The Greek here is *peri tês prôtês kai aneideou* (SB).

282. Reading *hautê* with (G)a. Vitelli prints *autê*.

283. The Aristotelian locutions *to hulêi einai* and *to hudati* are often translated according the pattern 'being X' rather than 'being for X', so the translation 'it is one thing for it to be matter and another <for it to be> water' might be preferred to 'the being that belongs to matter' and 'that which belongs to water'.

284. My phrase 'the composite thing' translates *tôi sunthetôi*, which is Aristotle regular name for the concrete object, the combination of matter and form. [De Haas points out that this distinction of two senses of being 'in' something is, in Philoponus' view, an attempt by Aristotle at distinguishing the matter of growth from that of generation: *John Philoponus' New Definition of Prime Matter*, pp. 150-1 (SB).]

285. See below, 84,27.

286. Namely, the view that it is points which are the matter of growing things.

287. For example, a sphere can be produced in thought by rotating a circle round its diameter.

288. *Cael.* 3.1, 299a6ff.

289. Vitelli suggests reading *oute* instead of *oude* here, without actually adopting the emendation. The fact that *oude* has occurred twice in the previous sentence might explain the corruption.

290. Again, Vitelli suggests tidying up the Greek by reading *auto kath' hauto* for *autas kath' hautas*, without actually incorporating the emendation in his text.

291. sc. from chapter 3.

292. In chapter 3.

293. Perhaps 'a this something' and 'a this' are to be regarded as equivalent to variables whose substitution instances are, respectively, sortals and proper names.

294. What Aristotle actually says, of course, is 'But points cannot be posited as the body's matter either, nor can lines.'

295. I follow Vitelli in printing a lacuna here. The words from 'to teach' to the end of the sentence seem unintelligible. The quotation is from 320b22, although Philoponus has *epeidê* where the MSS apparently have *epei d'* for 'since'.

296. I have used 'form' in this sentence to translate *morphên* and 'kind' to translate *eidos*.

297. De Haas takes Philoponus to think that either interpretation of Aristotle would work here: see *John Philoponus' New Definition of Prime Matter*, pp. 142-3 (SB).

298. sc. in chapter 3.

299. Book 1.7.

300. In his Clarendon edition, Williams prints the last parenthesis in square brackets, following Joachim, who suggests that it should either be treated as an insertion or read after 'same genus': see Joachim, *Aristotle On Coming-to-be and Passing-away*, pp. 120-1. Joachim refers the reader to *Metaph.* 1032a12ff. for the doctrine that the efficient cause of coming-to-be is either an actual thing or an actuality, i.e. a form. Philoponus both accepts the text in his commentary, and thinks it worth attention: see the following note (SB).

301. The MSS of Philoponus have *pantêi gar adunaton*, which, if correct would have to be translated 'impossible in every way'. This, however, would leave *ekhein* (to have) without a subject. Plato's text (*Timaeus* 28A) has *panti adunaton* which is much easier, and following Vitelli's suggestion I have decided to treat it as the correct reading.

302. Richard Sorabji highlights the importance of this recognition that cause is not always like effect in his Preface to this volume. Alexander P.D. Mourelatos discusses Philoponus' challenge to what he calls, following A.C. Lloyd, the transmission model of causality, in his paper 'Aristotle's rationalist account of qualitative interaction', *Phronesis* 29, 1984, 1-16. Other instances of Philoponus refining Aristotle's model of change will be apparent in the companion volume (SB).

303. On Aristotle's theory of spontaneous generation, see D.M. Balme, 'The development of biology in Aristotle and Theophrastus: the theory of spontaneous generation', *Phronesis* 7, 1962, 91-104 (SB).

304. Literally 'do not have their coming-to-be from'.

305. In Greek *dêmiourgikoi logoi*. [This phrase is a Neoplatonist term for Platonic forms: see e.g. Asclepius *in Metaph.* 44,33; 48,6, where the forms are expressly described as *dêmiourgikoi logoi*. While the term seems relatively rare, Philoponus uses it frequently in his *Aet.* See also 85,12.16, below, n. 339 and the companion volume. The translation 'rational principles' for *logoi* here is proposed by Frans de Haas (SB).]

306. sc. as opposed to a mathematical object.

307. The MSS we have of Aristotle's text seem divided between the two readings *kenon* and *koinon*, and Philoponus' remarks indicate that both readings were current in his day too.

308. *Phys.* 4.6-9.

309. Williams suggests reading 'the argument does <not> succeed'; De Haas thinks the text can be read as is, if we remember that the argument is a *reductio ad absurdum* (SB).

310. *Phys.* 4.6, 213a16. [Vitelli gives this reference: the view reported by Aristotle there is not his own. The term *khôristos* can be translated either 'separable' or 'separated' (SB)].

311. See above, n. 307.

312. Vitelli here prints *atopô*, but this must be a misprint for *atopôi*.

313. Again Philoponus was aware of different readings of Aristotle's text; and indeed the MSS available today are still split between the readings *auxomenon* and *gignomenon*.

314. The MSS of Philoponus omit the words *hulês dei einai tên auxêsin eis entelekheian megethous*. Vitelli prints a lacuna.

315. Vitelli does not punctuate at this point, no doubt taking the repeated *kapi*, which I have translated at its first occurrence as 'in the case of' and at its second occurrence as 'in terms of', as coordinate. But a new point is being made.

316. A common Aristotelian practice is to list common views on a topic as part of the data to be explained. At *Physics* 4.1, Aristotle begins his examination of *topos*, which can mean either 'place' or 'space': see above, nn. 10 and 275 (SB).

317. Vitelli marks a lacuna in the text at the beginning of this sentence, but notes that the Aldine edition prints the words *ta dê kata koinên ennoian* in the place occupied by the lacuna, and my translation includes a rendering of these words, and a further word such as *ektithetai* which I have supplied to make grammatical sense of the sentence.

318. Vitelli follows the Aldine editor in inserting *hôste* here, presumably to avoid asyndeton.

319. Vitelli adds a reference at this point to 505,21ff. of Philoponus' own commentary on the *Physics*.

320. The Greek, *adunaton hulên megethous einai khôristên*, can have the sense conveyed in the translation just given or as meaning 'It is impossible for matter to be separable from size', as Philoponus goes on to point out.

321. Philoponus here speaks as though we were already informed that there was a dispute about Aristotle's text at 321a6, *koinon* (common) being a variant reading to the received *kenon* (void).

322. See above, n. 320, for the two interpretations Philoponus gives of the Greek original of this phrase. The alternative interpretation is required in the next sentence but one.

323. The Stoics embrace the idea that bodies can be completely diffused throughout each other: see Alexander *On Mixture* or Plutarch *On Common Conceptions* 1078B-D for the famous hyperbole of a sea battle taking place within the leg of a man which had been severed and putrified in the sea. However, the problem concerns not only complete intermixing, but also the claim that two bodies can take the space that previously was occupied by one: if this is possible, the process could be repeated until a large body like the sea would fit into a teacup: see Richard Sorabji, *Matter, Space and Motion*, London and Ithaca N.Y. 1988, pp. 73, 101 (SB).

324. Vitelli follows the Aldine editor in supplying *gar* here to avoid asyndeton.

325. A third option, that the universe bulges, is offered by Xuthus: see *Physics* 4.9, 216b25 (SB).

326. Vitelli does not print this sentence as a question. [Philoponus is trying to find an account that will make it seem reasonable that compensatory compression and rarefaction do in fact take place. What he seems to be resisting is the idea of action at a distance, that some bodies change to compensate for changes in distant bodies with which they could not be affected by contact (SB).]

327. Philoponus seems to be referring to *Meteor*. 1.12, 349a5-9, although there changes of temperature are involved. For the idea that volumes of air move to fill available space, cf. Theophrastus *de Ventis*, esp. 5,33-5 and the Aristotelian *Problemata*; H.B. Gottschalk, 'Strato of Lampsacus: some texts', *Proceedings of the Leeds Philosophical and Literary Society* 9, 1965, 95-182, pp. 159-60 (SB).

328. cf. David Sedley, 'Philoponus' conception of space', in Richard Sorabji (ed.), *Philoponus and the Rejection of Aristotelian Science*, London 1987, p. 143ff. [Cases typically attributed to the 'power of the void' involve the movement or unusual retention of liquids to prevent voids forming, as in siphons. Philoponus applies the same principle here to account for the reciprocal compression and expansion of elements to fill a determinate quantity of space. The phenomenon has a long history in the medical schools and in mechanics, and seems to have been discussed among Aristotle's early followers. For further literature, see, e.g., H. B. Gottschalk, 'Strato of Lampsacus: some texts', *Proceedings of the Leeds Philosophical and Literary Society* 9, 1965, 95-182; David J. Furley and J.S. Wilkie, *Galen on Respiration and the Arteries*, Princeton 1984; David Furley, 'Strato's theory of void', in *Cosmic Problems: Essays on Greek and Roman Philosophy of Nature*, Cambridge 1989, 149-60; Sylvia Berryman, '*Horror vacui* in the third century B.C.E.: when is a theory not a theory?' in Richard Sorabji (ed.) *Aristotle and After: Bulletin of the Institute of Classical Studies* suppl. vol. 2, 1997, 147-57 (SB).]

329. The text here has only the definite article (*legô dê tên tou aeros*), which it would be natural to translate 'that' (I mean that of air). But this would have to refer back to the word just translated 'bulk', a masculine noun, and the article is in fact feminine. Grammatically it could refer back to the word translated 'change', which is feminine, but 'I mean the change of air' makes no sense. We can suppose either that the feminine article is a mistake for the masculine, and emend to *ton*, so that it can indeed refer back to 'bulk', or that the feminine word *genesin* (coming-to-be) has been omitted from the parenthesis, giving the sense I have expressed in my translation, assuming that what Philoponus meant to write was *legô dê tên tou aeros genesin*.

330. Vitelli indicates a lacuna at this point. Sense would be obtained by supplying the words *hê trophê* (the nourishment).

331. The Greek word used by Philoponus here is *energeia*, which echoes the word *ergon* which Aristotle himself uses. [The adjective here translated 'pure' is *eilikrinês*, a term that will play an important role in Philoponus' account of mixture in chapter 1.10. The contrast is drawn there between unimpeded functioning and the restrained activity of the powers of substances in a mixture: see Frans de Haas, 'Mixture and recollection in Philoponus: encounters with a third kind of potentiality', forthcoming, and the companion volume for more on this (SB).]

332. It is not clear what Philoponus is referring to by 'it' (*autou*) here.

333. The word translated 'efficient', *poiêtikê*, might in other contexts be translated 'active' or 'agent'. It belongs to the root *poiein* (to act) regularly contrasted with *paskhein* (to undergo) to give rise to the contrasting pairs 'active/passive', 'agent/patient', etc.

334. In English the verb 'alter', like the verbs 'change' and 'move', has both an intransitive and a transitive sense. This causes ambiguities which are absent from the Greek equivalents which use the active voice of these verbs to express the transitive sense and the passive to express the intransitive. This is why I have used the circumlocution 'the thing which does the altering' to translate what is merely that active participle of the verb *alloioun*.

335. See previous note. It would be more natural in English to talk of a 'capacity', rather than a 'power', for being altered; but it is not desirable to use different words to translate *dunamis* from one sentence to another.

336. Vitelli prints *to dunamei* here, which I find it impossible to construe. There is no indication in his apparatus of an alternative reading, but one must suppose that *to dunamei* is written in error here for *tên dunamin*.

337. The Greek is *tôi poiounti*. See above, n. 333.

338. The Greek, *hê poiêtikê aitia*, is the same as we have had before. Here one is tempted to translate it 'the agent cause' to give expression to the hint of paradox in the juxtaposition of *poiêtikê* and *paskhonti*. See above, n. 333.

339. I use the phrase 'that which fashions it' to translate *to dêmiourgoun*, the word used by Plato to describe the Master Craftsman or Creator of the World.

340. The Greek translated 'the maker' is *to poioun*, the participle of this same word *poiein* which can also mean 'act' or 'do'. Yet again, see above, n. 333.

341. Aristotle makes this claim later on in this work: *GC* 2.10, 336b27-9. [In the later passage Aristotle is trying to justify the claim that the process of coming-to-be and perishing persists, and says, in Williams' translation, 'for we say that nature in all cases desires what is better, and that being is better than not being'. The principle Aristotle uses needn't be taken to imply that nature always does what is best for the individual thing (SB).]

342. As usual I use 'substratum' to translate *hupokeimenon*. One of its meanings is 'subject of predication', and it it is this sense that it is used here to indicate that of which we say that it grows.

343. This word, *kinêsis*, which I usually translate 'change', since its extension is certainly greater than that of 'change' in English, I here give its more traditional translation to leave 'change' free to render *metabolê*, which, together with the verb *metaballein*, from which it is formed, occurs later in the sentence and frequently in the lines which follow. Unlike *kinein*, the verb from which *kinêsis* is formed, *metaballein* can be used in an intransitive as well as in a transitive sense (see above, n. 73). It is so used in most of its occurrences here.

344. Aristotle considers a view that only the qualified thing admits of degree while the quality itself is never 'more or less' (*Cat.* 10b26-11a4). Iamblichus argues that if there is a close correspondence between the quality and what is qualified, the quality ought to undergo the same affections as the qualified thing: Simplicius *in Cat.* 288,18-30; cf. 284,14ff., forthcoming in this series in a new translation by Barrie Fleet as *Simplicius: On Aristotle Categories 6-8*. Hence the idea that a quality undergoes intensification and relaxation – *epitasis* and *anesis*. See Nelly Tsouyopoulos, 'Die Entstehung physikalischer Terminologie aus der neoplatonischen Metaphysik', *Archiv für Begriffsgeschichte* 13, 1969, 7-33; Katerina Ierodiakonou, 'Aspasius on perfect and imperfect virtues', in R.W. Sharples (ed.), *Aspasius*, Berlin, forthcoming. R.B. Todd points to another Aristotelian source for the notion of a *epitasis* and *anesis* in a discussion of motion in *Cael.* 288a19: 'Some concepts in physical theory in John Philoponus' Aristotelian Commentaries', *Archiv für Begriffsgeschichte* 24, 1980, 151-70, pp. 168-9. Philoponus makes more use of this notion in his discussion of mixture: see the companion volume (SB).

345. Literally, 'as a consequence of the natural mixture'.

346. The Aldine editor inserted *eis* here.

347. Philoponus explains the relevant sense of '*per se* affection' in the following paragraph, and cf. my commentary on Aristotle's *De Gen. et Corr.*, p. 100.

348. This is hendiadys, in Aristotle and in Philoponus, since the phrase 'the what it is' indicates the answer that should be given to the question 'What is it?', i.e. the appropriate predicate in the category of substance: the appropriate answer in the case envisaged is 'flesh', so the meaning is 'keeping its property of being flesh and remaining flesh'.

349. The Aldine editor, according to Vitelli, proceeded at this point straight to 321b5 (although Vitelli prints '521b5'). Vitelli adds, and I can do no better, *turbatam seriem quomodo corrigam non habeo.*

350. The logic of the sentence which begins here does not end until 102,20. Before that, however, Philoponus seems to forget the structure he originally intended for the sentence. Its overall structure should be determined by 'Just as ... ' and an answering 'so ... '. In fact, when the time comes for the 'so ... ' part, Philoponus begins a new sentence 'The same must be said also ... '. The 'just as' clause is subdivided into two subordinate conditional propositions, contrasted with each other in the Greek by *men* and *mentoi*: 'if the cause of alteration is proportionate ... ' and 'if, however (*mentoi*), the incoming food is disproportionate ... '. But before moving from the first to the second conditional, Philoponus jumps the gun by introducing a further conditional which draws an analogy with the case of growth – the very analogy which it was the purpose of the 'just as ... so ... ' arrangement to express. This intrusive conditional sentence I have printed as a parenthesis. However, the disturbance it introduces to the overall thought of the passage is not limited to this parenthesis, because, when Philoponus returns to the second of contrasted conditional sentences (the one introduced by *mentoi*), he forgets that he is still in the 'just as ...' clause and supposedly talking about alteration and speaks of 'the incoming <things>', which must be understood as food, which is appropriate, not to alteration, but to growth, to which the analogy is to be applied in the 'so ...' clause.

351. See above, n. 350.

352. There is anacoluthon here. See above, n. 350. [On the idea that quantity as well as the quality of nutriment needs to be suitable, see De Haas, *John Philoponus' New Definition of Prime Matter*, p. 157 and n. 224; 'Mixture in Philoponus: An encounter with a third kind of potentiality', in Hans Thijssen (ed.), forthcoming proceedings of a conference on the commentary tradition on *GC* due to appear with Brepols (Turnhout). For more on Philoponus' concept of suitability, see the companion volume (SB).]

353. The word I have translated 'matter' is *hupokeimenon*, which I usually render 'substratum', see Proem, n. 17. As I remark there, *hupokeimenon* often bears the sense 'that from which', which is also used to explain the sense of *hulê*, regularly translated 'matter'. In this chapter both the thing before growth and the nourishment is called by Aristotle that from which a thing grows or *hulê*, i.e. matter (cf. 321a7). It is not surprising, therefore, that *hupokeimenon*, in this sense the synonym of *hulê*, is used here of what a growing thing feeds on.

354. Notably in chapter 7.

355. The Greek is literally 'the whole of the growing thing is passage (*poron*) and void'.

356. The word which I have translated 'penetrable' here and in the next sentence is *poros*, a noun meaning 'passage' or 'way through'. (It is the origin of the English word 'pore'.) See above, n. 355.

357. sc. form and matter.

358. The Greek is *ousiôdê.*

359. In Greek, *hupokeimenôi*. See above, n. 353.

360. The Greek is *ousiôdes.*

361. See above, n. 353.

362. This phrase renders *horistikos ôn*. *horistikos logos*, in line 30 below, has been rendered 'defining formula'. It is unfortunate that the same English word cannot be found to translate *horistikos* at both places.

363. See previous note.

364. The phrase '*qua* something endowed with quantity' translates *hêi peposôtai*.

365. See above, n. 353.

366. sc. the form.

367. sc. in the way in which a person who has had a leg amputated is mutilated.

368. The word thus translated, *diaphorêseôs*, can mean evaporation or perspiration, but seems to be intended here in a more general sense than either of these would indicate.

369. Philoponus is talking about two different problems here, and perhaps using the term *sunekheia*, continuity, in two different senses. One is the metaphysical problem of identity through change, common to both the growing argument and the ship of Theseus problem: why we say that an individual is numerically identical when its matter changes. The other is the physical problem about the mechanism by which gaps are closed to prevent void spaces forming. The physical continuity of matter, apparently used to explain its resistance to gaps, may provide a *de facto* guarantee that individuals will in fact be continuous through time, but hardly solves the metaphysical problem. On the resistance of matter to gaps, see above, n. 327 and Introduction (SB).

370. *surrhoia mia, sumpnoia mia, panta sumpathea*: *de Alim.* 9 106n23 (Littr.)

371. Or substratum, see above, n. 353.

372. The phrase 'as a complete whole' translates *holon di' holou*.

373. Vitelli prints *epeisousa*, but it is difficult to believe that this is not a mistake for *epeisiousa*. Cf. *epeision* at 107,29.

374. Literally, 'nature'. [Todd points to the influence of Galen's account of nutrition in this section of the commentary: 'Galenic medical ideas in the Greek Aristotelian Commentators', *Symbolae Osloenses* 52 (1976), 117-34. Galen sees himself as working within a Hippocratic and Aristotelian framework in contrast to an antiteleological approach represented by Erasistratean medicine: see Galen *On the Natural Faculties* trans. A.J. Brock, London 1916 (SB).]

375. sc. the ultimate subject of predication, i.e. that which is in each case said to grow.

376. See previous note.

377. The Greek is *huph'*, so that the phrase literally means 'the matter under every part of the form'.

378. sc. of matter and form. [Todd notes a similarity to Galen's idea that there are 'powers' or faculties of attraction and expulsion governing the movement of nutrients and waste products in the body: 'Galenic medical ideas in the Greek Aristotelian Commentators', *Symbolae Osloenses* 52 (1976), 117-34, pp. 119-20. For attraction in Hippocratic treatises, see, e.g., I.M. Lonie, *The Hippocratic Treatises 'On Generation', 'On the Nature of the Child', 'Diseases IV': A Commentary*, Berlin 1981, esp. pp. 266-68, 301-2 (SB).]

379. Aristotle regarded every homoeomer, such as flesh or bone, as a mixture of the four elements, earth, water, air and fire in some ratio or other. The word translated 'moisture' is a standard way of referring to the element of water.

380. In the sense described in the last note

381. The Greek word translated 'of its substance' is *ousiôdes*.

382. i.e. the subject of which growing is predicated, namely the bone.

383. The Greek is *proüpokeimenou*.

384. The word *hupokeimenon* is here used in the way that earlier (see above, n.

93) prompted me to translated it as 'matter', but so to translate it here would be to make this sentence more obviously than it is a mere repetition of the previous sentence.

385. sc. matter and form.

386. Literally, 'the being'.

387. Philoponus does not seem to have obtained a satisfactory understanding of this difficult but highly important passage. For enlightenment the reader is advised to consult G.E.M. Anscombe, *Collected Philosophical Papers* vol. I, Oxford 1981, pp. 64ff.

388. Literally, 'their being'.

389. Philoponus seems to forget that he has already written 'again' once in the sentence.

390. Here Philoponus refers to the problem today know at 'Ackrill's paradox': see Introduction for references to this problem in recent literature. Although Aristotle does seem to think that this extends to homoeomeries at *GA* 2.1, both at this point and in *Meteor*. 4.12 he suggests that the case is less clear for homoeomeries. The term translated 'evident' is *traneis* (SB).

391. I use 'of itself' to render *kath' hautên*, but its meaning in this context is probably to be gathered from the words which follow.

392. David Furley notes that while this renders the Greek, Philoponus needs to make the point that if something is potentially X now, it must be actually something else (contrary to X) now. It *will be* actually X, not something other than X (SB).

393. Perishing *per se* should be contrasted with perishing *per alium* – perishing in virtue of itself perishing vs. perishing in virtue of something else perishing. But when I eat an oyster it seems that the oyster perishes, and there is nothing else which perishes in virtue of which we say that the oyster perishes. But the perishing of the oyster is not, from Aristotle's point of view, a classic case of perishing, which would demand that the perishing of one substance was the coming-to-be of another. And when I eat the oyster nothing comes to be. What happens is that I grow bigger – I, who existed already, so that neither I nor any other substance comes to be in the transaction.

394. By 'the matter' here he means the nourishment, that by which something grows. See above, n. 353.

395. In Joachim's edition of the modern text, he brackets *êuxêthê*: in his Clarendon translation, Williams follows this and translates 'How affected by the growing thing?' (SB).

396. There is no question mark here in the lemma as printed by Vitelli. Joachim is surely right to print a question mark, as he does in his edition of Aristotle's text.

397. The Aldine editor prints *meta touto* in place of *meta toutou*, thus changing 'together with this' to 'after this', which makes better sense.

398. Philoponus here contrasts 'the form associated with shape' (*to eidos to kata to skhêma*) with 'the substantial form' (*to ousiôdes eidos*), mentioned four lines below.

399. The words translated 'as bone' are added to the text by Vitelli.

400. The phrase 'is endowed with a form' represents the word *eidopepoiêtai* in the Greek.

401. Vitelli prints: *holon men gar hôs holon ouketi. oude gar panti moriôi tês sarkos hê prosthêkê meizôn gegonen, hekaston mentoi morion tês hulês gegonen;* The text I have translated is the reading of R, which transposes *ouketi ... prosthêkê* to follow *mentoi morion*. I can make no sense of the text as printed by Vitelli.

402. Vitelli follows the Aldine editor in adding *dei* here.

403. sc. the form associated with shape.

404. sc. the thing which is nourished and grows.

405. In Greek: *epi tou ousiôdous*.

406. The word I have translated 'character' is *idean*.

407. The MSS have *kai hoti kai*. Vitelli brackets *kai hoti*. I suggest that the text should be amended to *kai hotioun*, and have translated accordingly.

408. He means that he is not saying, e.g., that Alexander comes to be from what is not Alexander but *is* Philip, but that what Alexander comes to be from is not a human being at all.

409. For Philoponus' notion of 'the three-dimensionally extended', see Richard Sorabji, *Matter, Space and Motion*, London and Ithaca N.Y. 1987, ch. 2.

410. The word translated 'immaterial' is *aülos*. Joachim prints *aulos* and translates 'duct'.

411. In his Clarendon translation, Williams follows Joachim in reading 'this form, like a pipe, is a sort of power in matter', but despairs of making this passage intelligible. Philoponus' gloss at 122,4 shows that he reads the term as 'immaterial' (SB).

412. See above, n. 409.

413. Alexander and Philoponus read this passage as a reminder that the true nature of *tropê* is to be an immaterial power that sometimes causes growth, sometimes doesn't. Whether it does in fact do so depends on the quantity of what is being nourished, not on the nutriment itself (SB).

414. Philoponus reads this phrase (*megethous aüloi*) as claiming that what grows is not the matter but the form of that to which the nutriment is added. A nutriment is presumably only able to cause actual quantitative change when the increase caused by the nutriment is greater than the diminution (SB).

English-Greek Glossary

absence of knowledge: *agnoia*
absence of perception: *anaisthêsia*
absence: *apousia*
absurdity: *atopia*
accede to: *prosienai*
accidental: *sumbebêkos*
accompany: *parakolouthein*
accomplish: *epitelesthai*
account: *logos*
accretion: *proskrisis*
act upon: *poiein*
active: *poiêtikos*
actualisation, actuality: *energeia*
actuality: *entelekheia*
ad infinitum: *eis apeiron, ep' apeiron*
add: *prostithenai*
addition: *prosthêkê, prosthesis, prostithêsis*
admission: *eiskrisis*
affect in return: *antipaskhein*
affected: *paskhein*
affection: *pathos*
affective: *pathêtikos*
agent: *poioun*
aggregate: *sunkrinein*
aggregation: *sunkrisis*
aim: *skopos*
alteration: *alloiôsis, ameipsis*
altered: *alloios*
analyse: *dialuein*
anhomeoemerous: *anomoiomerês*
animate: *empsukhos*
anywhere: *hopêioun*
appearance: *phantasia*
apply: *harmottein*
appropiate: *oikeios*
argument: *logos*
arrangement: *metataxis, taxis*
assimilate(d)(to be): *proskrinesthai*
assimilate: *oikeioun*
assimilation: *proskrisis*
at once: *hama*
atom: *atomos*
attack: *enstasis*

beaten out: *elaunesthai*
being: *ousia*
belong: *huparkhein*
bestow: *apotithesthai*
birth: *phusis*
boundary: *horistikos*
bring about: *ergazesthai*
brought into being (to be): *gennasthai*

category: *katêgoria*
cause: *aitia, aition*
ceasing-to-be: *phthora*
change (to): *metaballein*
change: *metabolê*
character: *idea*
choice: *proairesis*
combine: *sunduazesthai*
come to be: *gignesthai*
coming together: *mixis*
coming-to-be: *genesis*
commentator: *exêgêtos*
common: *koinos*
complete: *teleios*
complex: *sunthetos*
composed: *sunkeisthai*
composite: *sunthetos*
composition: *sustasis*
concept: *ennoia, logos*
conclude: *sumperainein*
connect: *suneirein*
contact: *haphê*
contiguous: *ephexês*
continuing sequence: *heirmos*
continuity: *sunekheia*
continuous: *sunekhês*
contract (to): *sustellesthai*
contrariety: *enantiôsis, enantiotês*
contrary: *enantios*
contribute: *suntelein*
contributing form: *eidopoios*
corporeal: *sômatikos*

magnitude: *megethos*
manner: *tropos*
marked off: *diorizesthai*
material, matter-like: *hulikos*
matter: *hulê, hupokeimenon*
middle (at the): *kata meson*
mingling, mixture: *krasis*
mix(ing): *mignunai, mixis*
mode: *tropos*
model: *hupodeigma, paradeigma*
movement: *kinêsis*

natural: *phusikos*
nature, natural power: *phusis*
next: *ephexês*
nourishment: *threpsis, trophê*
number: *arithmos*

objection: *aporia*
obviousness: *enargeia*
occupy: *katekhein*
occur: *huphistanai*
occur previously: *proüparkhein*
onkos: *bulk*
operation: *ergon*
opposed: *antikeisthai*
origin: *arkhê*
other: *allos*
outflow: *aporrhoê*
outside: *exôthen*
own: *idios*

panspermia: *panspermia*
part: *meros, morion*
partial: *kata meros*
participate: *metekhein*
particular things: *kath' hekasta*
particularity: *idiotês*
pass through: *diienai*
pass: *khôrein*
passage: *lexis, poros*
passive: *pathêtikos*
per se: *kath' hauto*
perceptible: *aisthêtos*
perception: *aisthêsis*
perfecting: *teleiôtikos*
perishing: *phthora,*
physical: *phusikos*
place: *topos*
plenum: *plêres*
point of agreement: *homologêma*
point: *sêmeion, stigmê*
position: *metathesis, sêmeion, thesis*
positive characteristic: *hexis*
posterior: *husteros*
potentiality: *dunamis*
potentially: *dunamei*
power: *dunamis*
pre-exist: *enuparkhein, proüphestanai*
preservation: *phulakê*
prime, primary: *prôtos*
principle: *arkhê*
prior: *proteros*
privation: *sterêsis*
privative: *stêrêtikos*
problem: *aporia*
produce: *apergazesthai, apotelein*
productive: *poiêtikos*
progress: *epidosis*
proof: *apodeixis*
proportionally: *analogon*
proportionate: *summetros*
proximate: *prosekhês*

qualitatively different: *alloios*
quality: *poiotês*
quantitative: *kata poson*
quantity: *poson*

reality: *huparxis*
really: *phusei*
receptive (to be): *anadekhesthai*
recognised: *epistêtos*
reduce: *agein*
refute: *elenkhein*
relation(ship): *skhesis*
relation: *logos*
relatives (cateogory of): *pros ti*
remain: *hupomenein, menein*
replace: *anteiserkhesthai*
resistance: *antitupia*
rest: *êremia*

same in genus: *homogenos*
same in name and definition: *sunônumos*
same in species: *homoeidês*
scientific: *phusikos*
segregation: *diakrisis*
self-subsistent: *authupostatos*
sensible: *aisthêtos*
sentient: *aisthêtikos*
separable, separate: *khôristos*
separating: *ekkrisis*

separation: *diallaxis*
shape: *morphê, skhêma*
simple, *simpliciter*: *haplous*
size: *megethos*
sizeless: *amegethês*
skill: *tekhnê*
solid: *stereos*
solve: *luein*
soul: *psukhê*
source: *arkhê*
species-determining: *eidopoios*
specifically identical: *homoeidês*
specifically: *kat' eidos*
specifying characteristic: *eidopoios, eidos*
spherical: *sphairoeidês*
spontaneously: *automatôs*
starting point: *pothen, arkhê*
state: *skhesis*
subject to quantity: *peposômenon*
subsist: *huposthênai*
subsistence: *hupostasis*
subsistent: *huphestêkos, huphestôs*
substance: *ousia*
substantial: *ousiôdês*
substratum: *hupokeimenon*
subsume: *anagein*
such and such: *poios*
supposition: *hupolêpsis*
surface: *epipedos, epiphaneia*
surrounding: *periektikos*

take on: *prosepilambanein*
tendency: *rhopê*
theory: *dogma, prosêgoria*
thought: *ennoia*
together: *athroos*
touch (to): *haptesthai*
transparency: *diaphaneia*
triangular: *trigônos*

uncapable of being affected: *apathos*
unchangeable: *ametablêtos*
underly previously: *proüpokeisthai*
underly: *hupokeisthai*
undifferentiated: *adiaphoros*
unification: *henôsis*
universal: *katholos*
unserviceable: *anepitêdeios*

vacuum: *kenos*
vain: *matên*
void: *kenos*

whole: *holon, holotês*
width: *platos*
work: *ergon*
world: *kosmos*

Greek-English Index

adiairetos, indivisible, 25,12
adiaphoros, undifferentiated, 19,14
agein, to reduce, 58,2
agnoia, absence of knowledge, 57,30
aïdios, eternal, 1,11
ainittesthai, to hint at, 44,19
aisthêsis, perception, 57,13
aisthêtikos, sentient, 2,8
perceiver, 16,29
aisthêtos, sensible, 16,30
perceptible, 36,35
aitia, cause, 7,18; 45,7; 49,25
aitios, explanation, 51,23
cause, 83,28
akhronos, instantaneous, 92,30
akinêsia, immobility, 31,29
akinêtos, (remaining) the same, 16,24
immobile, 31,30
akolouthein, to follow, 82,11
akros, most opposed, 67,5
alloios, altered, 9,2
qualitatively different, 72,6
alloiôsis, alteration, 8,30
alloiousthai, to suffer alteration, 97a2
allos, other, 9,2
amegethês, sizeless, not possessed of size, 85,22; 72,28
ameibein, to exchange, 71,20
ameipsis, alteration, 51,22
ametablêtos, unchangeable, 9,23
anadekhesthai, to be receptive, 50,20
anagein, to include, 44,4
to subsume, 70,30
anaisthêsia, absence of perception, 57,16
anaisthêtos, insentient, 2,9
imperceptible, 67,20
analogon, proportionally, 114,2
analuesthai, to disintegrate, 58,9
aneideos, without form, formless, 5,21; 45,18;
anepistêmosunê, lack of knowledge, 57,13
anepitêdeios, unserviceable, 102,22
anomoiomerês, anhomeoemerous, 12,1
antanaplêrôsis, mutual filling up, 92,15
anteiserkhesthai, to replace, 106,15
antikeisthai, to be opposed, 46,2
antiparakhôrein, to give up one's place in turn, 92,16
antipaskhein, to affect in return, 96,33
antitupia, resistance, 67,20
apathos, incapable of being affected, 17,6
apeiron, infinite, 35,18, 36,13
apeiros, infinite, 12,9
apeiros, inexperienced, 25,20
apergazesthai, to produce, 8,14
aperilêptos, indefinite, 12,8
aphthartos, imperishable, 1,10
apoballein, to get rid of, 45,14
apodeixis, proof, 7,4
apodidonai, explain, 26,17
apodosis, explanation, 8,15
apoios, without quality, 20,17
devoid of quality, 73,22
apophasis, denial, 46,10
aporia, problem, 48,19
objection, 90,26
aporrhoê, outflow, 23,25
apotelein, produce, 20,9
apotithesthai, to bestow, 19,33
apousia, absence, 56,4
apsukhos, inanimate, 2,8
arkhê, principle, 20,17
source, 49,26
starting-point, 88,18
origin, 97,28
arithmos, number, 45,5
asômatos, incorporeal, 37,25
athroos, together, 106,8

Subject Index